Communication Realities in a "Post Racial" Society

LEXINGTON STUDIES IN POLITICAL COMMUNICATION

Series Editor: Robert E. Denton, Jr.,
Virginia Polytechnic Institute and State University

This series encourages focused work examining the role and function of communication in the realm of politics including campaigns and elections, media, and political institutions.

RECENT TITLES IN THE SERIES:

Seen and Heard: The Women of Television News, By Nichola D. Gutgold

Nuclear Legacies: Communication, Controversy, and the U. S. Nuclear Weapons Complex, Edited by Bryan C. Taylor, William J. Kinsella, Stephen P. Depoe, Maribeth S. Metzler

Conditional Press Influence in Politics, By Adam J. Schiffer

Telling Political Lives: The Rhetorical Autobiographies of Women Leaders in the United States, Edited by Brenda DeVore Marshall and Molly A. Mayhead

Media Bias? A Comparative Study of Time, Newsweek, the National Review, and the Progressive, 1975–2000, By Tawnya J. Adkins Covert and Philo C. Wasburn

Navigating the Post–Cold War World: President Clinton's Foreign Policy Rhetoric, By Jason A. Edwards

The Rhetoric of Pope John Paul II, Edited by Joseph R. Blaney and Joseph P. Zompetti

Stagecraft and Statecraft: Advance and Media Events in Political Communication, By Dan Schill

Rhetorical Criticism: Perspectives in Action, Edited by Jim A. Kuypers

Almost *Madam President: Why Hillary Clinton "Won" in 2008*, By Nichola D. Gutgold

Cracked But Not Shattered: Hillary Rodham Clinton's Unsuccessful Run for the Presidency, Edited by Theodore F. Sheckels

Gender and Political Communication in America: Rhetoric, Representation, and Display, Edited by Janis L. Edwards

Communicator-in-Chief: How Barack Obama Used New Media Technology to Win the White House, Edited by John Allen Hendricks and Robert E. Denton, Jr.

Centrist Rhetoric: The Production of Political Transcendence in the Clinton Presidency, By Antonio de Velasco

Studies of Identity in the 2008 Presidential Campaign, Edited by Robert E. Denton, Jr.

Campaign Finance Reform: The Political Shell Game, By Melissa M. Smith, Glenda C. Williams, Larry Powell, and Gary A. Copeland

Us against Them: The Political Culture of Talk Radio, By Randy Bobbitt

Internet Policy in China: A Field Study of Internet Cafés, By Helen Sun

A Communication Universe: Manifestations of Meaning, Stagings of Significance, By Igor E. Klyukanov

The Perfect Response: Studies of the Rhetorical Personality, By Gary C. Woodward

Presidential Campaign Rhetoric in an Age of Confessional Politics, By Brian T. Kaylor

Manipulating Images: World War II Mobilization of Women through Magazine Advertising, By Tawnya J. Adkins Covert

The Politics of Style and the Style of Politics, Edited by Barry Brummett

Communication Realities in a "Post-Racial" Society: What the U.S. Public Really Thinks about Barack Obama, By Mark P. Orbe

Communication Realities in a "Post Racial" Society

What the U.S. Public Really Thinks about Barack Obama

Mark P. Orbe

LEXINGTON BOOKS
Lanham • Boulder • New York • Toronto • Plymouth, UK

Published by Lexington Books
A wholly owned subsidiary of The Rowman & Littlefield Publishing Group, Inc.
4501 Forbes Boulevard, Suite 200, Lanham, Maryland 20706
www.lexingtonbooks.com

Estover Road, Plymouth PL6 7PY, United Kingdom

Copyright © 2011 by Lexington Books

All rights reserved. No part of this book may be reproduced in any form or by any electronic or mechanical means, including information storage and retrieval systems, without written permission from the publisher, except by a reviewer who may quote passages in a review.

British Library Cataloguing in Publication Information Available

Library of Congress Cataloging-in-Publication Data

Orbe, Mark P.
  Communication realities in a "post-racial" society : what the U.S. public really thinks about Barack Obama / Mark P. Orbe.
    p. cm.
  Includes bibliographical references.
  ISBN 978-0-7391-6990-2 (cloth : alk. paper)—ISBN 978-0-7391-6991-9 (pbk. : alk. paper)—ISBN 978-0-7391-6992-6 (ebook)
  1. Obama, Barack—Oratory—Public opinion. 2. Obama, Barack—Political and social views—Public opinion. 3. Post-racialism—United States—Public opinion. 4. Communication in politics—United States—Public opinion. 5. Mass media—Political aspects—United States—Public opinion. 6. Public relations and politics—United States—Public opinion. 7. Presidents—United States—Election—2008—Public opinion. 8. United States—Race relations—Political aspects—Public opinion. 9. United States—Politics and government—2009—Public opinion. 10. Public opinion—United States . I. Title.
  E901.1.O23O73 2011
  973.932092—dc23   2011030857

∞™ The paper used in this publication meets the minimum requirements of American National Standard for Information Sciences—Permanence of Paper for Printed Library Materials, ANSI/NISO Z39.48-1992.

Printed in the United States of America

Contents

PART I	**INTRODUCTION**	
Chapter 1	Barack Obama, Communication, and Race	3
Chapter 2	Descriptions of the Study	17
PART II	**BARACK OBAMA AS COMMUNICATOR**	
Chapter 3	Perceptions of Barack Obama's Communication Style	33
Chapter 4	Shifts in Perception: The Campaign Versus the Presidency	51
Chapter 5	"Presidential Communication"	69
PART III	**RACE MATTERS IN A "POST-RACIAL" SOCIETY**	
Chapter 6	The Role of Race in "Post-Racial" Politics	91
Chapter 7	Black Pride in, and Allegiance to, President Obama	109
Chapter 8	White Opposition to President Obama	129
Chapter 9	Gates/Crowley Conflict and the "Beer Summit"	149

PART IV	THE MEDIA MACHINE	
Chapter 10	Media Influences	169
Chapter 11	The Celebrity President	189
PART V	**CONCLUSION**	
Chapter 12	Critical Reflections and Concluding Thoughts	209
Appendixes		225
References		229
Index		239
About the Author		245

Part I

Introduction

Chapter 1

Barack Obama, Communication, and Race

Barack Obama's improbable journey from Illinois state senator to president of the United States of America is documented within an abundance of national, and international, media outlets. In no uncertain terms, President Obama's election is regarded as "the election of our lifetimes" (Todd and Gawiser, 2009, p. 4) and "one that transformed how race and politics intersect in our society" (Ifill, 2009, p. 1). According to Hertzberg (2009),

> The presidential election that put Barack Obama in the White House has been variously called the most important, the most exciting, the most surprising, the most significant, the most consequential, and the most expensive in the modern history of the United States. The most expensive it certainly was, as was the one before and the one before that. (p. 1)

Hertzberg goes on to state that the 2008 election is "so extraordinary in so many ways that its meaning will take many years to play out and many more to be understood" (p. 313). Others also note that the historic nature of the election requires examination:

> "This is our moment. This is our time," Barack Obama declared in his victory speech on November 4, 2008. Such a moment is an opportunity to explore who we are, where we've been, and what the emergence of a leader like Obama can tell us about our culture, our politics, and our future. (Asim, 2009, p. 3)

This book describes the findings of a national study that explores public perceptions of Barack Obama's communication competence and rhetoric regarding race matters. A rapidly growing body of literature, in and outside of the academic community, is fast emerging. In the vast majority of cases, this literature presents statistical data from public polls, analyses from political pundits, and commentary from a host of cultural critics. What is missing from these publications is a qualitative investigation of what everyday individuals from diverse backgrounds think about Barack Obama. In this regard, I engage in a research project that seeks to use personal voices to provide a more holistic picture of public perceptions—something that is limited with descriptive statistics.

Taking a qualitative approach to explore public perceptions of Barack Obama's communication competence and rhetoric regarding race matters is of great significance in its own right. In addition identity politics continue to gain saliency within various aspects of U.S. culture so a comprehensive study must involve a diverse group of participants based on age, gender, race and ethnicity, socioeconomic status, political affiliation, and geographical region. Given this, academic scholars have a responsibility to utilize their research expertise to extend existing literature, as well as provide findings that have clear practical value for political scientists and communication consultants. This project represents a study that holds great potential in advancing how we understand the inextricable relationship between race, communication, and power.

The purpose of this book is to explicate the diversity of public perceptions of Barack Obama in general, and his communication style and approaches to race more specifically, which were gathered through a 2010 national study. Three research questions guide the project: (1) What is the general public perception of Barack Obama's communication competence—both it terms of effectiveness and appropriateness?; (2) What is the general public perception of his rhetoric regarding race matters?; and (3) How are these perceptions similar or different in terms of age, gender, race and ethnicity, political affiliation, region, and time (pre-/post-election)?

This first chapter provides an introduction to the topic of focus as well as this particular book project. First, I provide a brief overview of existing resources that describe public perceptions of Barack Obama, his communication, and how his presidency is regarded as symbolic of a "post-racial" society. Second, I share how this research intersects with my academic, personal, and political interests. Third, and finally, I offer a preview of the remaining sections and chapters of the book.

PRESIDENT BARACK OBAMA

The election of Barack Obama as the forty-fourth president of the United States is widely recognized as one of "historic proportions" (Leanne, 2009, xvii), so much so that *Newsweek* dubs the present era, "The Age of

Obama." As such, several biographies and autobiographies on President Obama exist (e.g., Obama, 2006), as well as a growing number of social, cultural, and political analyses that have recently been released (e.g., Asim, 2009; Ifill, 2009; Todd and Gawiser, 2009). These books provide a great deal of information about President Obama's personal life, educational and professional accomplishments, political journey, campaign strategies, and policies on various issues.

Significant survey data exists regarding public opinion of President Obama's popularity, policy, credibility, and other key characteristics (e.g., Kohut, 2008; Todd and Gawiser, 2009). The vast majority of this data comes from public polls generated by a large number of news agencies, research think tanks, and a host of public and private organizations. Over the past several years, polls have documented the ever shifting—and contrasting—opinions of President Obama that exist across the public sector (e.g., Stolberg and Connelly, 2009). While public perceptions of his job performance are largely aligned with political affiliation (e.g., Fram, 2010; Sidoti, 2011), one particular 2010 survey generates a number of interesting findings.

A national survey of 2,230 Americans (as reported in Laney, 2010) is widely reported in news outlets across the United States. The study finds that a significant number of individuals believe that President Obama is a socialist (40 percent), a Muslim (32 percent), not born in the United States—and therefore ineligible for the presidency—(25 percent), "doing many of the things that Hitler did" (20 percent), or "may be the anti-Christ" (14 percent). While none of these statistics represent majority opinions, they help to illustrate the great diversity that exists within public perceptions of President Obama. The research within this book seeks to gain more in-depth insight into these, and other, perceptions.

Studies by university researchers also provide valuable insight into how the public regards President Obama. Given the communication focus of this particular project, I review research by communication scholars (although scholars across a wide variety of academic areas have produced a growing body of publications in this area). Articles on Barack Obama began to appear in communication journals and edited books in 2007. Since that time, he has been the focus of research from scholars who engage Obama through rhetorical, political, critical, and explicitly cultural perspectives. More specifically, communication' scholarship centers on particular speeches (e.g., Frank, 2009; Rowland and Jones, 2007; Terrill, 2009), his use of social media (e.g., Harris, 2010; Ng, 2010a), celebrity endorsements during Obama's election (e.g., Pease and Brewer, 2008), persistence of rumors regarding his authentic self (e.g., Hollander, 2010; Spicer, 2010) and what his election means to the United States. (e.g., Darsey, 2009).This growing body of literature joins other research that explicitly engages the politics of race that surround Barack Obama's election as the forty-fourth U.S. president (Lee and Morin, 2009; Pasek et al., 2009; Philpot, Shaw, and McGowen, 2009).

Two major books—*The Obama Effect: Multidisciplinary Renderings of the 2008 Campaign* (Harris, Moffitt, and Squires, 2010) and *The Obama Victory: How Media, Money, and Message Shaped the 2008 Election* (Kenski, Hardy, and Jamieson, 2010)—offer great insight into various issues that were central to President Obama's election. In particular, Harris, et al. feature an eclectic collection of thought-provoking essays that explore rhetoric, new media, identities, public spheres, and representations. These recent publications are grounded in existing political communication scholarship, an area of study with deep traditions in the field (Nimmo and Sanders, 1981). More specifically, they continue to advance more recent efforts to understand the dynamics of race within contemporary politics (Connaughton, 2004; Cushman, 2005; Flores, Moon, and Nakayama, 2006; Kinder and McConnaughy, 2006). This book extends this existing research by focusing on Barack Obama's communication before, during, and after this election.

A COMMUNICATION APPROACH

President Obama's reputation as a master communicator is prevalent, so much so that his outstanding communication skills are recognized as a key source for his rapid political ascension (Leanne, 2009). Because of his winning rhetoric, he is described as "Kennedy-esque" and compared to Reagan, the man known as "The Great Communicator" (Freddoso, 2008, p. 55). Authors, editors, and speechwriters agree Obama is a gifted and effective speechmaker and has an uncanny ability to connect with individuals from varied backgrounds.

One of the most praised aspects of Barack Obama's communication mastery is his ability to speak to diverse audiences without losing any authenticity. According to one writer,

> Obama could change styles without relinquishing his genuineness. He subtly shifted accent and cadences depending on the audience: a more straight-up delivery for a luncheon of businesspeople in the loop; a folksier approach at a downstate V.F.W.; echoes of the pastors of the black church when he was in one. . . . Like the child of immigrants who could speak one language at home, another at school, and another with his friends—and still be himself—Obama crafted his speech to fit the moment. It was a skill that had taken years to develop. (Remnick, 2010, p. 18)

In this regard, President Obama is considered a highly competent communicator in different settings—someone who is "sometimes feisty, sometimes conciliatory, sometimes thoughtful, sometimes spirited, sometimes optimistic, sometimes steeped in severity (MacGillis, 2009).

Even those who disagree with his politics recognize President Obama's communication abilities (Steele, 2008). Many political opponents applaud his skill at delivering speeches with unrivaled inspiration and motivation.

> We all know Obama's style, his regal, visionary bearing, his above-the-fray persona, his inspired—and give him his due, inspiring—performances, his "Audacity of Hope," and his hypnotic, upbeat, unifying message. He is skilled. If we were voting for a chief motivational speaker or a political "American Idol," even I'd be on board. (Abraham Katsman, quoted in Corsi, 2008, p. 215)

Some critics, however, see President Obama's flexibility and willingness to code-switch in negative terms. Several negative advertisements criticize him for changing positions that help him win support. One specifically says that Obama shouldn't be called a flip-flopper because that term can only be used when a person actually holds one position at a time. Obama, according to one campaign message, holds two contrasting opinions on several key issues including banning handguns, public campaign financing, and withdrawing from Iraq (Kenski et al., 2010).

Other critics describe President Obama's communication as masterfully deceptive and largely drawing on people's emotions. According to Freddoso (2008), he demonstrates great skill in delivering speeches that have been carefully written, parsed, and tested to achieve maximum emotional impact. The reality—according to critics—is that Obama is all style and no substance. Rush (2009) writes:

> Obama possesses the rare gift of being able to speak with authority on issues about which he knows nothing. . . . He can propose measures that are frightening to the informed among us—such as imposing new, restrictive manufacturing standards on an auto industry in imminent danger of imploding—and do so conveying the absolute certainty that they are prudent, even brilliant acts. (p. 9)

Others see his communication as similar to "cotton candy:" "You might even enjoy watching him speak sometimes, but you know there's nothing to any of it" (Freddoso, 2008, p. 75).

The perceptions of President Obama's communication, not surprisingly, are as diverse as the public perceptions of him as a national leader. The trend of contrasting opinions is also seen within how the public regards the racial symbolism of his presidency.

PRESIDENT OBAMA AND A "POST-RACIAL" UNITED STATES

For many, Barack Obama's ascension to the pinnacle of political power in the U.S. vindicates Rev. Dr. Martin Luther King, Jr.'s vision of a color-blind democracy (Ifill, 2009). His campaign, from the start, drew on the idea that his candidacy transcends race. According to Joseph (2010), Obama

> Sought to appeal to white Americans by stressing commonalities over difference, unity over division, and the potential for racial rapprochement over racial war. Regardless of his efforts, however, from the beginning, race formed the underlying focus of the intense fascination and eventual scrutiny of Obama's candidacy. (p. 18)

Issues regarding race emerged throughout Barack Obama's campaign for the Democratic nomination and the U.S. presidency. These include the racially charged remarks by his former pastor, Rev. Jeremiah Wright (Hurst, 2010), and his highly touted "race speech" in response to the controversy (Isaksen, 2011). Racial issues also arose from comments from fellow Democrats—like President Bill Clinton, presidential candidate Joe Biden, and Senator Harry Reid—which were explicitly or implicitly racial (e.g., Hurst, 2010; Robinson, 2010).

During the presidential campaign, Barack Obama's comments regarding race drew praise, particularly for the sensitive ways in which he views "the race issue through the eyes of both black and white America" (Todd and Gawiser, 2009, p. 12). His ability to transcend race prompts descriptions such as "nonracial," "postracial," and even "supraracial"—terms that are frequently used, but seldom defined (Ifill, 2009). According to Todd and Gawiser (2009):

> Obama had treaded carefully on the race issue for much of the campaign, doing what he could to be "postracial." It's not as if he ran away from his ethnicity; it's that he didn't dwell on it. But he didn't have to; everyone else did in every profile of him written early in his political career. Of course, his unique background, being an African American with no U.S. black roots, meant many white voters viewed him through a different prism than they had other [black] presidential candidates. (p. 12)

Following his election, most Americans report that race relations are progressing in a positive direction. In fact, a 2009 New York Times/CBS News poll finds that President Obama's election alters public perceptions in positive ways, especially for African Americans (Stolberg and Connelly, 2009). For some, his election signifies the emergence of a "post-racial" society—a period in the U.S. when the public has moved beyond race. This is evidenced by voters who reportedly cast their ballots for a presidential candidate with little (if any) attention to race and how President Obama's race increasingly is a non-issue after the election. Comments following his first State of the Union address by MSNBC host, Chris Matthews, illustrate this new-found reality:

> He is post-racial, by all appearances. . . . I forgot he was black tonight for an hour. You know, he's gone a long way to become a leader of this country, and past so much history, in just a year or two. I mean, it's something we don't even think about. (quoted in Washington, 2010, p. A10)

While no longer noticing someone's race may translate to a "post-racial" society for some, scholars are quick to point out that that does not necessarily mean that we have not worked through all issues related to race.

According to Cho (2009), "post-racialism" assumes that significant racial progress has gotten us to the point where race is no longer a salient issue. Many critics insist that President Obama's election to the U.S. presidency—while historic—does not equate with an official end of racial prejudice, racial discrimination, or racism. For instance, Sugrue (2010) describes his presence as a "paradox of race:"

> Obama represents the paradox of race in early twenty-first century America: He embodies the fluidity and opportunity of racial identity in a time of transition. He also captures the ambiguities of a racial order that denies racism yet is rife with racial inequality; that celebrates progress when celebration is not always warranted. (p. 136)

Individuals, like Sugrue, critique those who make assertions of a "post-racial" society prematurely. Instead, they recognize the symbolic value of Barack Obama's election but point to the ways in which the election means little to the quality of life for everyday people. Still others point to how race emerges within public responses to a number of occurrences involving President Obama, like the Tea Party's racialized criticisms (Fram, 2010), and the public's response to his involvement (or lack thereof) in controversies involving African American citizens like Harvard Professor Henry Louis Gates (Guy, 2010) and federal employee Shirley Sherrod (Wickham, 2010). Following his election, race has seemingly taken a back seat to other more pressing issues like the economy, the war on terrorism, and environmental disasters. However, issues of race continue to exist on some level which makes for an interesting point of inquiry.

MY INTEREST(S) WITH THE TOPIC

My motivation for studying public perceptions of President Obama's communication style reflects an intersection of my scholarly, personal, and political interests. In order to provide readers with some background information on the project, each of these is briefly described here. My intention in sharing these motivations is to be transparent in how I—as a scholar, person, and political activist—am positioned in regards to the topic.

Scholarly Interests

In 1993, I earned my Ph.D. in interpersonal and intercultural communication from Ohio University. Since that time, my research and teaching have focused around the inextricable relationship between culture and communication. In other words, I am interested in exploring how culture impacts the ways in which we communicate and how all communication is best understood through a cultural lens. For over fifteen years, I have been actively engaged in teaching and research in the areas of interpersonal and intercultural communication. Specifically, I teach undergraduate and graduate classes in interpersonal communication, intercultural communication, interracial communication, gender and communication, as well as those focusing on communication theory and methods. My research interests overlap with the classes that I teach. In particular, my research focuses on culture and communication issues across a wide variety of contexts. These projects are in the areas of intergroup relations, biracial and multiracial families, mass media representations of diverse populations, interracial conflict, civil rights issues, diversity issues in the classroom, and first-generation college students.

The common thread running through all of my research accomplishments are explorations of culture and communication. Historically, I examined this connection by focusing on different cultural groups (e.g., African Americans, multiracial persons, LGBT persons, persons with disabilities) in different contexts (e.g., college campus, family, corporate America, local community, mass media). Over time, however, I have come to realize the inherent value of studying multiple cultural group experiences within a single context. Currently, my scholarly interests are in exploring the diverse ways in which public perceptions are guided by cultural similarities and differences. This emerging point of analysis, coupled with my existing scholarly accomplishments, provides a solid foundation for exploring public perceptions of Barack Obama's communication competence in general, and his rhetoric regarding race matters in particular. My primary motivation for this project, then, is to use it as a means to contribute to existing literature and my ability to provide powerful examples to students in my undergraduate and graduate classes.

Personal Interests

I believe that people typically research subject areas that are steeped in some personal, cultural, organizational, or social experience. This is definitely the case for my research agenda as a communication scholar, and this particular project on public perceptions of Barack Obama's communication. In fact, all of the topics outlined in the previous paragraph reflect areas of research that have personal salience in my life.

The connections between the topic of this book and my scholarly interests, given what I've shared earlier, should be apparent. In a similar vein, I want to acknowledge the personal interest that motivates my focus on President Obama, something that is grounded in the unique cultural perspective that comes from being a biracial or multiracial person. Like millions of other U.S. Americans, I am a person who embraces a biracial and multiethnic identity. My lived experiences are certainly not identical with those of Barack Obama. However, the similarities across several aspects of identity piqued my interest in President Obama on a personal level.

Like President Obama, my life journey has traveled along a path where racial and cultural identity is a constant point of negotiation. I was born in the mid-1960s (a couple years after Obama) and raised in a diverse low-income housing project located in a northeastern U.S. city. My father's father came to the United States from the Philippines in the early 1900s; the Spanish lineage is clear given our family names (Orbe, Ortega). Some of my mother's ancestors reportedly came over on the Mayflower. Like many Whites, she traces her European heritage to different cultures (Swiss, French, English). Being part of a multiracial family was not necessarily the norm; however it seemed to be less of an issue given that my neighborhood was predominantly African American and Puerto Rican. In very real ways, in-group and out-group differences were steeped more in class differences than racial or ethnic ones. My educational experiences, both in high school and through three different college degrees, expanded my cultural perspective in ways that parallel that which President Obama experienced. Currently, my wife (who comes from a multiracial lineage—African, European, and Native American—but has always identified as a black woman) and I are proud parents of three teenagers who continue to negotiate their multiple racial and ethnic identities in realities that are constantly changing. I believe that President Obama's election as the first U.S. president of African descent significantly impacts those realities and opens up a whole new world of possibilities for them and other multiracial children like them.

Political Interests

Although I had read about and watched some clips of Barack Obama's speech at the Democratic National Convention on July 27, 2004, my first real introduction to him came via *The Oprah Winfrey Show* on October 19, 2006. I watched this show with my wife, as Winfrey articulated her support for his yet-to-be-determined presidential campaign. After hearing him talk about a variety of topics, including his relationship with his wife and daughters, I distinctly remember turning to my wife and saying, "If he runs for president, I will take some time off of work in order to volunteer for his campaign." My wife's immediate response was a question, "Time off from work and volunteer without pay?" Unfortunately, I was not in a financial position to volunteer full time. Yet, my work with Obama's Campaign for Change organization was more involved than for any other past candidate.

Over the course of about a year, I spent hundreds of hours volunteering with different aspects of Obama's election efforts in three different Midwestern states (Michigan, Ohio, and Indiana). This included traditional activities that I had done before for other Democratic candidates: voter registration, phone banks, and door-to-door canvassing. This time, however, my involvement with the Obama campaign also included more intensive activities like donating significant amounts of money to the cause, coordinating voter registration drives, training volunteers, working behind the scenes at rallies and town hall meetings, and using online campaign features to raise thousands of dollars from family, friends, and colleagues. Like many of the millions of other volunteers, my experiences working on the campaign are some of the most memorable and moving that I have ever had. In many ways, they help to renew some of the optimism that had vanished from my political perspectives.

While I feel it important to be transparent regarding my personal and political interests in studying public perceptions of President Obama, my objective in conducting this research project is not directly related to his multiracial heritage or how the findings can be used to enhance the likelihood of his re-election in 2012. Instead, my primary motivation for engaging in this line of research is to facilitate an in-depth understanding of the diverse perspectives that exist in regards to Barack Obama's election and presidency. Working in different capacities for the Obama campaign gave me the opportunity to interact with hundreds of supporters. However, these experiences also put me face-to-face with countless individuals whose opposition to Barack Obama's candidacy (presidency) was (is) just as passionate as that which I encountered from supporters. I find the media representations of the drastically diverse perceptions of President Obama to be largely uni-dimensional, producing mass generalizations based on demographic markers such as political affiliation, race, gender, spirituality, age, and geographical region. Using his communication style (a fairly less taboo topic than focusing on politics or race) as a point of entry, I embark on this research project to come to a better understanding—for myself—of the hows and whys regarding diverse public perceptions of Barack Obama explicitly and issues regarding politics, race, and difference more implicitly. My hope is that the thematic insights in this book also help readers deepen their understanding as well.

KEY ACKNOWLEDGMENTS

A project of this magnitude can never be possible without the support, assistance, and encouragement of many people. First, and foremost, I would like to thank Western Michigan University (WMU), the School of Communication and College of Arts and Sciences for their support for my sabbatical leave (Fall 2010). The opportunity to focus my efforts on data collection and transcription during this time was invaluable for a timely completion of this book. Second, my gratitude to the WMU Office of the Vice President for Research who supported the research project through a 2010–2011 Faculty Research and Creative Activities Award (FRACAA). This internal grant provided key financial backing for the travel, lodging, and other expenses associated with data collection, analysis, and ultimate production of this book. I also appreciate the WMU Human Subjects Institutional Review Board's timely support of the project. Finally, many thanks to Siobhan Keenan in the WMU School of Communication who served as the account manager for FRACAA grant and Victoria Orbe who helped proofread, edit, and check references.

From a purely logistical perspective, the research in this book would not have been possible without all of the extraordinary efforts of site coordinators across the United States. As explained in chapter 2, these individuals were instrumental in recruiting potential participants, organizing focus group sessions, and working to ensure that everything went as smoothly as possible. I'm especially grateful for individuals who went above and beyond the "call of duty" to make sure that I was able to engage people from all different walks of life. So, a big heart-felt thank you to: Jake Arndt, Paula Orbe, Laurie Longo, Dawn Orbe, Jamel Santa Cruz Bell, Angela Cooke-Jackson, Tony Johnson, Katrina Bell-Jordan, Tony Adams, Wilfredo Alvarez, Etsuko Kinefuchi, Michele Matthews, Michaela Meyer, Ken Burks, Karen Deardorff, Jordan Soliz, Kiesha Warren-Gordon, Damon Scott, Sakile Camara, Sonja Brown-Givens, and R. Rennae Elliott.

Sincere gratitude goes to Rebecca J. McCary, editorial acquisitions, communication and education, at Lexington Books. From our very first email correspondence, she embraced the spirit of the book project and worked diligently to ensure its success. Thank you, Becca, for making the publication of this book so smooth, timely, and enjoyable!

On a more personal level, this book project was made possible through a tremendous amount of love, encouragement, support, and understanding from my wife, Natalie Jones Orbe, and children, Gabrielle, Isaiah, and Victoria. Extensive travel and extended blocks of writing time away from home meant sacrificing key "family time." The few times that I felt guilty about my absence were overwhelmed by all of the support that you all showed for me personally and the project as an extension of my professional life. Finally, I want to give a big "shout-out" to all of my extended family members, friends, colleagues, and other supporters who encouraged me at every step of the project. The fact that many of you used email, text messages, phone calls, and Facebook messages to check in with me and ask about the progress of the book was key in motivating me toward timely completion. I appreciate you all!

OVERVIEW

This book is organized into twelve different chapters. This first chapter introduces the reader to the origins of the research project that serves as the foundation for the book. The remainder of the chapters is separated into three sections. The first section, "Barack Obama as Communicator," focuses on public perceptions of his communication style with a specific emphasis on how (if at all) perceptions have changed over time. Particular attention is paid to how participants from diverse backgrounds regard what is commonly perceived as President Obama's "masterful communication style." This section also includes a specific chapter on exploring how public perceptions are influenced by existing standards of what is considered "presidential communication."

The next section explores contemporary "race matters"—a phrase that refers both to how race *matters* in the United States, and various matters related to what is commonly understood as *race* in the United States (West, 1993). Within this section, I describe the various ways in which study participants perceive the role of race in public perceptions of President Obama. While most participants believe that race is becoming less and less important over time, thematic insights within this section help the reader to critically understand how different perceptions are influenced by a person's age, race or ethnicity, and/or geographical origin. This section also explores public perceptions of

African Americans and Caucasian Americans and uses the infamous "Beer Summit" as a case study to demonstrate how participants evaluate President Obama's communication competency when engaging race-related issues.

The final section of the book focuses on the role that the media plays in public perceptions of President Obama generally, and his communication more specifically. News media, entertainment programming, and social media are all examined as important factors in understanding the diversity of public perceptions. Within this section, I also explore the common perception—especially among younger participants—of President Obama as the first "celebrity president" and how this affects evaluations of his communication with the public.

For each of the chapters in this book, I make the conscious decision to present dominant themes of participant responses in ways that are explicitly descriptive (as opposed to evaluative). This approach is consistent with the qualitative research design of the project (described in detail in the next chapter), which is grounded in an interpretive framework. As you will see, each chapter draws heavily from participant voices to represent each key idea—with little commentary except that which was necessary to create a smooth flow for readers. In this regard, I attempt to serve as a conduit for the hundreds of individuals across the United States who took time out to contribute their insight to the project. While largely descriptive in nature, the final chapter of the book contextualizes the book's larger themes within contemporary research and mainstream writings. The concluding chapter also outlines ways in which this line of research can be used to generate future research studies, impact practical decisions regarding political communication, and improve intergroup relations steeped in assumed difference.

Chapter 2

Descriptions of the Study

This chapter describes the nuts and bolts of the national study of public perceptions of President Barack Obama's communication that I conducted from June through December in 2010. The study was qualitative in nature, meaning that it sought to gather perceptions of diverse individuals in an open, unrestricted manner. Unlike many of the existing books on President Obama, the study wasn't interested in collecting and reporting statistical data from public polls (e.g., Kenski et al., 2010), conducting rhetorical analyses of various speeches, rhetoric, or mass media texts (e.g., Wolfgang, 2009), or providing political commentary analyzing the strategies, criticisms, and effects of President Obama's election (e.g., Hendricks and Denton, 2010; Mattera, 2010). Instead, I focused on creating opportunities for participants from diverse backgrounds to articulate their ideas in ways in which they were most comfortable. Before reading the different thematic insights from this study, it is important to first understand the methodological framework. This helps to contextualize the findings for the reader.

The core of this chapter concentrates on providing key information regarding different aspects of the study. First, I describe the process through which participants were recruited. Second, I explain the instrumental role that site coordinators played in the participant recruitment process. Third, I summarize the demographic data (in terms of age, gender, race and ethnicity, education, socioeconomic status, and political affiliation) for participants as reported through their written responses. Fourth, I explain how forty-two focus groups were used to gather public perceptions of President Obama from 333 participants. The fifth and sixth sections outline the process through which focus group audiotapes were transcribed and analyzed to produce the thematic findings described in subsequent chapters.

Chapter 2

PARTICIPANT RECRUITMENT

For the study, I sought participants in order to fulfill one specific objective: gain insight into diverse perspectives of Barack Obama's communication. In order to meet this objective, I worked to secure a sample that was convenient, but also strategically purposeful (Hunt, 1970). The sample of participants was convenient in that I drew from my personal, social, and professional networks to recruit potential participants. Like many college professors who conduct research, undergraduate students were a potential group that was readily accessible, available, and willing to participate. However, the sample was also strategically purposeful in that I consciously incorporated efforts that would attract a diverse set of individuals to the project. As such, participant recruitment targeted individuals with no college experience and other characteristics that are not represented in most traditionally aged college students (e.g., older participants, Republicans, and those from a lower socioeconomic status).

Participant demographics, in terms of age, gender, race and ethnicity, education, socioeconomic status, and political affiliation, were collected via an open-ended questionnaire prior to each focus group. This information was gathered as a systematic means to determine which perspectives were (un)represented in the data set. Initially, the study was designed to include one hundred to one hundred twenty-five participants in twenty to twenty-five different focus groups. However, as the data collection process unfolded it became clear that some groups (i.e., Democrats, women, twenty-year-olds, and college-educated persons) remained over-represented in the focus groups and other groups (i.e., Republicans, men, older individuals, and non-college-educated persons) were not being reached in equal proportions through established recruitment processes.

In order to accommodate a greater diversity of individuals—and simultaneously not exclude interested persons who wanted to be involved—333 individuals were successfully recruited to participate in the study. Ultimately, this large number of participants was necessary in order to generate a data set where both diversity of experience and saturation of data would be achieved. Within qualitative research projects, saturation occurs when researchers get to the point where repetition of information is seen within each new focus group (Wertz, 2005). In this study, the number of participants in the study extended significantly beyond my initial plans. This was necessary to ensure that saturation was reached with all of the different cultural groups. For example, saturation was reached with my traditionally college-aged participants and those identifying as Democrats fairly early in the data collection process. Consequently, I made conscious attempts to work with site coordinators to recruit older or non-Democratic participants. While these efforts were successful, it also meant that the numbers for all groups continued to increase, simply because the site coordinators and I did not want to exclude anyone who wanted to participate in the study. So, in the end, the number of participants from certain groups is larger than their U.S. population representation. However, the goal of saturation for each cultural group was accomplished. Having site coordinators throughout the United States was crucial in implementing an effective participant recruitment process, both in terms of sheer numbers and diversity.

SITE COORDINATORS

One of the requirements designated by my university's Human Subject Institutional Review Board (HSIRB) was that each data collection site had to have a site coordinator. These individuals had the responsibility of closely following the established procedures to recruit and organize potential participants into different focus group sessions in their respective areas. In addition, each site coordinator provided logistical support for my visit in terms of the project (e.g., obtaining approval from their respective schools or organizations, securing a space conducive for focus groups, arranging refreshments). Many also went above and beyond the "normal call of duty" to ensure that my visit was as productive and enjoyable as possible—opening their homes to me, arranging for ground transportation, providing home-cooked meals, and showing me around their local communities.

In order to identify potential site coordinators, I used my personal, familial, social, and professional networks to locate people living in various U.S. geographical locales that could provide a diverse pool of potential participants. In just about every case all it took was a simple email to have people agree to serve in this role. Subsequent emails and telephone conservations served as instrumental in maximizing the time that I spent at each data collection site. In the end, twenty-one individuals served as site coordinators for the project. Many were professional colleagues (both university faculty and administrators) who recruited students from their campuses as well as local community members. Others were family members and long-time friends who used their non-academic connections to help ensure that the participant pool had individuals with various socioeconomic backgrounds and educational levels.

In reflection, the site coordinators for the project were crucial to the study's ultimate success. Without any financial compensation, they were diligent in helping me reach a large, diverse group of participants from all walks of life. These amazingly generous individuals served as my liaisons to segments of communities that would have remained inaccessible without them. From the start of my project, I recognized that it would be relatively easy to secure current college students as potential participants. Yet, the site coordinators ensured that I was able to speak with college students from a great variety of campuses across the United States, including community colleges, small private liberal arts colleges, large state public universities, as well as institutions of higher learning whose mission is tied to serving African American and Hispanic/Latino students.

More importantly, site coordinators also used their connections in local communities to recruit participants whose life experiences did not necessarily include the college experience. In this regard, the study included people who could bring amazingly diverse perspectives to the study. In many cases, community focus groups discussions were held with participants who shared a key aspect of identity, like age, race and ethnicity, socioeconomic status, or regional location. The result was a unique opportunity to observe and learn from discussions that are often only heard by in-group members. For instance, site coordinators were invaluable in helping me facilitate focus groups with people from a poor or working class and non-college educated background (Connecticut), white senior citizens (North Carolina), African American military families (Virginia), rural non-college educated volunteer fire fighters (Ohio), African American men (California), Latino/as at a Hispanic Serving Institution of Higher Learning (Illinois), older community and business leaders (North Carolina), Libertarian and Tea Party members (Nebraska), and Seventh Day Adventists (Alabama). Without question, this study benefited greatly from the substantial amount of diversity in its participant pool. As described in the next section, participants vary in terms of multiple aspects of identity—all of which worked to create a study that highlights the diversity that is inherent in how the public perceives Barack Obama.

PARTICIPANT DEMOGRAPHICS

As summarized in appendix A, this study features a diverse participant pool. Based on the self-report data collected, the participants were individuals from diverse experiences based on a variety of demographic markers. A couple of the categories are relatively straightforward and do not require any explanation. For instance, in terms of gender, the pool of participants was approximately 58 percent female and 42 percent male. Age also is easily represented with little need for clarification: 57 percent of participants were 18 to 30, 30 percent were 31 to 50 years of age, and 13 percent were 51 and over. The level of education of participants was skewed toward individuals with some college experience; however, some significant representation across this category was achieved:

- Some high school: 1 percent
- High school graduate/GED: 15 percent
- Some college classes (including trade schools): 65 percent
- Bachelor's degree: 10 percent
- Graduate degree: 9 percent

Racial and ethnic information was also gathered from participants. This information was important given that the study is interested in exploring public perceptions of Barack Obama's communication—especially given the idea that he represents, to some, a "post-racial" leader. Existing research has determined that racial and ethnic identity influences one's perception of the world (Orbe and Camara, 2010). However, collecting this information is difficult given that race and ethnicity are socio-political constructions that have no scientific basis (Orbe and Harris, 2008). Because of this, I chose to give participants total freedom in describing themselves (as opposed to providing pre-determined boxes which they could check off). Based on the self-report data, the racial or ethnic composition of the sample can be summarized as follows:

- African American/black: 27 percent
- Asian American/Pacific Islander: 3 percent
- Caucasian/white: 50 percent
- Latino/Hispanic: 11 percent
- Middle Eastern American: 3 percent
- Native American: 1 percent
- Biracial/Multiracial: 4 percent

While these numbers appear fairly straightforward, some clarification is warranted. First, a number of individuals who self-described themselves as "black" also included more specific labels such as "Haitian," "Dominican," and "West Indian." Similar designations were found for Latinos (e.g., "Mexican American" or "Puerto Rican") and Middle Easterners (e.g., "Persian" or "Syrian"). For reporting these statistics, these particular labels were included in the larger group. However, within subsequent chapters they are used—whenever possible—to identify different quotes from these individuals. Second, in several cases, the information that participants provided on the demographic questionnaire did not match with how they described themselves within the focus group discussion. I first noticed this with a man from New England who listed his race or ethnicity as "black, white, Native American (Human Being)." During the focus group, he made several comments which referenced his identity "as a black man." A similar dynamic was seen in other focus groups where biracial and multiracial participants, as well as Middle Eastern Americans verbalized racial and ethnic identities that did not coincide with what they provided on written documents. So, for clarification purposes, the statistical summary provided here is based on categorizing information based on what was submitted in writing. Whenever possible, more specific racial and ethnic labels are used to identify participant comments.

Without question, participants had the most difficulty in filling out the question about their "Class Background/Socioeconomic Status." A significant number asked me questions about how they should describe themselves. Several college students, for instance, asked what they should put if they were raised in the upper or middle class but were now "dirt poor college students." Many participants appeared to be drawn to describing themselves as "middle class" (despite how much money they were earning). However, in one particular group that was comprised of people from lower socioeconomic backgrounds, an impromptu discussion about class issues erupted as people were completing the demographic questionnaire. In this exchange, one middle-aged white woman chastised one of the participants who had asked if he should list himself as "middle class." "Don't kid yourself, there is no such thing as middle class—you are either rich or poor in this country!" I raise this issue, and share these particular comments, to caution readers who might read these demographic statistics without a critical eye. Based on the information provided by participants:

- 31 percent were lower, lower-middle, or working class
- 50 percent were middle class
- 14 percent were upper-middle or upper class

Political affiliation was another aspect of demographic data that was openly discussed within different focus groups. Many participants—especially those in their twenties—expressed significant difficulty identifying with only one particular political party. One participant in Michigan captured the essence of this sentiment when he said, "I kinda feel like specific political affiliations are ending with our generation. We are all about right is right and wrong is wrong, regardless of political party." Consequently, close to 40 percent of all participants described themselves as Independent (16 percent), Unaffiliated (16 percent), or declined to provide any political affiliation (7 percent). For many, the resistance to adjoin themselves with a specific political party goes along with a primary political principle: "I vote for the specific person who is going to do what is best for the country, I don't care which party they are part of" (young white female participant from California).

Interestingly, some participants suggested that the hesitancy to identify with a political party may not reflect rejection of a specific ideology. Instead, it may be indicative of a desire to avoid whatever social stigmas are associated with different political labels. One young Caucasian male participant in southern Virginia, for example, says:

> For me, filling out the form about political affiliation was hard because I don't really identify with one or the other. The same is true for other people I know. So, when I talk to other people about the issues, they are typically in line with one ideology—although they resist identifying with one ideology or the other. They want to resist the label, but still have consistent ideas about politics.

Based on this possibility, it may be that a number of those who failed to list a particular political party actually do actively support the ideals of one specific party. This appears to be the case given some of the participant comments within different focus groups. Still, a majority of individuals reported having one political affiliation. Of those participants, 39 percent described themselves as Democrats, 16 percent Republican, 5 percent Libertarian or Tea Party members, and 1 percent Green Party members. In the end, it appears that I was able to accomplish my goal of including a diversity of political affiliations within the participant pool—including those that explicitly and implicitly identified with various political parties.

The demographic statistics are provided here to demonstrate the diversity of the participant pool. As illustrated through the discussion of race and ethnicity, socioeconomic status, and political affiliation, readers should recognize that this information was self-reported and, in many cases, reflects the perception of the particular individual. These perceptions may or may not match up with how the readers define certain concepts such as "middle class," "Republican," and "Biracial." In this regard, the demographic information provided here should be used only for general information purposes.

PROCESS OF DISCOVERY: FOCUS GROUPS

By definition, focus groups have two core elements: (1) a skilled facilitator who uses prepared questions, and (2) the explicit goal of gathering perceptions about a selected topic (Vaughn, Schumm, and Sinagub, 1996). Focus groups are used as a research tool by both researchers and professionals in a variety of fields including academic, market research, and political settings (Puchta and Potter, 2004). Depending on the particular project, they can be used to achieve a variety of objectives (Krueger and Casey, 2000). For this project, they were instrumental in exploring a general topical area that promised to generate diverse responses.

According to Morgan (1997), researchers use focus groups as an efficient means to gather data in relatively structured or unstructured formats. From a qualitative research perspective, the purpose of focus groups is to collect data where participants can consider their own views in the context of the views of others (Patton, 2002). Using focus groups provides researchers the opportunity to gain insight from the unrestrained vantage point of participants (Durgee, 1987)—especially when facilitators use a general conversational approach whereby participants can describe their experiences with only a general focus toward the phenomenon under study (Wertz, 2005). This particular use of focus groups to collect data is best characterized as flexible, probing, and synergistic, the results of which are not possible through individual interviews (Staley, 1990).

I used focus group discussions in this research project for a number of reasons. First, focus groups represent a time-efficient means to draw on several persons' perceptions at once. Embarking on a research project with hundreds of participants across the United States requires a significant time and travel commitment. I sought out opportunities to gather in-depth information from participants; conducting one-on-one interviews with over three hundred individuals is not feasible given existing time and travel constraints. Second, I have extensive experience with focus group research, which I was able to draw from as I engaged in a research project that addresses controversial issues such as politics and race. Multiple research projects on a variety of topics, over the past twenty-plus years, generated much insight that proved invaluable for facilitating discussions where all individuals—including those with minority opinions—could participate in meaningful ways. Third, and finally, focus groups can generate insights not possible through other forms of data collection. When focus groups are conducted by experienced facilitators discussions are engaging, lively, and synergistically insightful. For example, focus group discussions can provide the researcher with immediate, multidimensional feedback on a participant's comments, as well as descriptions that dig deeper than what is possible through other methods of data collection (Orbe, 2000).

A total of forty-two focus groups were facilitated for this study. Through the various site coordinators, groups strategically were held across various U.S. geographical regions. According to national designations (Overberg, 2010), the United States can be divided up into nine different U.S. regions. Focus groups were held in twelve different states in six of these geographical areas:

- Michigan, Illinois, Ohio, and Indiana (East North Central)
- Connecticut, Massachusetts, and Rhode Island (New England)
- Virginia and North Carolina (South Atlantic)

- Nebraska (West North Central)
- California (Pacific)
- Alabama (East South Central)

Conscious attempts were made to recruit approximately fifty participants per region. While this was largely achieved for four of the six regions (New England, South Atlantic, Pacific, and East South Central), the availability of site coordinators and magnitude of participant recruitment in two regions (East North Central and West North Central) made this target unobtainable. For similar reasons, three U.S. geographical regions—Middle Atlantic, Mountain, and West South Central—were not represented in the study.

Following existing guidelines (e.g., Patton, 2002), I facilitated each focus group discussion using a general conversational approach with open-ended questions designed to elicit fairly straightforward descriptions. This included a conscious effort to create and maintain a sense of informality where participants felt comfortable sharing their perceptions (Puchta and Potter, 2004). My goal for each focus group was to engage participants in ways that appeared natural and spontaneous—not awkward, forced, or premeditated—so that they would become less and less concerned with the fact that the discussion was being recorded for research purposes.

Each focus group began with general questions regarding participant perceptions of Barack Obama as a communicator. Three introductory questions were used in each focus group: Can you describe the first time that you were introduced to Barack Obama? What were your first impressions of his communication? Have your perceptions of him changed over time? These initial questions were useful in getting participants to start talking. While each focus group covered the majority of questions included in the Topical Protocol (see appendix B), they were incorporated into each group in ways that were cohesive with the flow of discussion. Since the goal was to gather descriptions through an open, unrestricted manner, I avoided any attempts to guide participants to pre-determined topical areas. Instead, I focused on following the conversational flow of the group, incorporating questions from the Topical Protocol when they were raised by participants. In order to gather significant depth into the issues at hand, I also was quick to use different follow-up questions ("Can you give a specific example?" "Can you explain what you meant when you said . . . ?" or "What else should I know about that"). This approach, as Patton (2002) argues, ensures that focus group discussions are productive while at the same time allowing participants flexibility in determining the issues that they consider most relevant. At the same time, this approach prevents researchers from probing participants to delve into topics that they do not want to talk about or think are unimportant (Anderson and Jack, 1991).

DATA TRANSCRIPTION

Many researchers who use in-depth interviews or focus groups to collect qualitative data utilize professional services or undergraduate and graduate students to transcribe them. However, since my dissertation, I have always transcribed qualitative data myself. While extremely time-consuming (and tedious!), I have found that this process is extremely important in providing the researcher a chance to get closer to the data and guarantees that the richness of participant narratives is not lost in the transcription process. Having said that, however, given the sheer number in the study, I had secured grant money to hire a graduate student to transcribe the focus group discussions. My plan was to have each focus group transcribed by the graduate student and then give it a close review as I listened to each audiotape. This process would provide me the opportunity to ensure that the transcript accurately reflected the focus group.

While this was the plan, the graduate student was not available to begin working with the project data until August, approximately five or six weeks after the first group was facilitated. I thought that it was important to transcribe these initial focus groups and evaluate the process before doing the next round of groups. Consequently, I transcribed the first four groups and quickly came to the conclusion that I needed to complete all of the transcription myself. In addition to losing much of the meaning of participants' comments, I also realized that trying to document a conversation with several different people engaging in a discussion with multiple interruptions, side comments, and people talking over one another would be impossible for someone who was not present in the original discussion. So, in the end, I personally transcribed all forty-two focus group discussions.

In order to maximize the accuracy and quality of each transcript, I was committed to transcribing each audiotape within seventy-two hours after the focus group was completed. In most cases, I scheduled time the very next day—many times in my hotel room or a room on the campus that I was visiting—so that the conversations were fresh in my mind. I found this practice extremely helpful in accurately capturing the essence of each focus group. For instance, while listening to the tape and transcribing the discussion, I was able to maintain a mental picture of each person who spoke including who they were, where they were sitting, what they were wearing, and the nonverbal cues that they used while speaking. I transcribed each focus group discussion verbatim, carefully documenting participant responses to different questions and the exchanges that emerged among each group. Participant comments were also designated with generic descriptors (e.g., "YBM" was used to indicate when a young black male was speaking) whenever possible. Transcripts also include notations that indicated meaning that was communicated nonverbally. For instance, I included descriptions of times when participants raised or lowered their voices, laughed to themselves, pounded the table while speaking, used dramatic pauses, or spoke in sarcastic tones. This proved to be extremely helpful in creating a document that captured the essence of each focus group discussion.

After all of the focus groups were transcribed, the data set was 385 single-spaced pages. The shortest focus group was six pages; the longest was fifteen pages (average length was just over nine pages). As required by HSIRB guidelines, focus group audiotapes were destroyed once they were transcribed. The next section documents the process by which this large qualitative data set was analyzed.

DATA ANALYSIS

Quantitative research studies collect numerical data that result in data analysis that is fairly straightforward and clean. In comparison, data analysis in qualitative studies is oftentimes characterized as non-linear, discovery-oriented, and messy (van Manen, 1990). The final section of this chapter outlines the process through which I analyzed hundreds of pages of focus group transcripts.

In order to gain insight into the communicative lived experiences of a diverse set of individuals, the data was analyzed through established qualitative methods. Specifically, I drew from guidelines (McCracken, 1988) that have proven valuable in thematic analyses of various qualitative data sets (e.g., Urban and Orbe, 2010). Following the five steps outlined by McCracken (1988), I read through all of the focus group transcripts and sorted out data into separate electronic files for each general sub-topic (as designated by the focal areas of chapters 3–11).This process resulted in data subsets that ranged from 7–14 pages of single-spaced excerpts from participants.

Second, I reviewed each data sub-set individually until preliminary themes began to emerge. For instance, in chapter 9 on the Gates/Crowley conflict and presidential "Beer Summit," participant comments were grouped in terms of their initial reactions to President Obama's comments, perceptions of race, influence of the media, the "Beer Summit" itself, and the prominent role that beer served in the meeting. As these thematic insights began to reveal themselves to me, I took special note to address logical relationships and contradictions within and across individual experiences.

The third and fourth stages of thematization were facilitated simultaneously. This involved engaging in a re-reading of transcripts to confirm or disconfirm emerging themes (Stage Three) and a continuous re-evaluation of how emerging themes continued to take form in context to one another (Stage Four). Pragmatically, this process included combining related themes into more broad categories and separating out specific themes whose meaningfulness was lost within larger thematic organization.

According to the guidelines outlined by McCracken (1988), the fifth stage of qualitative analysis features a synthesis of themes. Within this final stage of thematization, the goal is to understand the interrelationship of themes with specific attention to how they collectively work to capture the essence of the data. Given the study's specific objectives, this synthesis of themes highlights the ways in which public perceptions of President Obama are similar and different within and between different social groups based on age, race and ethnicity, political affiliation, and geographical location.

Throughout the thematic analysis process, I used Owen's (1984) three criteria of repetition, recurrence, and forcefulness to help focus on each of McCracken's (1988) five stages of analysis. These criteria helped me to identify those ideas, concepts, perspectives, and thematic insights that are especially relevant to the project. Some definitions from Owen's work might be helpful here. The *repetition* criterion refers to the repeating of key words and phrases, and words that are "special" or significant in describing a certain experience or feeling. In several instances, for example, I noted how specific words and phrases appeared consistently in focus groups regardless of age, race and ethnicity, gender, education level, political affiliation or geographical region. The *recurrence* criterion examines the meanings that were threaded throughout the transcript data, even when participants used different descriptors to represent the same meaning. This allowed me to understand how the same message might have been articulated differently by different participants. Given the cultural variation in communication that was apparent, this criterion was helpful to determine connections that qualitative data analysis software would fail to acknowledge. Finally, the *forcefulness* criterion allowed me to understand the importance or uniqueness of certain words or phrases. Forcefulness is traditionally displayed through the use of vocal inflection, volume, or emphasis through other forms of nonverbal communication. Within this analysis, examples of forcefulness were noted during the focus group discussion and incorporated into each transcript. For instance, transcripts included different codes (e.g., ALL CAPS), punctuation ! or ? or format (**bold** or *italics*) to reflect the ways in which participants used different vocal cues to emphasize certain words and phrases in particular ways. The transcripts also were written to include other notations that communicate key meaning. These included comments in parentheses or brackets that helped frame a participant's comments (e.g., [said sarcastically], [dramatic pause], [said as participant pounds his fist on the table], [laughs to herself], [lowers voice]).

SUMMARY

In summary, this chapter provides all of the pertinent information regarding the specifics of the study that generated the qualitative data that guides the thematic insights of this book. This chapter is important because it provides the reader with a detailed account of the research methods that served as a launching point for data collection and analysis. As such, readers can come to understand the information in subsequent chapters within a larger contextual frame that includes the role that site coordinators played in the process of participant recruitment, how data was collected via focus group discussions, transcribed, and analyzed through established qualitative thematic processes. Within this chapter, I also provide descriptions of the diversity within the participant pool, in terms of self-reported demographic data.

All of the content shared in chapter 2 should be kept in mind as readers move into topical chapters that come next. While the book features sections on "Race Matters in a 'Post-Racial' Society" and "The Media Machine," the next section focuses on public perceptions of "Barack Obama as Communicator." I begin this section by exploring how participants describes their initial perceptions of Barack Obama's communication.

Part II

Barack Obama as Communicator

Chapter 3

Perceptions of Barack Obama's Communication Style

"He is like a chess master in a world of checker players."

—Thirty-something-year-old African American man, Oakland, California

This opening quote captures the general sentiment of the U.S. public in terms of their perceptions of Barack Obama's communication skills. For the most part, supporters and non-supporters alike describe Barack Obama, the communicator, in overwhelmingly glowing terms. Across focus groups, participants from diverse backgrounds and political affiliations name a wide variety of positive communication characteristics in their descriptions: "confident, articulate, inspiring," "charismatic, well-spoken, and a natural communicator," "down to earth," "eloquent," "very intelligent, articulate, and well-informed," and "masterful in his use of language." Younger participants are more likely to add that he is "very handsome," a "strong, silent type," with "rock-star capabilities!" In comparison, older participants evaluate his communication in the context of other presidents who they regard as especially strong communicators. The most frequent comparison is with John F. Kennedy: "I think that he is one of the best speakers that we've had as a president, in all honesty, since Kennedy. . . . He's definitely one of the best that I've ever heard" (European American male from Michigan) and "I first compared him to John Kennedy; he also mobilized the young—my generation when I was young" (African American male from Massachusetts). Other participants invoke comparisons with other presidents, like one European American man from Ohio who says, "I saw him as a combination of Bill Clinton and Ronald Reagan. . . . He could connect to people like Clinton and was a great public speaker like Reagan." Several participants also portray him as the "anti-Bush" in terms of communication style.

This chapter focuses on explaining the ways in which individuals from across the United States perceive the communication style of Barack Obama. While much has been written about his communication prowess (e.g., Leanne, 2009; Wolfgang, 2009), I highlight particular points of insight that were raised by focus group participants. As such, what is included here has greater depth than that which is available through existing analyses of speeches, extensive poll data, or other political commentaries. As you will see, the power of everyday people describing different perspectives in their own words is invaluable in understanding this topic. I begin this explanation by highlighting the most common characteristics used to portray Barack Obama's communication.

CHARACTERISTICS OF A MASTERFUL COMMUNICATOR

"A Breath of Fresh Air"

For many participants one of the most compelling aspects of Barack Obama's communication is that it represents something different from the typical politician. He is seen, in this regard, as someone who the general public can trust. One fifty-something-year-old black woman from Rhode Island states it like this:

> You needed to see someone who came across in a trusting way. So many people came across as murky and dirty in the political world. And we had just come out of all that Bush mess. Obama was so clean, and fresh, and sooooooo genuine as a person. We really felt like we could trust him.

Another African American woman—a forty-two-year old nurse from Virginia—also comments on his integrity and positivity: "In my opinion, he had a very high level of integrity. He didn't want to bash people, he didn't want to say anything bad about people. He always wanted to be 'Mr. Positivity, Mr. Love, and Mr. Let's-Work-Together.'" Across different focus groups, participants portray President Obama as "full of positive energy" (twenty-something Latina from Massachusetts) and someone who strives to "stay above all of the negativity" (thirty-something-year-old white woman from Alabama).

Several participants also see President Obama's use of humor as a welcome aspect of his communication. According to one young white male from Connecticut who is currently working toward completing his high school diploma,

> He always seems to add humor when he is speaking, maybe not when he is addressing the nation, but on a smaller scale, he does. He feels more comfortable

just being himself. I saw him speak at a high school graduation (on TV), and he had lots of ad-libs. They were really good. He is quick on his feet. I think that he is witty.

President Obama's ability to "ad-lib" is also a topic commented on by other participants who by and large perceive most presidential communication as formal, stiff, and dry. Obama's willingness to go off script is something that many people appreciate. A forty-year-old white woman from Connecticut (in a different focus group than the eighteen-year-old male) describes her appreciation when she shares:

I had a conversation the other day with someone about [President Obama's] visit to Connecticut last week. And we were talking about his support for [U.S. Senator Richard] Blumenthal. . . . He was speaking and kinda made a joke about the fact Linda McMahon does have more money than Blumenthal. It's not that "she might, she definitely does." And I just think that—maybe it is scripted, but I don't think so . . . I just think that those off-the-cuff remarks are good. Everything seems so well-written, so moments when he makes off-the-cuff comments like that make him seem like a real person again—instead of a politician who is saying what he thinks you want to hear.

Motivational and Inspiring

The two words used to illustrate President Obama's communication that appear most frequently across all of the focus group transcripts are "motivational" and "inspiring." Most often, participants recall how they are moved by his speeches in ways that they had not been with past presidential candidates or presidents. His ability to move people from all types of backgrounds, in the words of one white male college student in Illinois, makes him a great speaker:

I remember thinking what a great speaker he was, but what I was most impressed with was his ability to move audiences, and motivate people. When I saw the audience's reactions to what he was saying, it would send chills up my spine. Somebody was doing something that I didn't see other leaders doing . . . Obama would go places and people would be falling out and screaming.

For many participants Barack Obama's rhetoric is filled with hope, something that is in short supply in Washington politics. One black male community college student from Michigan describes how "Obama had the communication skills to say things in a way that gave us hope that change could actually occur." This idea is echoed across different focus groups. In a Rhode Island focus group, an older black man—who describes himself as a political skeptic—gives praise for President Obama's communication: "He was such a great communicator that he actually convinced people that we should have hope . . . that we should have these high expectations that we could change the world." Several participants comment specifically on how President Obama's vision of change rejects existing social divisions. As articulated below, this is one of the most powerful aspects of his inspirational messages.

> With politics, things in general become really binary. It becomes us and them, Republicans and Democrats; and I felt there's so much divisiveness—even within different parties. I just thought that he was able to inspire people to be more than they were—to get out of the divisiveness and move toward a direction that included everyone. It just felt really amazing. It was inspiring and inclusive and uplifting. (Middle-aged white female from North Carolina)

As described in significant detail later in this chapter, some participants criticize President Obama's communication as overly emotional, strategically vague, and lacking in any real substance. However, most of the individuals involved in this study disagree. In general, they appreciate the precision in which he chooses certain words and phrases and utilizes dramatic pauses to enhance the power of his message. One young black male community college student in Michigan highlights President Obama's "ability for word play:"

> Words are powerful! How you use words, language, and what you say to people can inspire people to go a little higher or not. . . . Words can encourage positivity or focus on the negative. [Obama] has the ability for "word play"—he just doesn't stick to the book like a robot that you can program. But he uses what they give him, but at the same time, he has the sense and the soul to speak truthfully. From his heart, he can say, "You can do it." And we believe him.

Professional across Contexts

Another characteristic of President Obama's communication is his ability to maintain a professional demeanor across various contexts. This is something that struck many participants during the campaign. One Mexican American male college student from Illinois recalls how "he never really got rattled—ever." This perception is also evident in other focus groups. For instance, a twenty-something white woman from Michigan describes her thoughts during one of the presidential debates when she says:

> In terms of the McCain/Obama debate, McCain would kinda like make fun—not make fun, but sorta make fun of the things that Obama said. . . . But Obama would handle it all professionally. He wouldn't go back and make fun of things that McCain was saying. He just handled it all professionally.

"Professional" is a term used in several different focus group discussions. Interestingly, a similar sentiment is communicated differently in predominately or exclusively African American groups. In this context, President Obama is frequently referred to as the epitome of someone who is always "cool, calm, and collected." In the words of one young black female student attending a HBCU in Alabama,

> I can't remember the exact time when I first saw him, but I do remember my reactions. . . . He was always cool, calm, and collected. He didn't really have any extreme emotions, and he was able to answer all of these questions without any stress. That was my first reaction, and it continued as I watched him afterwards, during the political campaign as well as his presidency. He remains cool, calm, and collected.

"Classy" is another descriptor used to describe President Obama's approach to politics. For example, a young European American female student at a Michigan community college shares how impressed she was when she learned how then-Senator Obama would react to losing a primary.

> I remember seeing a documentary about him, and remember how he called all of the candidates when they won a state to congratulate them. No matter who they were . . . Hillary, McCain, everybody. I just thought that that was really classy. He is very likeable, super professional, and seemed genuinely respectful to others.

This particular set of comments continues to illustrate how President Obama's professionalism is seen across multiple contexts. Other participants extend this observation to times when he is more casual, yet remains professional.

One African American female undergraduate student at a state university in Michigan illustrates his ability to adapt when she states: "When he makes speeches, it seems like he is very professional, but when he goes on talk shows—he is more relaxed." She adds that "it shows that he can be more humorous, casual, and relatable but remain professional." This idea surfaces in focus groups in different states, like one at a college campus in Nebraska:

> Based off of just his speeches, he's a great public speaker. With different contexts, I would say so as well. I've seen him on different TV shows, and late night shows, he is still professional but he knows how to relate to different people and get his point across. (Twenty-something-year-old European American woman)

Other participants describe President Obama's professionalism in terms of his strategic adaptability in different settings. One young Middle Eastern American woman in California refers to him as someone "who knows when to be witty and he knows when to be serious." An African American woman from Virginia acknowledges that part of his versatility involves his ability to adapt to various communication styles in different settings. Referring to his "blackcent" (black accent) this college student observes: "He is also the master code-switcher . . . he knows when to emphasize it and when to pull it back. He doesn't sound like Al Sharpton or Jesse Jackson all of the time!" Being able to adapt his communication to specific audiences is seen as a skill of the "consummate professional"—a phrase that a middle-aged white woman from Connecticut uses when she says:

> I see him evaluate the audience constantly. . . . He is so fluid, and speaks so well, and I know that he is constantly evaluating what is going on. He always remains professional, but it is not the same professional in every setting.

Engaging

Through different focus group discussions, it is clear that Barack Obama is extremely skilled at engaging people in meaningful ways. People are highly impressed by this unique communication ability but also feel empowered, as evidenced by one young African American woman from Massachusetts who explains:

> I think that the impressive thing about Obama is that he speaks *with* you instead of *to* you. So, you feel like you are actually in the room listening to his ideas, his point of view. He actually understands that not everyone went to Harvard.

President Obama's ability to "speak *with* you instead of *to* you" is something that is alluded to in other focus groups as well, including one at a small private university in Virginia. In this particular group, a young white woman states:

> He is listening to you. Even in a big audience, you can see him listening . . . he is connecting with you one-on-one. He does that instead of making a big show of his points, his message. And he doesn't go off topic. I think that helps in getting his message across, and having us connect with him.

Many college students cite his engaging communication style as something that fuels their interest in politics and their desire to get involved in the campaign. For instance, at one Michigan state university a white woman describes the energy that President Obama's campaign had on campus:

> I think that he got the younger crowd to get involved. He communicated effectively especially to our age group. I don't know if it is because I am of

age now, but I just feel like, on the college campuses, everyone was involved. Everyone wanted to be involved—be a part of it. But with Bush, it was like we don't care.

Some Obama critics suggest that his outreach to young college students is a "political strategy" (see chapter 10). Yet, the vast majority of college students involved in this project found his engaging style as genuine and empowering. This is certainly the case for one young European American female college student in Ohio who shares:

> I've been to two of those rallies, and in the second one, I actually met him. I was working as an intern at a newspaper and got to talk to him. He just . . . I mean he put his arm around me, and he asked me where I was going to school . . . and he asked me what my major was. It was just like—he is so seductive [group laughter] . . . in such a good way, though. I left the room, and was just like, "YEAH!" I don't even know how to explain it, but I see him as very engaging in terms of his style. It made me feel empowered.

Interestingly, this woman is not the only participant who had a personal interaction with Barack Obama. Across the United States, people describe meeting him at campaign events and other local venues. At one focus group at an Indiana university, six of the nine participants describe meeting President Obama "up close and personal." All portray his engaging style in enduring terms.

Barack Obama's engaging communication style is not only praised by traditional-aged college students. At one New England college campus, a white female administrator in her forties speaks of the time when then-Senator Obama spoke at a campus event for incoming first-year students:

> I remember him from the FYE Convocation, and I found him even more impressive in person. It was . . . there was an energy about him. From my perspective, there was a focus on hope and change. And I think that was amazing. And when he spoke, he didn't lose me. He didn't lose me with political words . . . it just seemed like I could understand what he was saying. For me, that was big. He connected with me . . . and I could connect with what he was saying. Usually, when I hear a long political speech coming from a politician, I tend to zone out and think about what I need to buy in terms of groceries. But when he was talking, I paid attention the whole way through.

Other administrators, faculty, and community members in this group share similar comments. Most focus on the ways that his engaging style—regarded as a "gift" by one black woman—attract all types of individuals:

> I think that that is one of his gifts—to be able to draw an audience in, and almost like they are having an intimate conversation with him (as opposed to him

and two thousand people). And the students were so excited that it was really inspiring to me as an administrator. Typically we are usually concerned with the bad image, the bad things that [students] do, blah, blah, blah. But to see all of these kids—not just the college Democrats and Republicans—the regular, everyday kids trying to get tickets even though they weren't freshmen. That was a real hopeful piece. Because all of the sudden, he was the person to see. So that was really something.

For several participants, President Obama's communication is engaging because he isn't "talking down to them like they were stupid" (middle-aged Caucasian woman from Alabama). This sentiment is best captured in the comments from an African American woman (of similar age) from Rhode Island:

He treats us as adults and not as children. A lot of presidents do that—they almost act like we can't comprehend. He just makes it very plain, open, and honest to us, so that it is understandable. I appreciate that. He tells a story that is easy to understand, and he trusts the people to understand. If you make it clear and direct, this is what is happening, this is what we have to do, then it's clear. Don't treat us like we don't—or can't—understand.

Personable, Likeable, and Relatable

Participants see Barack Obama as highly engaging, in part, because he comes across as personable, likeable, and relatable. These qualities are only implicitly connected to his communication though; instead they appear to more directly reflect personal characteristics. One African American woman from Michigan puts it simply: "He is likeable. His tone is personable . . . how he carries himself, it is likeable and relatable." Many participants describe how his communication makes them feel. This includes a young Caucasian female from Ohio who says:

Obama has an extensive vocabulary, but he relates, so it is understandable. He doesn't use language that a common person can't understand. I'm sure that he doesn't write his own speeches but you feel like he does. You feel like he is the one talking to you.

Similar comments are seen across different focus groups; all refer to the ways in which his communication is perceived as reflecting certain personality traits that people find enduring.

For many participants, President Obama is seen as relatable because he is a "normal person." What is especially interesting is that he is described in this way by people from all walks of life. For instance, a middle-aged white woman is part of a group of unemployed/underemployed persons in Connecticut. She says: "He seems very likeable, with a normal, average-type-of-guy approach. That makes him definitely approachable." A younger African American woman from Michigan uses almost identical words to describe the same perception when she states: "He is like the average person; that makes him really likeable and relatable." Similar comments are found from a variety of people from Alabama, Ohio, North Carolina, Illinois, Nebraska, and Indiana. For many participants, Barack Obama's communication with the public isn't viewed as an act or a political strategy. It is genuine, as one young white male from California articulates:

> I don't think that he is trying to sound like a normal person . . . he is a normal person. I think that he is speaking genuinely, like he would when he goes home and talks to his wife. He is super bright, but I also think that he would be a nice guy to hang out with.

His connection is also personal; in fact, participants view him as "down-to-earth." This is seen in the comments of one young African American woman attending a HBCU, who describes how she likes how he is "just being himself:"

> Being that I'm from Maryland, I grew up very close to Washington, D.C., so I was familiar with different locations that he was visiting. Specifically, I remember that he went to Ben's Chili Bowl—and I remember thinking, "Oh, I know where that is—I've been there." To see that he is down to earth and does things like that shows that he is still human. He is a great communicator because he is able to connect with people through just being himself.

While some participants find Barack Obama personable, likeable, and relatable because he is seen as a "normal person," others believe his ability to "find common ground with everybody" is due to his unique upbringing. For one young African American man from Georgia who is finishing his college degree in Michigan, President Obama's ability to relate to everyone is because he is biracial: "I think that one reason why he relates so well with the different races is because he is mixed. He's not going to put one race over the other when it is pretty equal." Other participants thought that his racial identity is only part of it. A young Caucasian man from rural Ohio explains:

> I think that his personal history makes him so easy to relate to. There are pictures circulating of him smoking weed, and he has talked about using cocaine. And he had such a different childhood than all of these other presidents. He is a biracial child, growing up in Hawaii with his white grandparents. He has lived in Indonesia. And his mom married all of these different men. He has had such

a crazy different experience that makes him relatable to everyone else. He loves basketball . . . I just think that he is totally relatable to everyone.

The idea that President Obama's unique experiences allow him to relate to everyone is seen in other focus groups as well. Part of this is the fact that he was not born with a silver spoon in his mouth. As such, a small business owner (middle-aged Latina) in Michigan portrays him as someone who can understand what "middle-class people are going through." In similar ways, he is also described as someone who can relate to the poor and working class (forty-something-year-old woman in Connecticut). For others, Barack Obama's age and educational experiences are at the core of his ability to relate to everyone:

> This is probably very simple, but we are missing that he is young! It is not typical for presidential candidates to be this young, or look this young. There have been some younger presidential candidates, but they did not necessarily look young. But he looked even younger than he was. I found that to be a contradiction because he looks like "Joe average" but then you listen to him speak and he speaks like someone with advanced degrees. (Twenty-something European American male from Illinois)

Collectively, Barack Obama's relatability is regarded as instrumental in his ability to communicate with people from vastly different backgrounds. Again, part of this is due to his ability to adapt his language to his audience:

> The first time I heard him, he came off to me as someone who wanted to relate to every person, not just a certain type of person. His vocab was very basic; he doesn't speak like he is very intelligent. He just keeps it at a level where everyone can relate to him and understand what he is saying. It's easy to understand what he thinks is important. (Young white male college student from Indiana)

In addition, President Obama is also seen as a representation of "every person." Consequently he is seen as someone who transcends individual differences and focuses on the larger good. This perception is seen in the comments of a forty-eight-year-old white woman who is part of a group of working-class individuals in Connecticut.

> What stands out to me is that he really does talk to you as a person. He's speaking in terms of everyone coming together and working for the good of the country. And he doesn't single out that you should do this, and you should do that. You really feel like you could walk up to him and he would talk to you as a human, not as a Mexican, black, or a white person. Or even rich or poor, or young or old. I feel that he would treat you exactly the same way.

The personal connection that many participants feel with President Obama is undeniable. In one case, that of a twenty-something-year-old Puerto Rican woman from New England, it even transcends language.

> Most of my family has been able to connect with Obama in ways that they never have connected with other presidents at any time. Half of them don't even speak English well, but they are able to connect with him in an emotional way. He brings something out of them that goes beyond language . . . and they are able to understand, and feel positively about him without really understanding the language.

CRITICS OF OBAMA'S COMMUNICATION: A SMALL BUT VOCAL GROUP

As demonstrated throughout this chapter, the vast majority of participants portray Barack Obama as a "masterful communicator" whose style draws praise from individuals from all types of backgrounds. The praise is evident in every single focus group discussion, at least to some extent, including those which are exclusively or primarily comprised of Republican, Libertarian, and/ or Tea Party members. This is not to say, however, that criticism of President Obama's communication does not exist. This final section highlights the voices of those in the minority of the study's participants: vocal critics of his communication style.

A few participants describe President Obama's communication in negative terms. One white female Republican from Michigan uses the word "arrogant" to refer how she views his communication style. Other Tea Party members from Nebraska call him "pompous . . . quite full of himself—especially being the first African American male running for president." A white male Republican from North Carolina criticizes President Obama because, in his opinion, he is "too intellectual" in his communication with the general public. A third white participant from California, who also identifies himself as an Obama non-supporter, questions why I was conducting a national research project someone who he doesn't regard as "special" in terms of the way that he communicates:

> When I see him, I try to be open-minded because I actually didn't vote for him. When it comes to his communication, I must say that I don't think that he is all that special. Not to belittle him, but he isn't that different than many other people who are effective communicators.

The criticisms of these three participants occupy a fairly isolated existence within the transcripts. In other words, their comments are not repeated by any other participants in any of the other focus groups. However, another point of criticism relates to Obama's communication did get considerable attention from participants within a variety of focus group discussions: His use of teleprompters.

Teleprompter as Crutch

The most cited area where individuals criticize Obama's communication is related to his use of teleprompters. Many focus group participants acknowledge the necessity and effectiveness of using this technological advance, especially when the president is giving a speech of great significance. However, among the critics, Barack Obama's use of a teleprompter is problematic on several levels. First, the teleprompter is seen as a major distraction—one that makes listening to him speak, in the words of one fifty-year-old white male Tea Party member in Nebraska "excruciating."

> The biggest annoyance that I have in how he delivers his message is when he is on teleprompter, it is very distracting to have him looking from one side to the other, and then back to the other side, etc. Very seldom does he look up the middle, because the teleprompters are to the sides. It's excruciating watching him. It's basically like he's watching a tennis match. So, that's been one thing, as this process has happened. I agree that once it gets off of a teleprompter and is in a situation that he has to be impromptu, there's a lot of hesitation and thinking between thoughts. He slows down and you can see him trying to collect his thoughts. He has that . . . places where he has a lot of ums and ahs, that breaks things up quite a bit and that makes it difficult to follow him when he does that. I think that he uses that as a technique myself, because when you are doing that sort of thing, you are in your brain trying to figure out what you are going to say. And so all of these "ums" and "ahs" come in there to fill in that space while you are trying to figure out what you are going to say.

Second, teleprompters are a point of concern for participants who believe that it impacts his credibility and trustworthiness. For instance, a white male Independent voter who is part of a college student group in Michigan describes how his initial perception changed once he recognized his use of a teleprompter.

> The first time I saw him speak, my initial perception was that he wasn't looking at a teleprompter because he had a very natural delivery—he would look at one side and then the other. But then, later after he had been elected, a lot of camera angles would show a teleprompter on either side of him. So, that kinda ruined it for me. . . . That kinda hurt his credibility.

Several other participants interpret his—what they would say—overreliance on teleprompters as a sign that he is being deceptive with the general public.

For instance, an older African American woman in her sixties from Illinois questions the reasoning behind President Obama's teleprompter use.

> He uses that teleprompter, too. He just can't get up and speak from the top of his head. . . . Do you remember the debates? When they asked him about Jeremiah Wright and Farrakhan? He just couldn't come up with answers. He would just kinda hesitate, "What am I going to say? Am I going to say the wrong thing?" His ideas are not going to come to him, unless he has written those answers down.

This particular woman is concerned that what appears on the teleprompter is not President Obama's own ideas, but instead others who are "telling the president what to say . . . what to think."

This suspicion, which is seen as unique to President Obama, is also mentioned in a focus group discussion of Michigan community college students. In particular, one thirty-year old woman (who self-identified as an ultra-conservative Republican) states:

> He uses a teleprompter; none of the other presidents, to my knowledge, ever had those. It seems like everyone has one now. I think that it is kinda scary because I don't know if it is him who believes it, or the folks that are writing the papers for him.

The particular focus group that this woman is a part of is predominately white and Republican. Throughout the discussion, many participants are highly critical of President Obama, and at one point, disapprove of his off-the-cuff comments following the arrest of Professor Henry Louis Gates (see chapter 9). For much of the focus group discussion, the one African American woman in the group sits quietly and listens. Once the criticisms seem to magnify with every new speaker, she speaks out and asks:

> How many people were saying earlier that they really didn't like what he was saying because of the teleprompter? That you didn't believe what he was saying? One of the times that he doesn't have a teleprompter, and he is saying what he feels. People want to criticize that too. What do you really want? Do you want for him to read from a script or a screen and not really know if it is him? Or do you want him to be upfront and honest and just speak his mind? Which is it?

A similar exchange occurs within an Indiana focus group of college students. Within this particular discussion, a twenty-something white woman points out that this particular criticism appears to be fueled by the media:

> Before I came back to school, I was a community organizer and I dealt with issues that had to do with Indiana, but EVERYBODY wanted to talk to you about

what's going on in DC. So, I had a really wide range of opinions that I heard . . . I found that in a lot of older, Tea Party types. I found that a lot of the FOX News watchers want to talk about what a good orator he is, as if his ideas have no merit. It is just his speaking skills. He's not really saying anything. And he can't do it without a teleprompter, they always talk about that.

As seen within these comments, critics of President Obama's communication take great issue with his over-reliance on teleprompters. In their eyes, this form of technology represents cause for irritation, suspicion, and distrust. These participants point to his teleprompter use as a weakness of his communication effectiveness. Interestingly, others criticize President Obama—not because he is an ineffective communicator but—because he was *too masterful* in his communication competence.

President Obama: Smooth Talker and Trickster

For some participants, President Obama's communication with the general public is so effective that it automatically triggers suspicion. In one Michigan focus group, a thirty-something-year-old woman critiques the popularity of President Obama, especially with individuals who refuse to see beyond the "public performances" that he gives:

> I do think that there is a difference between coming off as being well liked, and actually being a likeable person. And that was the hardship for me. I wanted to like him. He is well spoken, he handles himself quite well, and has great mannerisms. But, there's something about him to be . . . something about his body language, the way that he emphasizes certain words, it just puts me off. Because I feel like he puts up a wall. He is soooooo well liked, and embraces everyone that, to me, that can't be realistic. I don't trust him.

In a Connecticut focus group, a white woman who describes herself as "too old to be part of the working poor," acknowledges the number of people who are suspicious of President Obama's communication skills. Specifically she says, "I've heard that people think that Obama is such a good communicator that he can pull the wool over everybody's eyes." She goes on to say, "Being a good communicator is a negative to them—it is how he tricks us."

For many critics of President Obama, his mastery of communication is seen as a tool he uses to manipulate the general public—many of which would not support his ideas if they could see "past all of the glitter." Several participants, across a couple different focus groups, describe President Obama as a "smooth talker": a masterful communicator who uses his oratory to please the public. One middle-aged white female from North Carolina shares:

> I think that he is a very smooth talker. I remember the first time that I heard him speak . . . to me, it felt like he would never commit to something. He kind of was wishy-washy—he would go with what would make everybody happy, not necessarily stand up for what he believed in. He would go with whatever would give him the most votes.

Many of these comments are offered in focus groups where Obama critics appear to outnumber supporters. However, in one Michigan focus group where participants describe President Obama's communication as "inspirational," a white male Independent voter in his twenties interrupts to say:

> I would say more like propaganda. I'm sorry [to previous speaker who described his use of words to motivate as inspiring]. . . . Because he is a good communicator, he is able to manipulate and influence us in a way that he uses his language—different loaded terms and repetition. Like his use of "hope" throughout the whole campaign, he was pounding, and pounding, and pounding it [hammers fist into his other hand]. What even was that hope talking about? But it was so vague, you could have put any type of hope that you wanted to in to that position. It was not necessarily a bad thing, but because of his good communication skills, he does have more influence on a normal person.

To these individuals, President Obama strategically uses his communication skills to get elected and remain popular. In the words of one white female participant from Ohio, he continues to do so:

> Even in his speeches now; he just gave one on Wall Street reform. Being Republican, I can hear everything that he is saying, and I'm going "Yeah. You know, yeah. I agree with that." He gets me all fired up. What he is saying is great. But knowing what is underneath what he is saying—because he is only touching the surface. It sounds good, but it means something so much different. He can just mislead you like no one else.

Mouthpiece or Evil Mastermind?

Generally speaking, the vast majority of focus group participants understand the power that comes with someone, like President Obama, who is a masterful communicator. As described earlier, most see this as a means to reach out and connect with people from diverse backgrounds. However, others perceive his strong, positive personality and strong communication skills as a smoke screen. One fifty-something-year-old white man from Nebraska reflects:

> I think that all of us were all so taken by him because he was so glamorous, down to earth, well liked, educated, attractive guy standing up on the podium,

you just wanted to melt when he talked. I don't know how many of us did actually listen to what he was saying or think critically about where the ideas came from of how much power it gave him.

Among the relatively small number of participants who regard President Obama's communication negatively, two particular points of concern exist.

The first concern relates to the great influence that President Obama has over the U.S. youth. Across focus groups, a substantial number of participants describe how Obama's campaign appeared to target, and win over, young voters (see chapter 10). However, a few perceive this in troubling ways. For instance, one white female community college student in Michigan states:

> He really targeted the youth. He is the most skilled speaker that I have ever listened to. You want to listen to him regardless of what your beliefs are. He even talks you into believing what he is saying. He has a certain power over people, especially young new voters.

In at least two different focus groups, participants are concerned that Obama's communication abilities and his influence over the youth are similar to the ways in which Adolph Hitler rose to power in early twentieth-century Germany. One twenty-something-year-old white woman in Connecticut shares that she has read several articles that promote these "extreme comments." In another focus group held at an Indiana college, an African American male participant describes a recent conversation that he had with several European American co-workers. The participant had recently traveled to the University of Michigan to hear President Obama speak at their graduation.

> I was arguing with some people I work with about Obama and tried to convince them to at least listen to what he has to say. I was recently at [University of Michigan's] graduation . . . and they were like, "Yeah, he's a really good speaker, but so was Hitler." It's a great point. Hitler was a great speaker. You may not agree with what he was saying, but he is a great speaker. So, sometimes an Obama strength can be turned against him because everyone is like, "Do you know how dangerous it is for someone to have that much power?"

The second concern represents the flip side of the first. Interestingly enough, other critics of Barack Obama do not feel that his communication effectiveness gives him too much power. Instead, they fear that his advanced abilities to communicate to the general public in masterful ways are being used by more powerful people behind the scenes. The idea that President Obama is a mere mouthpiece for others is stated directly by a white male Republican from Michigan:

He's the deliverer, the mouthpiece. All of it is put together by a team that researches the area and then they create a script that he follows. His speaking ability is stellar. He is a great mouthpiece. He portrays it well, if he believes it or not.

This perception is shared by other participants in Illinois, North Carolina, and Nebraska focus groups. In these groups, people articulate their suspicions that President Obama is being unduly influenced (and, in some ways, controlled) by a variety of political folks: Dick Durbin, Nancy Pelosi, Barney Frank, David Axelrod, and/or Rahm Emanuel. For one African American woman in her sixties from Illinois, President Obama is a "puppet" to others because "he doesn't have the knowledge and know-how to go about doing things." As one Asian/Pacific Islander unemployed male from North Carolina states, "There is a lot going on behind the scenes in terms of others trying to get him to think and communicate a certain way." The fact that this is "going on right in front of everyone's eyes," is described by participants as "disgusting," "ridiculous," and "horrible."

SUMMARY

This chapter focuses on explaining the perceptions that the general public has of President Obama's communication. As I illustrate throughout the chapter, the vast majority portray Barack Obama as a masterful communicator whose communication style is motivational, inspiring, and engaging. Compared to other politicians, his personable and relatable style is seen as a breath of fresh air. Despite this dominant perception, a vocal minority perceives his communication through a highly critical lens. Interestingly, some non-supporters regard Barack Obama as a masterful communicator who uses his oratory skills to deceive the general public. With this foundation set, chapter 4 highlights the ways in which participants evaluate President Obama's communication as he transitioned from presidential candidate into the Oval Office.

Chapter 4

Shifts in Perception

The Campaign versus the Presidency

> I think that the expectations were so high that it almost doomed him from the very beginning.
>
> —Older Caucasian female from Alabama

This chapter continues a focus on public perceptions of President Barack Obama's communication. In chapter 3, I share the diverse ways in which participants describe their impressions of his communication style. Within chapter 4, I extend the focus to how the public evaluates his communication competence during the 2008 presidential campaign and with his current performance as the forty-fourth U.S. president. For many, these perceptions are influenced strongly by the very first impressions that were formed. Consequently, that is the first topic that I cover in this chapter.

THE CONTEXTUALIZING NATURE OF FIRST IMPRESSIONS

The very first question I ask of focus group participants is regarding their first impressions of President Obama's communication. Some individuals have a difficult time remembering a specific instance; however, most are able to recall a specific time when they first heard him speak. The vast majority of these persons mention seeing his speech (or a tape of his speech) at the 2004 Democratic National Convention in Boston, Massachusetts. For instance, one young white female from North Carolina shares:

> The first time that I remember seeing him was at the Democratic National Convention . . . I don't exactly remember the year, but it was absolutely spellbinding. I could not take my eyes off of the screen, and I don't think that anyone else in the convention hall could either. It was simply magnificent. And you had to walk away, thinking that he was going to be something in the future.

For many, this initial exposure left quite an impression and planted the idea that Barack Obama would eventually live in the White House. This perception is a common one and best captured in the words of a middle-aged white female from Massachusetts,

> [I first saw him at] the DNC convention here in Boston, when he gave that speech, I was like "He's going to be the first black president." I didn't think that he would be the president this soon, but hands down, after that speech, I thought that he would be the first black president. I knew it a minute into the speech—it was really quick. Before that, I had never heard of the guy. I was like . . . really taken back by it. I was in awe. And the buzz in Boston about the convention really added to it. I had worked at an event and had some connection to it, so that helped. And then to see that on TV, I was blown away.

Other focus group participants recall specific instances when they were able to hear President Obama speak in person. These first impressions seem to be a precursor to what was yet to come. Consider the comments of a twenty-something-year-old African American college student from Illinois who says:

> He spoke in my church; I believe that he was running for senator. I was intrigued by what he was saying even then. And then I was really impressed when he was running for president. When I heard his acceptance speech, I was drawn to tears just because of how much emotion was behind his words. I felt like he was really trying . . . that he really wanted to be president. Then he was so pleased that he finally accomplished this goal and whatever he planned to do was going to be accomplished. And it wasn't going to be easy. I was intrigued by what he said [and] I felt a connection with him, from the first time that I heard him speak at my church, to this acceptance speech in Chicago.

Another participant—a Caucasian male—from the same Michigan focus group of undergraduate students also reports that he was really impressed with Obama's communication from the very start. However, for him, this led to a different set of emotions.

> I was actually mad—upset the first time that I heard him speak. I'm not Democrat or Republican but the first time I heard him, I was like, "Okay, he's gonna get elected just because he is very smooth—very likeable." But I didn't like him, because he didn't have a lot of political experience. I mean, he was a

senator for one term, the first time overseas was during his first campaign run or whatever . . . so I didn't really like that he didn't have a lot of experience. But on the other side of it, you had the crypt-keeper (McCain) running against him, so . . . I was more of a Mitt Romney guy, personally.

As seen in future sections, many participants' perceptions of President Obama's communication have changed over time. Even for those whose perceptions remain fairly consistent, they report a different reaction to hearing him speak as president. For instance, one young African American woman from Illinois states:

> I don't think that his communication has changed. I think that, now that he has been elected, people are feeling more comfortable with him being president. Back in the day, whenever he spoke, people were like "Hey, Obama is speaking." But now he is president . . . I know that, for me, whenever he makes a speech or goes somewhere to speak, I'm not as enthused as more. It's not a big deal. I no longer run to the TV whenever he is speaking.

A similar sentiment is articulated in different focus groups across the United States. One forty-year-old Caucasian man from Connecticut explains it as: "The more you hear him speak, the less effect it has on you. His message gets communicated very well; he is a very good speaker. But when you hear it all of the time. . . . It's like your favorite pizza. It's a great pizza. But if you have it every day, it kinda loses its luster after a while."

Other participants also acknowledge a change in communication, something that they attribute to the fact that Barack Obama is a politician. Within this perspective, despite his personal ideals, he has to adapt to the realities of an intense political world. The bottom line, in this regard, is that President Obama's communication must ultimately position him in a positive light with voters. This point is made evident in the comments of one white male senior citizen from Connecticut:

> I don't know if this is a style thing, or more of a content thing, but a politician's job is to get re-elected, so I think that he is started to move toward that goal. . . . I'm not saying that I agree that that is the way that it should be, but most politicians tend to want to get re-elected and their platform and communication is geared toward that.

The informal, personable speaker that people came to appreciate on the campaign trail has been transformed into something significantly different. Part of this seems to be the result of a presidential team of advisors: "I would like to see him in a more informal way . . . when I see a press conference or a speech, I just know that it is so much showmanship: Speech writers who decide what he should say, staff who have picked out what he was going to wear, etc. It is very formulaic, and I don't think that that inspires a lot of confidence in everyday people" (young white woman from Connecticut). For several participants, the formalities that come with the presidency limit President Obama's effectiveness. One thirty-something-year-old white woman from Massachusetts describes her desire to see more of Barack Obama and less of his "cronies":

> I think that now he has more people writing for him. So, sometimes I don't think that the messages that he is conveying are really his ideas. So, I think that a lot of other people have a hand in what he actually says and how he communicates to us. Sometimes, it doesn't seem like it is his actual personality, and it doesn't have the same effect than it had before . . . I see that as a negative thing. I mean, because I feel like we voted for you as the president. I voted for you, so I want you to direct us, not your cronies.

One participant—a middle-aged Caucasian female from Connecticut—describes how "she sees the politician more now" and "how the great speaker isn't there as much." One white female college student participant from Illinois voted for Obama but is increasingly critical of what she describes as his "typical politician shit":

> He dances around the issues now. Just give me a god damn fuckin' answer! He's more political now, he does the typical politician-shit. I feel like with all of the promises that he has broken, things that he has failed to stand up to. . . . I literally don't even want to hear his voice now. I want to know what he has to say, but I have to read it because if I hear his voice the first thing I do is get irritated.

Throughout the different focus group discussions, it became clear that many participants feel a personal connection to President Obama. When they feel betrayed, their reaction is filled with emotion (as was the case with the participant whose quote ended the previous paragraph). For several participants, the expectations that they have for President Obama were formed through their initial impressions of him. One of the more interesting examples of this is provided by a middle-aged Jewish American man living in Rhode Island. Within the extended quote below, he describes how he "fell in love" with Barack Obama but now feels like a "jilted lover."

> So, when I go back to the first time I heard him, I heard something for the first time that included all of the things that I would want—and more! So, I had a mental checklist of what I wished someone would say, and he covered them all. From the first moment, I was with him. But I thought that it was too good to be true. I was thinking "Maybe he had a good moment, I'm not going to get too emotionally involved." I know that Hillary was there and I was skeptical about his chance for success. But the first time that I heard him I got some reassurance that he got it.

He was the closest thing I've ever seen to a human being who gets it . . . and that followed me the entire election. And just that euphoria that we had, it was amazing. We couldn't believe that we were seeing something like this take place. Now, I feel like a jilted lover, in a way. Because I fell in love, and now we are in a separation mode—we are trying to resolve this. I am, at least, he doesn't know that we are in a relationship. [group laughter . . . people talking over one another]. When I see a man like Obama who I felt was the right person, and going through some of the stuff that he has (like the banking crisis) . . . I see him as being too soft in his approach. When I hear of the criticism, it is really difficult to hear that. And I don't like it . . . remember I'm chilled, teary-eyed listening to him, so much so that I fell in love with him. But now I see him communicating differently. It is different. I heard him speaking on NPR the other day, and he was talking about something and he got really emotional. And he made a really snide comment about the Republican opposition, a rude remark that during the election, he never would use. He was always above it. McCain would fly off the handle, and say outlandish things. But Obama wouldn't do that. He was better than that. He always kept his cool. Now he's gotten to a point where he is going after them. . . . Is he reacting in his own frustration? He is trying to overcompensate? It's hard to hear, frankly, because for me, he is better than that. Sorry for going on, but I'm trying to temper it with my own perceptions of him. My perceptions of him have changed. So, now when he gets up there and says something, I feel like he created really high expectations for a date, and now he is standing me up [group laughter].

This extended quote goes a long way to capture how one individual's first impressions of President Obama affect current perceptions in powerfully personal ways. It also touches on a number of key issues that are highlighted in this chapter. The remainder of this chapter continues exploring how the U.S. public perceptions of President Obama's communication have shifted over time. For some, the changes are natural in light of the different objectives of someone running for office versus serving in that office. Others describe his shifts in communication style as a reaction to the realities of the U.S. political system. All participants agree that current perceptions of President Obama are impacted by the expectations that were created during the 2008 presidential campaign. These, and other issues, help to guide the diverse sets of perceptions described in this chapter.

DIFFERENT ROLES, DIFFERENT COMMUNICATION STYLES

As I highlight in the previous chapter, President Obama is perceived as a masterful communicator when it comes to connecting with people and inspiring them to see things in new ways. This ability, for some participants, leads them to define him primarily as a "motivational speaker"—something that didn't automatically translate into an effective president.

> One of the things that struck me, as we've been talking about this, is that he comes across as more of a motivational speaker. He likes to motivate people. He likes to give speeches that motivate people. So, he is used to speaking to their feelings and those sorts of things—things that will motivate people to do specific things. But, now that he is in office, he has to communicate ideas and his policies where he wants people to go and how he wants people to get there. And that's not coming off quite so well.

This extended quote is from an older white man from Nebraska, who describes himself as someone who supports the Tea Party. Other participants, like a young African American man from Indiana, agree:

> During the campaign, his answers to questions just seemed to flow—even if it was a difficult question, he would just give a good answer. But now whenever he gets a question, there is a little bit bigger lapse of time before he answers. And you notice that he stutters a little. . . . It's not as easy to give the answers that everyone wants to hear because of the situation. It is completely different. You can say what you ARE going to do once you are in that position. But now that you are in that position, and it's not exactly working the way that you want it to, it's more different.

The idea that talking about change and actually enacting it are two drastically different things is articulated by a number of participants. It also is made explicitly clear by the comments of an older white male from North Carolina who uses the phrase, "the devil is in the details," to discuss the difficulties of enacting change.

> I think that [my perception] has definitely changed, and one of the reasons is that the goals of the campaign are entirely different than the goals when you have to actually run the country. In the campaign, you can paint with a broad brush. You don't have to get down with details, so you can exude with hope and confidence. You have handlers who help you do that every day. But when you get a daily briefing from the CIA about what is going on, and you worry about a factious and uncooperative Congress, and yet you have the task to get specific legislation through . . . you can't paint with a broad brush. So, he cannot exude the same values, and if he did, people would accuse him of being a Pollyanna. You know that the devil is in the details, and the details catch up with everybody.

For most of the individuals who share this perception, President Obama's lack of effectiveness as a president is due to a deficit in skills. The general idea is that he is an effective motivational speaker, but ineffective manager. Other participants, like a middle-aged white man from Massachusetts agree that his communication has changed, but emphasizes that the shift isn't due to a lack of ability.

> I think you have seen him scale it back with moderation. Someone who is such an inspirational speaker, you see him change a little bit. You know, talking to Democrats and Independents, he is sorta over the top with his policy and how he spoke to them. But now I think that you see him toning it back a lot. He is everyone's president now and I see how he communicates with more of a broad appeal. As president, I don't think that he can just say everything that he wants to say. He can't give these big, grand speeches; nor as president do I think that he thinks it is always appropriate to give speeches that way.

Other participants, including a number of Barack Obama supporters, agree with this assessment. For instance, a middle-aged white male community college student from Michigan states:

> His whole communicating ability makes you feel connected and that is spectacular. And whether it had substance or not, you were enthralled with what he was saying. That finesse, that polish that people have been talking about, really made a difference. But once the campaign was over, and he moved into the White House, the truck started backing up and that office is taking an effect on his communicating ability. Now he can't just focus in on how he sounds, it's more about substance now. It just can't be about the way that you are expressing yourself. It has to carry weight.

Being viewed as an inspiring communicator who can also articulate ideas with significant substance appears to be a challenge for a president who is regarded first and foremost as a masterful public communicator. Given his highly regarded performance as a presidential candidate, a shift in focusing in on particular policy objectives leaves certain participants with a less than positive perception. This is the case for an African American female student from Alabama:

> For me, before he became president, I think that he was much more . . . he was able to connect with people. He understood how to make grand, abstract concepts really possible and relatable. It came naturally to him. Now when I see him on the news or whatever . . . I understand that his role has changed . . . he is selling himself less and selling and explaining policies more. To me, his language is much more technical now, and it is policy-oriented. And I think that it has taken on a colder feel to it. Less of him comes through.

For another African American student, this one attending college in Massachusetts, this shift is not seen as such a negative thing. In her opinion, he is just showing a different side of his communication style.

> I don't think that his style has really changed, but you do get a different type of persona from him. Initially, he was reaching out to really young voters, so he used humor and stories to connect with us. That was his main goal—so he talked about things that we really enjoyed. He did it to reach young voters and minorities—that was his goal. So, now that he is actually in the White House and carrying that burden, he has to step into that role. Now his goal is different. His style has changed based on what he needs to get done.

Other participants describe Barack Obama's communication as largely consistent. However, several discuss how his optimistic communication style is being tested in the realities of the U.S. political world. A forty-something-year-old African American woman from northern California makes this point when she says:

> I met him as a senator early, very early. I visited Chicago, and my perception was that he was the "new kid in town" with so many ideas, and so very optimistic, and I just wanted to say, "Yeah, we will see how long that lasts." [laughs to self] The reality isn't as optimistic and that takes a lot out of you. You can look at him today and see the effects. . . . But at that time, and during the election, as well as now, I really feel like he believes that through communication anything is possible. He still believes that by working across the aisle good things can actually happen. I find that quite often, he communicates in a way that is still optimistic—but also frustrated.

In this perspective, Barack Obama's accomplishments as a masterful communicator remain intact. He is still viewed as an extremely competent communicator, but someone who also is facing tremendous challenges. According to an older Caucasian woman in North Carolina, she remains impressed with his communication efforts:

> My perception is that now he does an awful lot of explaining, which is different from his first speeches . . . I really respond to his visionary speeches and I'm very grateful that he has enough intelligence and the wherewithal to explain all of the things that are being done. So, my explanation of the shift in his communication, between the time he ran and the time he got elected, so much crap happened.

In this instance, the participant is not referring to the problems that President Obama inherited in terms of the economy, war, or the environment. "Crap" is used to describe the bipartisan division in U.S. politics, something that is viewed as extremely challenging for any new president—even those whom has masterful communication skills.

REACTING TO THE REALITIES OF BIPARTISAN POLITICS

A significant number of participants raise the issue of bipartisan politics in their descriptions of President Obama's communication effectiveness. Almost without exception, these participants are supporters of the president. Most often their comments accuse Republicans of creating opposition to any policy idea that President Obama, as a Democrat, supports. In one focus group of students attending a Hispanic-serving university in Illinois, most participants are vocal supporters of President Obama. Within this group, one young Latino male shares:

> It is sorta hard to do when he got elected, because everyone was saying—all of the Republicans were saying that they were going to shut him out. . . . We have been talking about people who supported him, but the people who were in opposition were just as moved by his message, but only in a negative way. And so, they are very united in their not-liking him. . . . He has been shut out. It's not like he hasn't been trying, but the bipartisan disagreements have hurt him. It is a huge problem—not just with his Presidency but how the system is run. The Republicans are refusing to agree to any Democratic initiative.

According to these participants, loyalty to one's political party seems to take priority over what is best for the country. Furthermore, the negativity and lack of respect between political party members is described as "horrible." One middle-aged Caucasian woman who is part of a Connecticut focus group of unemployed and underemployed individuals shows considerable anger with what she describes as the "ridiculous" way in which politicians behave. In particular, she focuses on the lack of respect on Capitol Hill.

> No matter how he communicates, he should be respected. Like with the congressman yelling out—calling him a liar. Congress never conducted business like that. Never. That's ridiculous. He is the president of the United States, and he deserves respect. And he isn't getting any respect. I think that something needs to be done about that . . . that just buuuurrrnnns me. I don't know . . . I don't know how they can't get order in Congress. He deserves respect . . . no matter what you think of him. He is president and deserves respect.

According to an older black woman in Rhode Island, the "Republican attacks are getting stronger and stronger." As such, many perceive the shifts in President Obama's communication as a reaction to nastiness of bipartisan politics.

Many participants interpret President Obama's shift in communication style (from presidential candidate to president) as a strategic move to negate the tensions associated with bipartisanship. One young white female undergraduate student from Massachusetts describes how "He has always been articulate, but now he has to be much more diplomatic and be sure that he doesn't rub anyone the wrong way." A Latina college student from Illinois agrees and notes how "He is much more careful about what he has to say. I can tell that he is holding his tongue sometimes when he speaks and keeping up his guard quite a bit." This Puerto Rican woman went on to ask: "Isn't he more moderate now, than when he was running? When he was running he was more assertive in his beliefs, and now it is more work to do stuff. He actually has to compromise to get stuff done; he has to be more moderate." Moderate, in this context, refers to his political stance. However, other participants describe his communication as more "moderate" as well:

> I think that it has to do with when you are running for president, you have to have the energy and give it your all. You have to go with that type of emotion. But when you actually become president, you kind of . . . you have to pull it back a little bit. He has the knowledge that he needs to get both parties together to make the government work. But it means not being so dominant. So, in a sense, that's why he's changed some. (White female college student from Illinois)

Other participants are critical of President Obama's more "moderate" communication. In their eyes, they wish that he would maintain the persona that was the hallmark of his successful presidential campaign. This includes, in the words of one middle-aged black man from Virginia, "getting into the ring a little more, putting on the gloves, and going for some blows." According to one unemployed white women in her forties, most people she knows "think that Obama is letting everyone push him around." Within her Connecticut focus group, many agree with her. She goes on to say, "He doesn't have that strong backbone that he showed us before the election. That's the Obama we want to see." One forty-something-year-old African American man—a self-proclaimed political junkie from Ohio—anticipates a return to the "old Obama" following the 2010 midterm elections.

> I think that Obama's communication style is going to change after what has happened with these midterm elections. I don't think that the message is going to change a whole lot, maybe some small tweaking. But I think that his communication is going to change in order to get things done. We are going to see Obama in his prime!

DOUBT AND LACK OF CONFIDENCE

One theme that emerges from the focus group transcripts suggests an alternative explanation for what is perceived as a shift in President Obama's communication: Self-doubt and lack of confidence. This is evident in the comments of several different focus group participants. One white male college student from North Carolina states, "He is a great speaker, but his tone has changed a little bit to me as well. It is not as really vibrant as it was before." A young white female in the same focus group describes President Obama as full of doubt: "He convinced us, 'Yes we can' but then we don't see that same spirit now." A fifty-something-year-old white man from rural southern Ohio mocks the fall in confidence by stating, "'Yes, we can' has become 'maybe we might.'" A young Caucasian woman from Massachusetts also comments on how he has lost some of his carefree attitude since becoming president.

> He also has gotten so much more serious. I saw him speak as a freshman, he was so upbeat, he was hilarious. I just remember laughing, and having a great time. My whole memory is of him being upbeat and him telling stories and being funny. Now that he has direct issues to work with in office, he seems much more serious . . . and at times, sad. He has aged an incredible amount in just two years. It just shocks me every time that I see him. He just looks older, a little bit more serious. It seems like the HOPE is a little bit gone . . . because it is such a harsh reality now.

For several participants, Barack Obama's communication abilities have not changed. What has changed are the larger circumstances, and these affect his confidence. This idea is articulated by an older black male from California who says:

> I see more anxiety in him now. I see a little bit more explaining and not being as direct. I mean, in some areas, he is direct, but not in other areas. I think that his campaign was pretty direct in what he wanted to do as president. But now, I don't see that as much. I don't see as much confidence. His speaking ability, his nonverbals are still the same; they haven't changed at all.

The idea that Barack Obama's communication as president fails to reflect the charisma, confidence, and certainty of his campaign trail rhetoric is the topic of several focus group discussions. One in particular seems to capture the essence of this perspective. It occurs within a group of Michigan community college students, most of whom describe themselves as moderate or conservative Republicans. What follows is an excerpt from a conversation between a Native American and several white female participants.

> NAF: When he was running for office and I got to know him as a public figure and speaker in general, I think that he was more direct in his statements. He would come across to the public, he knew we had questions and he had to answer those. And if he didn't answer those questions, we wouldn't have elected him—well at least some of us wouldn't. But now that he has been elected, he's got the prize—the goal that he has set out to accomplish, I feel that he is much more ambiguous in his statements. Now that the ball actually is in his court, I don't know if he actually knows what to do with it. And I think that that comes across in his speaking.
> WF#1: I think that now that the pressure is really on, we've put you on this pedestal that you've asked for, what are you going to do with it? I think that his speech has definitely been—especially this past year when he was been going through some things—his communication definitely lets on that he is not as sure of himself as he once was. And that is reflected in the public because we've noticed it so now we don't feel as sure of him as we once did.
> WF#2: I think you also see more of his temper coming out. I have seen several speeches where you see that he is getting annoyed with the redundancy and the stupid answers that he's already given, time and time again. "Okay, let's move on." He just doesn't seem to have confidence in how to get things done.
> WF#3: I think that in the beginning he was so polished, but now he is sounding less so especially because the approval rating is so low. I think that he is just searching for help, and he doesn't know where to get it from. So, I'm not really happy with him right now.
> WF#2: Before he didn't have to have all of the answers. He could make direct statements about what he was going to do . . . but now he's actually there and he's finding it hard to do so. So, to keep up with the approval ratings, I don't know if he is being more of a red herring, but I do think that he is being more ambiguous, and getting more angry, more frustrated. I don't know if he needs to come down to more of our level. It sounds like he is so used to being on this educated pedestal, but now . . .
> WF#1: He definitely doesn't seem as arrogant as he did before. Now he seems more desperate.

Shortly after this exchange, a white female Obama supporter in the group comments on how during the campaign some people in the focus group criticize President Obama for being too confident. She goes on to question how the same people also could be critical of a more cautious approach. Ultimately, she chides the rest of the group by saying, "I'm confused—and I'm sure that he's confused too—about how you want him to be." She then, looking at me adds, "People aren't happy with the way things are. People are just looking for someone to blame, and of course, it is easiest to blame the president."

UNREALISTICALLY HIGH EXPECTATIONS

As demonstrated in chapter 3, the general consensus among focus group participants is that Barack Obama proved himself to be a masterful communicator during the 2008 presidential election. For many participants, the election had a "magical feel" to it which resulted in increased voter involvement—especially among traditionally disenfranchised groups—and high expectations for the future. Some suggest that his masterful communication skills are at the core of such high expectations. This point is made by a young white male from Alabama when he says:

> Because he was such a good orator, a lot of people thought that he should have these super powers that can do everything at once. A lot of people don't truly understand what a president can, and cannot, do. It just seems that people had these huge expectations for President Obama—they wanted so much in so little time. Everybody wanted so much from him that now that he can't do everything, then they are disillusioned with him. I almost get this feeling that he is so isolated because of the high expectations.

A public perception that Barack Obama's communication abilities constitute a "super power" is discussed in several different public groups. For instance, the idea is raised by a first-time voter who describes how Obama's communication persona inspires so much hope for this generation:

> Compared to every other president, he has had the highest expectations from the people. I think that everyone put so much faith into him. I think that some people don't feel like he is doing enough, but he is not God . . . he doesn't have super powers to make everything change. But I do think that all of these expectations are also a burden at times. The expectations were so high because of where we were as a country and the way that he portrayed himself, he gave everyone faith and hope. We all had so much hope. Me, personally, had so much hope when Obama was running. I couldn't believe how he was able to bring all of us together to make a change. I thought that it was all going to get better, for us as college students, for people in the lower class, it would be better. For people, in general, it would be better. (Twenty-four-year old Middle Eastern American male from Illinois)

According to some participants, the wide appeal that Obama benefitted from during the presidential campaign resulted in expectations that were diverse as well. One young Mexican American male college student from Illinois declares:

> I think that, in part, is why he has such high expectations placed on him. The expectations come from all different types of people—all of the different types

of people that voted for him. So, for instance, black people will have a different set of expectations of him than what white people would expect. And even more so with different classes: upper class, middle class, lower class. As much as his appeal was an advantage, it is now a disadvantage because all of the expectations are so high.

The idea that an extremely successful presidential election results in unrealistic expectations is a consistent theme across focus groups. Some participants, especially those who are relatively new to politics, expect the positive energies of the campaign to continue. This is the sentiment of one twenty-seven-year-old Latino from Massachusetts:

> I voted for him because I thought that it was going to be in campaign mode for the four years . . . I thought that I would actually see him with his sleeves rolled up, talking about issues in very plain terms like he did in the campaign . . . I want him to be that motivator. Like with the economy, there are a lot of people hurting, but I don't see the reassurance from the president that we could get better. I think that he has to be that cheerleader for the country.

Many participants discuss how Obama supporters, especially those with little political experience, have unrealistically high expectations in terms of how fast change can occur. "The buzz words were hope and change. That's what he ran on, and that's what everyone latched on to," comments one young Caucasian male from Nebraska. He, like others, discusses how many people "don't realize that he can't magically change everything overnight." An older white male from Illinois also comments on this issue when he says: "If people were looking at him to make change like Roosevelt did with his 'first one hundred days in office,' that's not possible any more. The president doesn't have that much power any more. So much has been transferred to congressional power."

Several participants' comments reflect that President Obama also might have had unrealistic expectations about how quickly he could enact change. According to a sixty-something-year-old woman from Connecticut,

> I think that there was so much damage done before he even took office . . . and he thought that he could repair some of it quicker than he could actually do it. And he convinced a lot of people that he could do that . . . and um, he got dealt an awfully hard hand to deal with. People are holding him accountable for doing some of the things he wanted to do, but no one is helping him with it.

The perception that Barack Obama is idealistic is also a point of discussion in a Nebraska focus group. According to one older white man, "he actually got elected being an idealist, but that idealism didn't last very long." He adds that, "obviously this is supposition, but I think that he has realized that saying something and getting it done are two very different things."

The presence of unrealistically high expectations, according to several participants, causes the general public to view President Obama as a failure. A number of Obama supporters are adamant in pointing out that he has achieved several campaign promises (e.g., in health care, Wall Street reform, economic development). These accomplishments, however, are largely ignored given that people expect him to do much more quickly. One young Caucasian woman from Ohio shares:

> I think that the people had VERY high expectations for him . . . and that's why, at the beginning of the presidency and even now, they feel like "Oh, he's failing." But if we really think about it, he had a big job ahead of himself; and I knew that he wasn't going to be able to get everything done in one term. He's done some things already, but if he gets another term, that's when we will begin seeing real change . . . there will be even more improvement.

A similar idea is articulated by a middle-aged white male from New England. As seen below, he questions the general public's ability to understand how change works.

> His whole campaign was about change, and I really think that there have been some big changes but not necessarily those that we automatically feel in our everyday lives, though. What can he really do to change someone's everyday life? What can he really do in two years? Four years? Or even eight years? I think that so many Americans had such lofty expectations for him, that he can't win. I think that he is doing a good job, but it's hard to him to meet such unrealistic expectations.

According to a young Mexican American woman in California, "people are now giving him a hard time because they look at him as being a perfect president who was going to come and change the world instantly." Her focus group occurred a couple of weeks following the 2010 midterm elections. She goes on to criticize how so many people voted against President Obama's agenda after such a short amount of time: "There is no way that you are going to be able to change something so engrained in four years. In a year and a half, almost two years, he is going to completely change the United States? Really? Come on, people, be realistic!"

UNREALISTIC EXPECTATIONS: WHO'S TO BLAME?

Thus far, I have demonstrated how many participants describe how Barack Obama's communication effectiveness is criticized in light of the unrealistically high expectations that surround his presidency. Maybe not surprisingly, the vast majority of these participants are Democrats who actively support President Obama. In many of their comments, I see attempts to defend him against attacks that they consider unfair or overly critical. Interestingly, participants who self-identify as Republican, Libertarian, or Tea Party supporters have a different take on the issue.

According to some participants, Barack Obama and his campaign staff are to blame for creating such a high level of unrealistic expectations. According to one young white male Republican from Massachusetts, the expectations that we have of President Obama are "self-imposed":

> I think that a lot of the expectations that came with him were self-imposed. We were definitely coming off of a really bad situation, low approval rating from President Bush . . . and we wanted a superman. And he sold himself as that. He became a mythical, larger-than-life legend . . . before he was even designated as the Democratic nominee. His face was on hundreds of t-shirts and all over the Internet. He was just such the icon of change and hope. In part he sold himself to that level, and in turn, people were expecting him to perform at that level. You put your faith in what you perceive to be the best person for the entire nation, and want to see that come to fruition. So, yes I think that they are a lot more critical, but I think that it is because he set himself up that way.

This idea is also seen in the perceptions from a young white woman from Virginia who also comments on his choice to campaign on idealistic values: "His whole campaign was built on hope and change. And when you have those two goals, you hope that change will come. That's the platform that he ran on, and when you think of him, that is what you think of. So, of course, we are going to expect those things." These types of perceptions are most evident in groups that include primarily more conservative voters. However, they are also heard in groups where one or two Republican-leaning participants express their minority opinions. This is the case in an Illinois focus group where a young white female says: "I know that I'm not alone here, because I know a lot of people who feel the same way: He created such high expectations for himself to get things done. That's why so many people were duped into voting for him. Now we are just waiting, waiting, waiting."

Other participants place more of the blame on Obama's campaign staff. These are individuals who largely believe that he serves as a "puppet president" being controlled by more powerful Democrats in Washington. According to one older white male North Carolinian, "The Obama campaign didn't understand how they created all of these unrealistic expectations for Obama . . . they had put him on a Messiah pedestal in order to get him elected. That was the only way that he could win against another candidate who was so much more qualified." A middle-aged white male from Nebraska agrees with this assessment. Specifically, he criticizes how the campaign "used every trick in the book" to create the perception that Barack Obama was "nothing less than the Messiah."

Addressing other participants, he says: "Think about it. Axelrod and all his people used every trick in the book to convince the U.S. public that Obama was nothing less than the Messiah! They were in cahoots with the liberal media who focused on how shiny and new he was. We were led to believe that he was this perfect leader who could change the world." Within this perspective, President Obama deserves criticism for "promising people the moon" and not being able to deliver on those promises once he took office.

Supporters of President Obama, however, are quick to point out the fact that all political candidates make campaign promises that, once in office, prove impossible to keep. According to these participants, that is something that is simply accepted by the voters. However, several comment on how when President Obama was elected the perception was that he would accomplish everything that he talked about during the campaign. According to several participants, like the young biracial woman from Massachusetts quoted below, this is related to the expectations that President Obama and his campaign staff created:

> I think that we had such high expectations, because for one, he gave us those expectations. I felt motivated, had hope, and expected change with Obama. People thought that Obama was the greatest thing ever. . . . It's funny because people actually expect him to keep his campaign promises whereas that hasn't been the case in the past.

For this participant, the expectations for President Obama seem to be different than those for other presidents. One twenty-something-year-old Caucasian woman from Connecticut offers an interesting example of how these expectations affect people in different ways.

> Working in the pharmacy, I hear a lot of anti-Obama comments—especially when people have to pay a co-pay. It is often viewed as his fault, and I think that there is a huge difference between President Obama and other presidents. I mean, when President Bush was president I never heard anyone blame President Bush for their co-pay. Never. But the instant that somebody has to pay a co-pay that they weren't expecting now, it's Obama's fault. And I've heard it over and over again. So, it's instantly his fault when he doesn't do everything he promised. It is very interesting to me that people would instantly blame a president for their own small issue.

SUMMARY

Chapter 4 extends some of the thematic insights I describe in the previous chapter. In particular, I demonstrate how public perceptions of President Obama's communication are influenced by the larger political context (e.g.,

Barack Obama the presidential candidate versus Barack Obama the forty-fourth president of the United States). Within the chapter, I discuss the influential role that first impressions and unrealistically high expectations play for individual evaluations of his communication effectiveness. Finally, participant comments are used to illustrate how President Obama's changing communication style can be understood as a reflection of the realities of a bipartisan U.S. political landscape—something that according to some, drastically reduces his confidence that he could foster in meaningful societal change. Chapter 5 continues exploring public perceptions of President Obama's communication by examining how focus group participants react to specific events that garnered significant attention in recent years.

Chapter 5

"Presidential Communication"

> I think that we expect presidents to be a certain way and act a certain way. And when they don't, we evaluate them accordingly. We evaluate them a few notches down.
>
> —Young white male college student from California

Public perceptions of Barack Obama's communication are largely contextualized by how individuals believe he *should* communicate as president. In the previous chapters in this section, I focus on the diverse ways in which study participants evaluate President Obama's communication effectiveness. This chapter extends this point of analysis to include public perceptions of his communication competence. Within the field of communication, communication competence involves an evaluation where an individual is regarded as both: (1) effective (achieving a specific goal), and (2) appropriate (taking into account the other person's perspective) (Spitzberg and Cupach, 1989). Addressing issues related to perceptions of President Obama's communication competence is especially insightful given that participants have very different ideas regarding whether or not his communication is appropriate or not. Within the examples featured in this chapter, evaluations of appropriateness are most closely related to the standards for presidents that have been created over time. In this regard, the chapter focuses on how President Obama's communication is seen as succeeding or failing to follow existing perceptions of what constitutes communication that is "presidential." Alternatively, I explore the ways in which the public sees President Obama's communication as extending existing presidential standards in positive ways.

In their descriptions of the 2008 presidential election, participants recall how they evaluated candidates, in part, based on if they appeared "presidential" or not. Once candidates were narrowed down in terms of their policies, individuals then applied the "presidential" standard: Which candidate most closely matches up with the standards that they have for the office of the presidency of the United States? In terms of communication competence, participants generally regard Barack Obama as the candidate with the highest levels of communication effectiveness and appropriateness. While participants appreciate his ability to motivate and inspire individuals from all types of backgrounds, this skill is not the most important aspect in terms of their evaluation of whether or not he is the most "presidential." Instead, most participants point to instances when he is able to draw from his personal, educational, and professional experiences to provide leadership on important social issues. Several speeches during the presidential campaign are mentioned as examples of Barack Obama's "presidential-ness." However, one speech in particular stands out: his "A More Perfect Union" speech on race.

"A More Perfect Union" is the name of the speech that then-Senator Barack Obama gave at the National Constitution Center in Philadelphia, Pennsylvania on March 18, 2008. Borrowing a phrase from the U.S. Constitution preamble, this speech was a response to growing concern regarding Obama's relationship with his former pastor and mentor, Rev. Jeremiah Wright whose controversial comments regarding the United States received tremendous media exposure. The speech addressed a number of politically charged topics including race, racism, racial inequality, racial tensions, white privilege, black anger, and white resentment.

Across the board—including individuals from different political parties—participants regard "A More Perfect Union" as "one of Obama's shining moments." The vast majority of participants' comments are similar in that they applaud his ability, genuineness, and courage in addressing an issue that has long plagued the United States. In the words of one young African American man in Alabama,

> I think that his speech on race during the campaign was excellent. It was a speech to deal with the Reverend Wright situation. It was the most insightful speech on race that I've ever heard. He spoke about the issue in ways that I have never heard before. He did it in a straightforward kind of way. He covered a lot of important issues in a way that everyone can understand. He spoke truth to the issue of race in America.

Similar glowing accounts of his speech are provided by others, including a middle-aged Caucasian male from southern Virginia. In no uncertain terms, he says: "It seemed to come across as the most straightforward, intellectual discussion of race that any of our leaders had ever done." Other participants focus on how the speech took great courage and included significant risk.

> With the Reverend Wright thing, I know that his advisors were telling him, "Don't touch it." I clearly got that vibe. "Don't touch it." But he made a speech that addressed it as directly as anybody. He brought his experiences of living in a white world into the address, and then being a part of a black community as a community organizer. But his experiences were coming into play and the breadth of his experiences were right there for everybody to see. I thought that it was extremely impressive. (Seventy-something-year-old black male in California)

For many participants, when Barack Obama addresses the issue of race in such a honest, straightforward and productive manner it helps illustrate how he possesses the qualities necessary for the role of U.S. president. However, as established in chapter 4, his ability to meet and exceed the existing standards of "presidential communication" creates an expectation that he would be able to bring comparable levels of communication competence to all settings. When this doesn't occur, some participants are critical. For instance, one twenty-something-year-old Puerto Rican male attending school in Massachusetts states:

> I definitely think that he is composed. I think that he is charismatic. I think that he is really thoughtful. But I also think that all of these things have sort of waned as he took on this role of commander in chief . . . I think that he is more . . . at least the way that I perceive him on television, I see him as more calculating, more cerebral. I feel more of a disconnect, whereas before I felt like he was speaking from the gut. For example, when he gave the speech on race, I felt like he was speaking from the gut. When the Jeremiah scandal really blew up . . . not only did I watch that, but I think that a lot of people watched it and felt that he was speaking from the heart, what he really believed. Whereas now that he is actually governing the country, when he says something, I feel that the words are carefully chosen by his team. I think that you see that they are more scripted, and I almost feel that he is not being himself. He is being forced to go the political center, because of the tough times that we are in.

This participant is not the only one who wishes that President Obama could maintain the high level of communication competence—in terms of both his effectiveness and appropriateness—achieved during his speech on race. While many participants have this general expectation, one Californian Asian American man in his forties has a specific example of how President Obama can apply the principle to a contemporary issue.

> I mentioned the Reverend Wright thing because I think that that was a great form of communication. . . . It was obviously done for political reasons, he was

suffering politically at the time. He took on a major issue in the United States, the issue of race. I think the timing was good, and the content was good. I think that that was a great example of effective communication from the president. It just occurred to me that, since being president, he has maybe missed some of the timing and content. So, let's say that there's a problem with employment right now. I would like to see something very similar to what I saw with Rev. Wright around employment. The issue is not something new, it is not a problem because Barack Obama is president. It's not a problem because it is 2010. There have been unemployment problems since the United States split from Britain. So, it is something that can be talked about in terms of context in a similar way that the race issue was addressed. I don't think that I've heard that since the election. A difficult issue being addressed in timely manner and with the content that can get us thinking and talking about it.

This quote highlights how participants use established standards of what they perceive as "presidential communication" to evaluate Obama's communication competence. Next, I examine how President Obama's leadership style has veered from traditional approaches. Then, in the remainder of the chapter, I discuss participants' reactions to how President Obama communicates regarding several specific events: The BP oil spill, Kanye West's behavior at the MTV Music Awards, and the controversy involving a mosque near Ground Zero.

A MORE FEMININE APPROACH TO LEADERSHIP

The month that I began facilitating focus groups for the research project that is the basis for this book, an article appeared in *The Washington Post* that describes President Obama as "our first female president" (Parker, 2010, p. 17). In the article, the author argues that if President Clinton can be regarded as the first black president (a label initially given to him by African American author Toni Morrison), then President Obama can be viewed as our first female president. In particular, Parker lists several communication behaviors (e.g., listening, coalition building, passive-voice constructions) regarded as feminine in U.S. society. She makes it clear that she is not "calling Obama a girlie president," but questions if he is going to be the "first male president who pays a political price for acting too much like a woman" (p. 17). Several participants in several focus groups make direct references to Parker's article in discussions of public perceptions of President Obama's communication. The vast majority of participants, however, are not aware of the article. Yet, after the topic is introduced, they share the perception that President Obama's leadership style seems out of bounds of what is considered "presidential."

While the majority of participants view President Obama's communication style as an appreciated change, this perception is not universal. In fact, a number of participants are quite critical. This includes some individuals who want him to represent the United States in more powerful ways. According to one white male senior citizen from Connecticut, President Obama needs to be more "aggressive in his communication. We are the most powerful country in the world, and we need to tell countries what we want them to do." From his perspective, listening is a sign of weakness. "We should not always listen to them—they should be listening to us!," he goes on to say. Other participants also criticize the lack of power in his communication style, especially when he is interacting with leaders from other countries. After listening to other participants describe President Obama's communication style as powerful, a thirty-something-year-old Caucasian male from Massachusetts responds: "Well, I think that that is interesting, because I don't see him as a powerful communicator. I just don't at all. His look isn't powerful to me; I'm like 'Come on, you're being a wimp.' We are the most powerful country in the world, and I want someone to communicate like it! Don't back down from other countries."

Other participants are critical of the ways in which President Obama appears too connected to some of the issues that he is working on. This includes several instances when, in some participants' eyes, he is not able to maintain objectively detached from the issue. Allowing one's emotions to show, according to one Native American male college student attending a Michigan community college, is unprofessional and ineffective. In response to a conversation where participants describe how President Obama shows considerable frustration with a heckler, he asserts:

> You want detached professionalism . . . you want the communication where he's looking you in your eye and speaking to you objectively . . . But when it comes down to a situation and he is the president, he needs to get the job done professionally. It could be a national conflict, war, or whatever comes our way . . . he needs to do it with detached professionalism where he doesn't allow his emotions to take precedence over what needs to be done. But when he has a little break down when responding to someone in the crowd, that show a weakness that causes us to lose confidence in him in the bigger situations.

In another focus group on the same campus, some participants applaud President Obama's ability to practice empathy in his communication with others. However, a young white male Republican questions the value of this approach when he says: "But is that really what you want the president to do—feel empathy for everybody? In my mind, empathy and emotion should be totally eliminated from politics. Emotions should not be there, because once you allow emotion to get into these issues, it blows it all up." Within this perspective, President Obama's communication style is not "presidential" in that it lacks the necessary aggression, power and objectivity. According to others, he fails to enact a communication stance that intimidates others—something that reduces his overall effectiveness as the leader of the Free World. This issue is discussed at great length in a focus group with several white males (WM), a white female (WF) and African American female (AAF) and male (AAM) that took place at a large state university in Michigan. Within the extended excerpt provided below, take note of the different perceptions regarding "the intimidation factor" and how it is positioned in terms of what is considered "presidential."

>WM#1: I think that his nonverbal communication is actually pretty good. He really expresses emotion accurately and it goes along with what he is saying. Not only that, the gestures that he uses aren't overly aggressive. He doesn't point, he kinda makes this shape (shows hand open, fingers together). He doesn't really . . . some presidents bang their fists on the podium and stuff like that. He doesn't come across as overly aggressive, which I think is very effective especially if he is going to be communicating with representatives from other countries. I think that it is really important that he has that ability. I think that it is something that everyone should model.
>
>WF: I don't know really too much. But what I have seen is that a lot of other presidents who I've seen glimpses of on TV, I felt like they were intimidating so that you know that they are in charge. With Obama, I kinda forget that he is so powerful because when he talks I feel that he is just a person who is sharing his views. If I had a chance to talk with him, it would be easier to express my feelings with him because I would feel that he would understand me. As compared to trying to influence me and remind me that he is the president.
>
>WM#2: I kinda like the intimidation factor of the other presidents. I always feel that the president—if I voted for him or not—represents me. And, if you're going to another country, I don't want to be like "you're less of a country than us," but you're representing America. America—some people might disagree—but America is the greatest country on earth. You have to represent us with power, with authority. You have to be number one at everything that you do. So, I don't like how—I don't want to say that he is soft, but some of his body language sometimes (to me) isn't "presidential." It doesn't have the power that I like from president's past. Like a Reagan.
>
>AAF: I don't know. I think that when he enters a room, he's just like, "Yeah, bitches I'm here." [Group laughter]. He just gives off that essence, like "Yeah, I'm the man. I'm the one runnin' this."
>
>AAM: I think that that is what makes Obama so great. He is not intimidating—who wants to vote for someone who scares them? I think that, yes, he does a great job at sounding forceful. Because he has said, "We will NOT stand for this, we will do this," but he is not UUUURRRGGGHHH in

your face. Think about it: When parents yell at you, do we listen? No. But when they talk to us, we listen. Well, he talks to us: "This is wrong, this is right. This is what we are going to do and this is how we are going to do it." I think that is what makes him so great because he has learned how to master that communication skill. People feel like they can relate to him, and not like he is trying to make them do something. They want to do it because they want to.

Like that which is reflected in this one group interaction, most participants perceive President Obama's communication as a welcome shift in "presidential communication." For instance, his desire to embrace a more inclusive, democratic style of leadership is applauded by some participants including one older white male from North Carolina who says:

One of the things that made me really like him, was at his cabinet meetings, he wants to hear from everybody. If there is one person who hasn't spoken, he will say, "So, what do you think? What is your point of view? What do you have to say? I want to hear from you." In other words, he takes into account as much knowledge, as much information, as he can before he makes some of the most important decisions that a human being can make. I applaud that, and furthermore, I personally applaud people identifying him as feminine communicator. I think humanity has not adequately appreciated the value of women . . . we haven't adequately recognized the intellect and communication abilities of women.

Across different focus groups, participants view the fact that President Obama "is much less masculine than previous presidents" as "a nice change" (young white female from Virginia). In fact, one twenty-something-year-old European American woman from Connecticut embraces the idea that President Obama is our first female president. For her, his nurturing style is exactly what is needed:

I personally think that America needs a mother, at this point. Somebody needs to come and grab everybody up and say "Come on, I'll take care of you." I think that is what he is trying to do . . . like with Iraq, "come on, we've done all that we can do, let's go." Same thing with Afghanistan . . . "Let's take care of our people. Let's take that money and use it here." And I said, "Thank you, Lord, finally somebody wanting to use our money here." Finally. When I read that article, I thought "About time. We need a mother for America. There are all of these first ladies, but we need a woman president to be a mom around here." And that's the feeling that I get. By supporting the troops and bringing them home, we are going to have money to do things here. Let's solve our own problems before everyone's else's.

For a significant number of participants, President Obama's approach to world affairs is a welcome shift from the approach of previous U.S.

presidents. One young European American woman from California states: "I like that he wants to be a diplomat. I think that the whole chauvinistic mode of ruling the world is not working for us. Especially because we are the most powerful nation in the world, in our eyes, not necessarily how the rest of the world sees us." In particular, several participants openly criticize the approach taken by President Bush. This is the key idea of comments provided by an African American man from Virginia who is dedicating his life to military service.

> Look at President Bush. He was the guy who was all tough and said, "I'm gonna go in and find weapons of mass destruction, and do this and do that." To me, he had that tough guy image: "we are going by ourselves if necessary—we don't need anyone." For me, what I do for a living (traveling around the world in the military), I see people's views of America. People's view of us is that we are arrogant, lazy, ignorant. People do not hold us in high esteem. What they want from us is money. If they want something from us, then they will work with us. But their own personal perceptions are that we are arrogant, pompous, and that's it. And all that Bush did was solidify that.

Another African American man, of similar age but from Alabama, offers comments that reinforce the idea that President Obama doesn't have to embrace a "cowboy approach" to conquering the world to be effective. Specifically, he states:

> I think that he has been stern on some things, at some times. He isn't the cowboy guy, someone who is going to go in and rile things up. That's not his style. That's President Bush's style. He wasn't that smart, but Obama is smart. If you are smart, to me, you don't do certain things just because you can. You think through things more. Bush did things out of ignorance, not because he was an educated man. To me, Obama is better than that. He is smart so he doesn't have to use that style. I don't call Obama weak or feminine. I think that he knows how to do things through his own style.

The issues regarding President Obama's "feminine" communication style is an interesting point of analysis in terms of the standards associated with what is considered "presidential communication." I continue examining these issues through participant perceptions of President Obama's communication surrounding three recent events: (1) BP oil spill, (2) Kanye West's behaviors at the MTV Music Awards, and (3) the controversy over constructing a mosque near Ground Zero. Within each of these examples, I explore a different aspect of "presidential communication."

BP OIL SPILL

On April 20, 2010, a BP Oil Deepwater Horizon rig exploded off the U.S. coast killing eleven workers and pouring twenty-five to thirty-nine million gallons of oil into the Gulf of Mexico. According to the critics, President Obama's response was less than acceptable—both in terms of timeliness and forcefulness. The president was quick to defend his actions by citing the number of times he had visited the area and the time spent behind the scenes meeting with experts. He then said publicly, "I don't sit around just talking to experts because this is a college seminar. We talk to these folks because they potentially have the best answers, so I know whose ass to kick" (Sargent, 2010). President Obama's communication surrounding the BP oil spill is a topic of discussion in many different focus group discussions. In particular, participants use it as an example to illustrate their perceptions of his communication competence.

Timeliness of His Response

Within the different focus group discussions, only a few participants directly criticize the timeliness of President Obama's response to the BP oil spill. In fact, the couple of negative comments that appear are typically based on other people's perceptions. For instance, one young African American woman from Massachusetts shares that: "I'm really close to my aunt and my uncle, they are much more critical of Obama. . . . So like with the oil spill, my aunt was one of those people who said that he needs to get out and do something! And be quick about it! He needs to get angry and show some emotion." One participant, a Caucasian man from rural southern Ohio, suggests that his delayed response might have been due to ineptitude. "One thing that he did with the BP oil spill was that he kept his mouth shut . . . because he had no clue. He didn't know what to say, or what he was going to do with it. I mean we didn't hear anything out of him for three-to-four weeks . . . it was that long before he even made a comment or a statement," he states. For this particular issue, the most vocal critic is a young white male community college student from Michigan. Participating in a group of Democratic, Republican, and Independent voters, he urges others to compare and contrast the response to President Obama's delayed communication to what happened with President Bush.

> Not to take a time trip, but let's go back to New Orleans. Hurricane hits, President Bush hears about it, heads down, and does what he can. Everyone gave him crap out of the wazoo for it. Now BP's been leaking oil for two months, now it's okay. Now it's not so bad that someone isn't doing something. He's not bad that he isn't down there every weekend doing something—but its okay if you

fly down on Earth Day, from Washington, D.C., to California, that's fine. It's just interesting to see how this all plays out.

Immediately following these comments, other participants are quick to point out the differences between the two events. Most in the group defend President Obama's response.

In most focus groups, participants describe President Obama's communication regarding the BP oil spill as both appropriate and effective. In particular, they focus on two points. First, participants argue that President Obama's delayed response is effective given the circumstances. From the perspective of a young African American woman attending a HBCU in Alabama, "I wouldn't say that him not talking until Day 30 was ineffective, because he really didn't have anything to say. What is he supposed to do? Call a news conference and say nothing? I appreciated that he didn't waste my time saying something on Day 2: 'There is an oil spill.' I like that he waited and actually gave me the facts." Other participants focus their comments on how they appreciate that President Obama does not rush in and try to solve the problem with U.S. tax dollars. One middle-aged white male from southern Ohio advises:

> He done right by telling BP that they had to fix it. He told them "You know what you've done, now you have to solve it." If he had stepped in there, and tried to fix it using tax dollars, it would have been bad. I think that behind the scenes he was involved. But him and his advisors were advising BP that this is what the public deserves and this is what you need to do. They were doing things behind the scenes, we just didn't see it all.

For some participants, President Obama's delayed response is necessary to ensure that BP will take responsibility for the problem. The benefits of his actions are clear, as one older Caucasian woman from Massachusetts articulates:

> I think that everything that has happened with BP, he handled it very well. He was very effective. He managed to get the companies to step up and fund hundreds of millions of dollars. There were no court settlements, it was just them willing to give this money to help people who lost their jobs and the water/land that was destroyed. I think that he could definitely say that he helped with what happen so quickly. If it was Bush or someone else, he might have sided with the oil company or been a bit more lenient with them.

Interestingly, another white woman in the same group immediately disagrees.

> I kinda feel the opposite because he didn't really stand that strong of a stance . . . BP was kinda a really big contributor to his campaign . . . because of that. . . . He

did take a stand eventually, and he was really hard on them. But at first, I think that he was silent. Yes, he was addressing the issue, but he wasn't attacking BP. And now, it really ticks me off because I knew that they had made financial contributions to him and his campaign. And maybe his advisors told him to do that, or maybe it was a personal decision, but either way, I didn't like it. I thought that he needed to take action faster and be more decisive. He needed to be more critical with BP faster.

Like so many other issues covered throughout this book, the timeliness of President Obama's response to the BP oil spill is perceived quite differently by different individuals. Such is the also the case for the forcefulness of his response.

Forcefulness of His Response

Did President Obama display enough forcefulness in his response to the BP oil spill? Was his communication "presidential?" These two questions are at the heart of several focus group discussions. For some participants, President Obama's communication is "presidential" and strikes an effective balance in his handling of the situation. That is the conclusion drawn by one young white female from Nebraska who says:

Personally, I know that he has gotten a lot of grief about the whole Gulf Coast incident and how he is not being forceful enough—or how he is not doing enough. But I think that he has been pretty effective. He has been down there numerous times, talking with different professions—fisherman, senators, and other people down there—trying to figure out the right thing to do. And talking to BP about how to fix it. I don't think that he was not emotional enough, he's the president. What is he supposed to do? It's not like that he can personally fix the problem. He is doing all that he can. I think that he was effective in going down there and talking to different professions.

In terms of forcefulness, most participants focus on President Obama's comments where he references "whose ass to kick." Interestingly, this issue is raised in a number of focus groups including one in Virginia where a young European American woman shares:

Wasn't there a situation where he was talking about going down there, and he cussed on national TV? I thought that it was inappropriate. In one interview, he said, "I want more information about who was responsible, because I want to know whose ass to kick." I thought that that was effective but inappropriate. It made it show that he cared, but he could have used different language. It didn't seem that presidential to me.

While this participant interprets his use of language as effective—in that it achieves his goal of making sure people understood the seriousness of the matter—not everyone agrees. Several young and middle-aged white women, for instance, believe that it sends the wrong message to others including the participant who says:

> When we are teaching our children that you don't do that, and they are watching this from our president and he is doing it. . . . It is sending the wrong message to our kids—that it is okay to talk to anybody any way you want, and use whatever language that you want. Isn't he supposed to be a role model? (Michigan community college student)

All in all, most participants who weigh in on this subject perceive President Obama's language as a sign of forcefulness that might have been inappropriate but is highly effective. For many, like a middle-aged Mexican American woman from Michigan, "Using that word, it makes it seem that he is angry for the people. And that's effective for me." Others believe that President Obama had a "human moment where he said something that a lot of [people] were thinking" (young white woman from Nebraska). In this regard, his response is honest in its forcefulness. This was the point of one middle-aged African American woman from Alabama who says:

> If you ask him an honest question, then you are going to get an honest answer. At that moment, if you agree with it or not, he gave an honest answer. I feel like that he shouldn't be penalized for that. You've [another participant] said that he should be discretionary with all of these things but I would say that he doesn't have time for all of that. Clearly, if it is a serious matter with an ambassador or another president, or the king or queen of some country, of course, you want to be mindful for what you say. But I feel that what he said to BP was what everyone else was feeling. If my livelihood was being challenged, of course, I would want someone to be held accountable. There's always a time and place for nice words, to be really careful about what you say. But when he responded the way that he did, you got the point. You understood his overall message: "I'm about business and BP is going to be held accountable. Period. We are going to do whatever it takes to make sure that they get the job done." People wanted to hear that.

At least one other participant questions why everyone is focusing on that one word and not his overall message. In her view, President Obama is unfairly being criticized for something that most other leaders get "a pass for": "So what—he swore?! He didn't say any more than the rest. Clinton swore. Old man Bush did too. And Biden? He is the leader of the pack for crying out loud! (middle-aged white woman from Connecticut).

Several participants interpret President Obama's using such forceful language as a response to criticisms that he is being "too soft." One young African American college student from Illinois offers:

> Obama cussing about the oil spill might have been a little bit inappropriate. But at the same time, it was effective because everyone is always on Barack about being too soft on certain issues . . . how nice he is. So, when he slips up and says a minor curse word, don't get mad at him because he has been trying to handle things that polite way the entire time, and it's not happening.

In this regard, at least one participant questions if President Obama's response is part performance for the camera. This thirty-year-old Caucasian male from Nebraska begins his comments describing how the media influences public perceptions.

> I think that if you go back in history, you do see politicians being more emotional in terms of how they govern. I think that it is just since television has come around that presidents have become more robotic in terms of what they say and what they do. I mean some of our past presidents were nuts . . . [group laughter]. FDR was a nut! We've had figures in history like that. I'm comfortable with someone being real and genuine, if they are real and genuine—and not trying to manufacture realness and genuineness. I'm not sure if Obama's interview was genuine or manufactured for the camera.

The next section of this chapter explores public perceptions of President Obama's use of "jackass" in describing Kayne West's outburst at the 2010 MTV Music Awards. Within that discussion, many participants point out how race was a factor. Interestingly, a few participants also believe that race is an underlying factor in how people perceive President Obama's reaction to the BP oil spill. In fact, one young African American woman from California says:

> Like after the whole Gulf oil spill, all of the articles talked about how he wasn't angry enough. They were asking 'Where are you? Why aren't you more angry?' And, I think that his cool, calm, collective personality that people really loved when he was running—something that was not the typical black man. Those things helped him when he got elected, those same things now are negative. No matter what he did, everyone was looking for this huge angry reaction. And the fact that they didn't get it, now they see his personality as a negative.

KANYE WEST, TAYLOR SWIFT, AND PRESIDENT OBAMA

At the September 2009 MTV Video Music Awards, Taylor Swift wins the Best Female Video Award. As she begins to accept the award, rap artist Kanye West takes the stage—and the microphone—to interrupt Swift and let the audience know that Beyonce Knowles is more deserving of the award. The reaction to West's behavior is quick and universally negative. President Obama finds himself a part of the controversy when a reporter casually asks him his thoughts about the situation and another reporter tweets the president's off-the-record response.

> During a CNBC interview on Monday, President Obama called Kanye West a "jackass" regarding his behavior at the MTV Video Music Awards. Obama's colorful remark was actually made in an off-the-record portion of the interview that was tweeted—and then deleted—by ABC News reporter Terry Moran. "Pres. Obama just called Kanye West a 'jackass' for his outburst at VMAs when Taylor Swift won. Now THAT'S presidential," Moran wrote ("Obama: Kanye is a 'jackass,'" n.d.).

Like the BP oil spill, participants—especially traditionally-aged college students—are quick to use President Obama's comments about Kanye West to illustrate an example where the "presidential-ness" of his communication is in question. This section highlights some of the major themes of these discussions.

The language that President Obama uses in describing Kanye West is eerily similar to that which is used in response to the BP oil spill. However, the circumstances surrounding these two instances are very different and consequently evoke significantly different public perceptions. Two specific points of reference are made. First, participants are quick to criticize the media in terms of broadcasting comments taken off the record. This point is made dozens of times by many different participants. African American participants appear most vocal in their criticism of the media; such is the case with one thirty-something-year-old woman from Alabama:

> I thought that that was something taken out of context. It was recorded outside of an interview, so it was an improper, personal type of question/comment. It wasn't like he was going on CNN or *60 Minutes* and then making some comments about it. [group agreement.] That was more of a personal opinion than anything else. I don't see anything wrong with that at all. It wasn't like he was addressing the nation, calling a news conference, and then saying, "By the way everybody . . . "

The second thing that participants take issue with is why the question was even asked of the president in the first place. A young African American woman from California, for example, asks:

> Why would the media even ask him the question? It is like they are trying to get him to say something. . . . Why should he even have to comment? Why

was the question even posed to him? His own personal feelings should be his; he shouldn't have to be placed in that type of situation. It's not a political-type of thing. Now the oil spill is something different. That's something that he should communicate on . . . but Kanye West? What does he have to do with anything?

Other African American participants in several different focus groups provide a clear and concise answer to her question: Race. According to these participants, President Obama's identity as the first U.S. president of African-descent triggers differential treatment from the media. A fifty-something-year-old black woman from Massachusetts asserts:

> I think that people see him as a black president. There are questions that are asked of him that would NEVER have been asked of other presidents regardless who they are. NEVER have questions like that been asked of other presidents. Like the Kanye West question—who would have asked that of another president? And have the president actually answer it in a knowledgeable way? And not have people be shocked and appalled!? We should all be shocked and appalled that anyone who was part of the press corps would ask such a question—especially given the times that we are in. But, at the same time, this is part of his strategy, right? He has made himself to be the type of person that is in the know. He knows about these things. He knows what's going on with the young people, the Kayne West stuff. He knows what's going on with all of these different things.

The perception is that President Obama is expected to address issues related to race—something not necessarily included in traditional conceptualizations of "presidential communication." This issue is also an important aspect of the Prof. Gates/Sgt. Crowley conflict and subsequent "Beer Summit," the focus of chapter 9.

Once participants get past criticizing the circumstances that produced President Obama's response to Kanye West's outburst, they move to praising him for comments that are perceived as both appropriate and effective. For many participants, President Obama's honesty and realness are welcome additions to the way in which presidents communicate. Most of all, participants applaud how he didn't attempt to create a façade, and instead displayed his human side. A young Mexican American woman in California makes this point when she says: "I think that overall he is human just like everyone else. And he was talking one-on-one, person-to-person so he wasn't trying to be political or trying to worry about what everyone thought of him. He was being a person, and he should be able to do that. But, I don't think that everyone should make a big deal of it." A twenty-something-year-old African American in Michigan agrees, and also is critical with anyone who takes issue with it: "I heard that he called Kanye West a jackass after the MTV Music Awards . . . I don't think that that should be held against him . . . he is still human. A lot of people are always bashing him, but it is for the stupidest things. I think that it is all a part of being human."

Other participants praise President Obama for his blunt honesty concerning Kanye West's behavior. According to a young black female from California,

> He was just speaking the truth! He is a jackass! [group laughter]. First of all, the mic wasn't supposed to be on, so whoever did that was wrong. Everybody would have said that Kanye West was a jackass. How could you go up on stage and do that to that seventeen-year-old girl? Are you not a human being? . . . I think that President Obama said that—but we all were thinking it. I don't think that there is one person in this room that would have been, "Oh, poor Kanye!" No. I like Kanye. I like his music and everything. But when President Obama said that, I didn't say, "Oh my gosh, the president said that." I said, "Okaaaaaaaaaay." [group laughter]

For many participants, being "presidential" doesn't always include brutal honesty. However, one young white male college student in Alabama thinks that it should:

> I want an honest president. Even if he did go on CNN and make those comments, or describe the BP oil people as "dumb-fucks," I honestly don't see anything wrong with that. Because that shows his own personal opinion. I'd rather have that than just listen to what he thinks we want to hear. Of course, I don't want him to go on there and cuss all the time. But he's honest about it. Don't try to please everyone . . . I want someone to be honest.

For other participants, President Obama's response to Kanye West is interpreted as "keepin' it real." According to one thirty-something-year-old man in northern California, "Calling Kanye West an asshole shows me that he is still down. He's still one of us." A young black female from Alabama agrees with the assessment.

> With Kanye West, he was dead-on. He was just an asshole. I feel like, you know, sometimes . . . I think that because he is the president people want his ways to be way up here, but he is an average everyday person, number one. Number two, sometimes it is okay to call a spade, a spade. I think that American people, we don't always want to hear the truth. We want to hear what sounds good. And sometimes I think that he needs to call a spade, a spade.

African American participants are not the only ones who appreciate President Obama's realness. A Caucasian woman in her late-twenties shares the following comments in a Connecticut focus group discussion:

One of the first media attacks against him that I remember was when he mumbled "jackass" during an interview. It was caught on tape, and of course, it was torn apart by a whole bunch of media stations. But, I think that to me, that shows that he is very real. Like with President Bush, I felt that he was always . . . he wasn't true to himself. He always said what he had to say, what he thought that the American people wanted to hear, and he went with that. With Obama, he is very real. He is real with his family, he is real with what he says. If he wants to swear, he'll swear. And that's just the end of it, and that's it.

BUILDING A MOSQUE NEAR GROUND ZERO

Focus group participants also discuss President Obama's comments regarding the proposal to build a mosque near the site of the terrorist attacks in New York City on September 11, 2001. During comments shared during a dinner in celebration of the Muslim holiday of Ramadan, President Obama cite the right to freedom of speech and offers support for the Muslim group's right to build the mosque. After some public criticism, he reiterates that he had "no regrets" about his comments but does clarify that he is not commenting on the "wisdom" of the decision (Jackson, 2010).

Public perceptions of the final scenario in this chapter offer another viewpoint on what participants view as the most "presidential" way to communicate about such issues. On one hand, participants call for President Obama, as the country's leader, to take a stand on controversial issues. A twenty-something-year-old European American male college student from Illinois criticizes President Obama on this element:

> Even the mosque that is being built at Ground Zero, that's another example of the problem where he doesn't necessarily take a stand on an issue that people want him to take a stand on. I can't remember who was interviewing him, but he was asked about whether he supported the mosque situation. And he didn't give a definitive answer. And a lot of people were upset about that. They were more upset that he didn't take a stand, more so than the fact that he didn't take a certain stand. This is an important enough issue that he had to take one side or the other. We wanted him to say something that was definitive, and he didn't.

Another participant, a middle-aged Caucasian woman from California, criticizes President Obama for being defensive when taking an unpopular stand: "With the mosque at Ground Zero, I've noticed that when he is saying something that the majority disagrees with, he kinda comes across as defensive more so than other people would." She then adds, "and that comes across as unpresidential." A white male in the same focus group takes issue with the condescending tone of President Obama's comments:

I remember him saying, "This is America, they can do whatever they want." . . . He didn't really go into any depth. . . . It was like he was dumbing it down for all of us. I think that it should dumb it down a little bit, but it was like he used "Kindergarten English." He could have presented his arguments a little better, he could have explained it more . . . don't talk to us like we are children.

On the other hand, participants perceive President Obama's comments regarding the mosque proposal near Ground Zero as representative of "presidential communication." These individuals describe his response as "diplomatic," an important quality for any president to possess. Such is the case for a white man in his seventies who shares the following comments during a North Carolina focus group discussion:

I think that freedom of religion is crucial to people getting along . . . so I think that he did the right thing. He said that it is part of our Constitution, it is part of our fundamental rights in the United States to practice different religions. Nevertheless, we do have this freedom of religion and if the mosque advocated terrorism, then we have problems there. But I don't think that the Muslims should be judged by the militant Islamic group that had no respect for human life. Nevertheless, I do think that it is extremely important for us to practice what we preach. . . . But I think that because of the diversity of opinion, he got it just about right. He said that we have a right to build that Mosque there subject to the local zoning laws; whether they build it there or not is a question of wisdom—which is another issue that he didn't get into. And I think that that is fine. He shouldn't have to get into that. I do think that he should have said that they have a right, subject to the local zoning laws, to build that there (assuming that they can finance it and so on).

In this focus group, participants also critique the role that the media plays in making this an issue. Several people, for instance, point out that the sound bite (mosque at Ground Zero) is not accurate. One older white woman provides the following insight:

I don't want to get into the mosque too much, but my understanding is that it is not a mosque, it is a community center and not *actually at* Ground Zero. . . . I could be wrong . . . but what I do want to say is that this was a time, among many others, that I felt that Obama waffled a little bit. I cannot imagine anybody being in the position that he is in . . . to have absolutely every word be under a magnifying glass. What you say you have to be so careful about, everything that comes out of your mouth . . . yet, in general, he just seems able to flow. The population, in my mind, has been turned against him by the media. I really firmly believe that. I think that he has been . . . he has waffled here and there in terms of his communication. For example, initially he did support the right of the mosque to be there. Then, at a later time—not too long, maybe the next day—he said that he didn't think that it was a good idea.... My sense was that it was an implication so that he was covering himself. I suppose that that is a strength of a good communicator, right? Because they know how to respond to whatever comes up in a careful way, so that everyone's ideas are included. And I really think that he is an artist in that, in my mind. But I suppose that that is part of the political process. You can't just say what you want to . . . you have to be vague with your comments so that most people agree with you. That's part of being president.

Within these comments, she indirectly makes the argument that part of practicing diplomacy is considering all sides of an issue. This may come off as "waffling"; however, it represents a communication skill that is regarded as "presidential."

SUMMARY

This chapter provides glimpses into how participants perceive President Obama's communication competence through implicit and explicit standards of what is viewed as "presidential communication." Throughout the chapter, I highlight the ways in which public perceptions regard his communication as in/appropriate and in/effective in terms of his responses to a number of specific events including the BP oil spill, Kanye West's outburst at the MTV Music Video Awards, and the controversial proposal to build a mosque near Ground Zero. These occurrences are all identified and discussed by a significant number of focus group participants, whose comments provide insight into how perceptions are informed by expectations of what is considered appropriate and effective. Chapter 9 continues this path of exploration with yet another event that garnered international attention: the conflict between Professor Gates/Sergeant Crowley, which triggered a presidential "Beer Summit." Without question, this series of events is the single-most discussed topic among participants, marking it as something deserving substantial attention. However, prior to focusing on President Obama's communication regarding the Gates/Crowley conflict, some preliminary analyses of race are covered in chapters 6, 7, and 8.

Part III

Race Matters in a "Post-Racial" Society

Chapter 6

The Role of Race in "Post-Racial" Politics

> Barack Obama represents a transitional bridge. The United States wasn't entirely ready for a black president. But they could be ready for Obama.
>
> —Young Caucasian woman from Massachusetts

As I wrote in chapter 1, my primary objective for this project is to investigate public perceptions of Barack Obama's communication. I am explicitly interested in getting the perspectives from individuals from diverse backgrounds across the United States. This is important because I suspect that individual perceptions are going to vary significantly depending on the person's cultural identity. Race, racial identity, and racism represent one topical area that I want to cover during focus groups discussions. As someone who teaches classes on interracial communication and communicating about taboo topics, I recognize that public discussions about race—especially amidst acquaintances and strangers—are oftentimes a challenge to facilitate because people are fearful of saying something ignorant, offensive, or inflammatory. Consequently, my strategy in each focus group is to concentrate on Barack Obama's communication until a participant (or participants) broaches the topic of race. Once issues related to race are raised, I embark on a series of questions regarding Barack Obama's race, the role of race and racism in the electoral process, and whether or not the United States has reached a "post-racial" existence. This strategy is effective in that it eases focus group participants into discussions regarding this taboo topic in a seamless manner as participants became more comfortable with one another.

One of the questions that I include in my list of questions for each focus group is, "Do you think that the general public sees President Obama as an African American U.S. president, or a U.S. president that happens to be

92   *Chapter 6*

African American?" I pose this specific question to generate a discussion regarding the media's claim that the election of the U.S.'s first president of African descent signals the existence of a "post-racial" society (Cooper, 2010). Chapter 6 focuses in on the analyzing responses to this question; in particular it explores the role of race in the election and presidency of Barack Obama.

BARACK OBAMA TRANSCENDS RACE

According to many participants, President Obama was elected in part because he is able to transcend race for voters who are ready to move beyond traditional racial divisions. However, as demonstrated here, European American participants (of all ages and backgrounds) are most likely to make this assertion. One young white woman from California explains how President Obama's personal characteristics and accomplishments are instrumental in transcending race:

> I think that he goes beyond race. Yes, he is black but actually he is mixed. But so often people generalize your race based on the color of your skin, not actually science. Because he is president, though, he goes above and beyond race. Not only that though, but his "black characteristics" (if you will) are not there. The way that African Americans speak, the way that they behave—a lot of things about him radiate "white" not "black." And maybe that's why I don't even think about his race.

The idea that President Obama's mass appeal transcends race among European Americans is discussed in a couple different focus groups, including one comprised of all African Americans in California. Within that discussion, a middle-aged black male jokingly states that "For most whites, Obama is the Bob Marley of politics." Bob Marley was dedicated to making great music that transcended race, and participants describe President Obama as doing the same thing in politics. In one of the most unique comparisons in the project, one young Caucasian woman from Indiana describe the irrelevance of race in Obama's politics by when she says:

> I think about the fact that he is a black man, our first black president as often, about as often as I think about the fact that he is our first president with fantastic abs. I'm serious. I really don't feel that he isn't up there with "The Situation" [from MTV's *Jersey Shore*] with his shirt off all of the time. He hasn't named his abs or anything, he doesn't make a big deal of it. And he does the same thing with his race. He sticks to business and doesn't focus on that, and I appreciate that about him. He's all about good politics.

Some participants (but clearly not the majority) see Barack Obama's election as a sign of a "post-racial" United States. One twenty-six-year-old woman from California who describes her own race as "human," asserts that "at this point, the whole race thing is over . . . it doesn't matter anymore. We've transcended it. Now we have a black president, so clearly we are not racist." Other participants offer additional evidence for this. Such is the case for one middle-aged white male from Massachusetts who says:

> I was going to say that when I hear him, I hear him as The president. And I have to remind myself that he is black. He speaks to me as a person, and it didn't bother me. Same thing for my daughter; she says 'Obama, he is the president.' She doesn't see a black president.

To these participants, a racist society could never elect an African American president. As such, his election is a message to others that:

> With the issue of race, I think that the message that he is conveying is that there are no longer any boundaries when it comes to race. They shouldn't be any barriers; you can do whatever you want. You shouldn't be held back by it. (Thirty-something-year-old Caucasian woman from Michigan)

The idea that President Obama transcends race, according to some participants, makes any discussion of race irrelevant. Consequently, a few—like the young white female student from a state university in Alabama I quote here—are critical of my questions regarding race:

> Can I make a comment? Or ask a question? I can't wrap my mind around why it matters that he is a black or white president. Why does it matter? Every president that we have in office you should want them to be the best president that we've ever had in office. That's what I want to say when people describe him as a black president. He's your president. Support him, or vote differently next time. Don't bring up race, because it doesn't matter.

Several European American participants are quick to point out that President Obama's ability to transcend race does not always erase his race, it just isn't as important as other things. One young white male graduate student from Massachusetts makes this point when he says:

> If you talk to people eighteen to twenty-five, I don't think that we see him as the first black president. Well, he is the first black president, but I don't necessarily see him as a black president. When I watched him speak, I never really identified him as the black candidate. He wasn't Jesse Jackson, he wasn't that type of candidate. He really didn't speak like that. A lot of the buzz about

him as a candidate wasn't about him being the first black president. It was more about his policies, and his issues. And a lot of people agreed with him on the issues, agreed with him personally . . . race wasn't important.

A seventy-something-year-old white male from North Carolina agrees. Within his comments he acknowledges the history of race in the United States, but describes how President Obama's communication brings out the best of human qualities:

> When I was a little kid in Detroit, the kids from my school would stand out on the street, and see black people on the bus run by, they would use words that were not proper to use . . . I thought that that was a grievous mistake—and I was probably only nine or ten years old. But, I . . . as I have grown up, and acquired more knowledge, I've learned that race should be irrelevant. Now I appreciate that frequently it isn't, especially with the working class. And my background is as working class as you can be. You know it's always there. But intellectually, it really doesn't belong there, it is not relevant. When I look at him, Obama as president, I don't think of him in terms of race. To me, he is a thoughtful, human being who is trying to do a good job. He is an excellent communicator, in my view. He tries to take into account multiple points of view that resonate with all of us as human beings.

Given the perception that President Obama is able to transcend race, several participants point to the role of the media in making race a central issue. According to these individuals, the media plays up the issue of race because it "sells well with the general public." According to one young white female college student from Ohio: "I feel like race was hit on way too hard during election—not by him because he was never like, 'Vote for me because I'm African American.' It was the media that made such a big deal out of it." A number of other European American participants launch similar criticisms. A twenty-year-old white male from California, for instance, compares President Obama's ability to transcend race in politics with what is happening in sports and music.

> If it wasn't for the media, I would not even think about it. It wouldn't even cross my mind . . . his race wouldn't even have been on my radar. I think that black people dominate the United States right now—like in sports and music, why not the presidency? Some of my favorite athletes and artists are black, but I don't ever think about their race. So race wouldn't have even crossed my mind if the media hadn't made it such a big deal of it.

Other participants also discuss how media influences impact personal perceptions of the role of race and Barack Obama's election. For instance, one middle-aged white male from Rhode Island discloses how family members' ideas appear to be directly informed by certain media outlets.

> I have to tell you, I had some family gather not too long ago. It's kinda embarrassing, though. I was with someone who I am related to who said, "Obama—he chose his race box." And I said, "What?" I've heard a lot of stuff but this is a new one. So, I said "What do you mean?" She said "Well, they asked him to check a box, and he checked off that box. He could have picked white or black and he chose black." Do you think that he had a choice in America to be part black and not be black? First of all. And secondly, what does that mean? Do you think that he had a conscious choice to be black? Is that what you mean? I couldn't even get what they were trying to say. They hear this stuff on FOX News or from Rush Limbaugh, and then they repeat it without even making sense of it.

BARACK OBAMA'S SELF-TALK ABOUT RACE

When it comes to the role of race in current politics, many participants describe how they attempt to ignore media messages and base their perceptions on Barack Obama's own self-talk about race. For these participants, the most frequent perception is that he communicates in ways that make race a non-issue, a stance that seems appropriate and productive. One young white female college student from Indiana declares: "I never saw race to be an issue of any kind. I never looked at him as our first black president. He was just another president. And I don't think that he ever made it a big deal . . . and he shouldn't have." Other participants also applaud this approach: "He does a really good job at being race-neutral. Race doesn't come up that often" (white male college student from Michigan community college). Another young white female participant from the same focus group adds:

> President Obama has gotten it right. He doesn't make it a race thing. By him doing that, he is showing the rest of the country and even the rest of the world to think and act in that way. I mean, we are different, but we are also the same.

Within this perspective, the issue of race is discussed as something that is present but not especially relevant. This is the meaning behind the comments of one middle-aged white woman from Connecticut when she says:

> I don't think that Obama focuses on the race thing, because it is what it is and you have to get over it. I don't think . . . he knows what he is and we all know what he is . . . It's not like he is walking around saying "I'm the BLACK president!" People need to move past the whole race thing.

Participants seem to appreciate President Obama's focus on other issues (e.g., the economy) that are regarded as more important than race. In the words of one fifty-something-year-old (African American female) participant,

> I think that he has done a good job at not focusing his presidency on just race. I think that he has done a good job at focusing on his job as the president. . . . Race is not his number one priority right now. He has a lot of things on his plate, and that may be one of them but it is not the only thing he is focused on.

Other black participants express their perception that President Obama's downplaying of race does not necessarily mean that he is ignoring it all together. For several individuals, issues of race are always present at some level.

> I wanna say that I did view him as being the first black president. But at the same time, I feel like he never really made it apparent during this campaign. He never made it seem like, "Vote for me, I'm going to be the first black president." People can look at it either way—they can either agree or disagree, but he never addressed it formally in his speeches. He might have talked about minorities or about socio-economic status and the economy but he never really brought it to Blacks or Hispanics specifically. I think that he keeps it on the level that it is kinda subliminal. (young black female student from Illinois)

For at least one older black woman from Massachusetts, President Obama's communication is conscious and purposeful:

> I think that when he sought out the presidency, he knew that race was going to be an issue that followed him, and one that he was going to have to deal with—he had to accept that. And I think that he did a really good job at not making it a main issue, while making sure that he is addressing problems that are going on in the African American community. His whole thing about fatherhood, and being a good father, that's something that is a big issue in the African American community. He addressed it, but didn't make it something that was on his agenda. But I think that he has done a good job at using his role to address issues like that.

Not all participants describe Obama's self-talk regarding race in a positive light. In contrast to other participants whose comments were shared earlier, some believe that President Obama focuses too much on race. At least a couple of people comment on how they think that his constant reference to being bi-racial or black is an overplayed strategy. For instance, one twenty-nine-year-old European American woman from Nebraska complains: "When I first heard him speak, I heard him say—over and over again—my mom is a white woman from Kansas and my dad is a black man from Kenya. I got really sick of hearing that." A similar criticism is brought up in other focus groups, like one at a community college in Michigan where one thirty-something-year-old white woman says:

> In the beginning, when they were deciding who was going to be the Democratic nominee, he said that race wasn't going to be an issue at all and that he wasn't going to speak about it. Then, a couple of months later, it was all about race.

In the eyes of one young white woman from Illinois, President Obama's tendency to highlight his race is a strategic move to silence critics who want to avoid being labeled as racists.

> The way that it has been handled by him, it's sometimes shoved down our throats in a way that it makes me excited for the *next* black president. That way we can get it out of the way now. That way we can concentrate on the job that you're doing, not the color of your skin. Sometimes that just keeps coming up . . . it's because he is black. . . . No, it's not. I'm not criticizing what you're doing because you're black. Don't play the race card at all . . . I don't know what other people feel like, but I know that sometimes I feel like I may not be able to criticize what he is saying because I am white and I don't want somebody saying that I'm a racist or something.

A traditionally aged white female college student from Alabama points out how attention to race is unavoidable, but President Obama's heightened attention to the issue is divisive.

> I think that it is difficult to handle, because he will constantly refer to himself as black. . . . In his speeches, he said that he wasn't going to bring it up, but he has brought it up. And it is an unavoidable subject, it's right there on the surface. To hide it, I think, would almost be impossible. But I think that he has embraced that a little bit too much which is a disservice to the country. Instead of uniting the people, it's led to some division.

One older white male from Nebraska simply puts it as follows: "By giving so much attention to it [the fact that he is the first African American president], he feeds fuel to the fire by making it such a big issue."

Given all of these things, I seek insight from participants in terms of what role race plays in President Obama's election and current perceptions of his presidency. Interestingly, but perhaps not surprisingly, participants have various opinions on the issue.

BARACK OBAMA'S RACE AS A DEFICIT

Not a single focus group participant explicitly states that President Obama's race is the reason why they did not vote for, or support, him. Yet, a significant number of individuals do describe other people that fit that description. One outspoken African American female college administrator from Massachusetts discusses how others seem to treat President Obama differently as a black man. This differential treatment includes treating him "like that black man who somehow got control of the country, but people don't want to give him the respect of being the president. From her, and others' perspective, some U.S. Americans never give him a "fair shot" because he is African American.

In one Connecticut focus group of individuals from a lower socioeconomic status, several individuals acknowledge that race negatively affects some perceptions of President Obama. Their discussion includes the following exchange:

> WM#1: I know folks who don't like him because he is black.
>
> WM#2: I know also people who are against him because he is black . . . or because he is Muslim, or because he wasn't born here. There's always something. Basically it is because he is not like them.
>
> WF: Yes, there are a whole group of people who don't focus in on his job. Instead, they focus on his race, religion, or where he was born. "Is he really this? Is he really that?"
>
> WM#3: I have that as my view . . . again, when we are talking about the population, we are talking about some people who think he is Muslim, they don't know that he is Christian. They have all of this stuff. Let's say that these are things that people are fearful of . . . him being black, him being a Muslim. So, if you are on the other side, people are going to play off of those fears.

These comments demonstrate how race negatively impacts certain public perceptions. However, they also highlight the ways that other points of difference are used to criticize President Obama so that people can avoid the stigma of being accused of racism. In a different Connecticut focus group, a white male senior citizen highlights this issue when he says:

> There are folks who really believe that he wasn't the right guy to elect . . . what is interesting is that when I listen to these people—the people that I know and talk to—they never used that word, black. They talk about a lot of his opinions on issues, but race isn't a major thing that they talk about. They never use the race card. Not all Americans, but the ones that I hear who are negative about him don't. It is about him as president, it seems like they do everything possible to avoid talking about his race.

Whenever racial prejudice and discrimination is discussed as an issue, focus group participants consistently describe it in terms of *others*—firmly differentiated from their own opinions. Most often, individuals describe the South as a place where existing racist ideologies work against President Obama. This point is brought up in several different group discussions, but is most explicit in the words of a twenty-something Middle Eastern American man from California:

> I would say that the more Southern people—who may be more racist—I'm sure that they see him as a black president, but they wouldn't use that exact word. That Southern population sees him as the "N-word" president, in their eyes that's obviously not a compliment. And with people on the West Coast and East Coast, there is more of an integrated population. They probably see him as more of a post-racial president.

Several participants from the South also acknowledge the likelihood that this is the case, yet interestingly, they also describe it as a problem for others. For instance, one younger white male from North Carolina says:

> There is probably a large demographic in the South especially, from a lower socioeconomic class of white males, that see him as a black man who happens to be president . . . instead of actually giving him the respect of being a black president or a president who happens to be black. He is just a black man who happens to be president. I'm just generalizing but I'm not even sure that they would acknowledge the fact that he is biracial. Because even though he is biracial, he still isn't white.

In another focus group discussion in North Carolina, an older white male describes how age is also a factor:

> And that will also depend with different age groups. In my age group (70s), they look at him just like blue collar white males do, from the South. They go back and still hang on to the southern view of African Americans. They think that he just got lucky, he's not worthy of that office. To them, he is just a black man who just happens to be president. I think that that is pretty pervasive of people my age in the South.

Older Americans are identified as the most likely group to see President Obama's race as a deficit to his ability to run the United States competently. Most often, participants feel that this is most relevant for those living in the South and other rural areas. In the words of one young white woman from Nebraska,

> When it comes to my parents and grandparents, it's a totally different story. My grandparents definitely see a race issue [let's out an audible sigh]. They are very

Republican, and from a small rural town. It definitely didn't help that he wasn't white. So, they are VERY judgmental in that sense. But between my grandparents and I . . . we have completely different opinions. Everything changes, we are more accepting than our grandparents were . . . we are more accepting than our parents are. Our children will be more accepting than we are.

For this participant, younger voters are considerably less likely to see race as a deficit. Instead, given the substantial number of younger voters in the 2008 presidential election, President Obama's race could be seen as an asset. This idea is the focus of the next section of this chapter.

BARACK OBAMA'S RACE AS AN ASSET

According to one young black male from Illinois, Barack Obama's race is an asset because it serves as a motivating factor for people to get involved in politics.

> I think what really helped Obama was that he was black. You got people who are black but don't usually vote at all, saying "Shoot, we got a brotha running, so let me vote." And we have young people who are getting more involved . . . the next time we are gonna have even more young people voting, so I think that it will just continue to increase, and increase, and increase.

This idea is also seen in the comments of a young Native American and white man from Indiana who discusses his motivation for supporting President Obama.

> I'm looking around and seeing a lot of people from my intercultural communication class and our professor . . . she always tells us that the problem with society is that we are always trying to be politically correct. We are trying to say that the world is black and white. But that's not how you should go about it. It is okay that he is African American and for me to be white . . . that's one of the reasons why I wanted him to be president. I knew that he would bring about a lot of social change and that is exactly what I think that our country needed. So, it is not about differentiating one another, it is about accepting our differences. I think that he is taking our country forward to a place where it needs to go, and I think that it continues to do that. And that's why I wanted him in office.

In addition to motivating new voters, especially younger, black, and Latino persons who historically had been political inactive, several participants believe that President Obama's race also creates a "buzz" given that his presidency is making U.S. history. In one Massachusetts focus group, three African American women in their thirties and forties discuss this issue. One explains how his "unique candidacy attracted lots of media attention and the number of people that all of a sudden followed politics." She believes these individuals outnumbered those that refuse to support for him because he is African American. A second black woman followed by saying:

> I agree that it actually helped him because it sorta gave him a celebrity status. He was the first African American person that had that much chance to get elected in history. So, even when negative things about him were put out there by the media, it became the center discussion of the news. And it didn't matter if people were arguing for or against him, it was just the fact that his name was out there like that. And people were just that avidly discussing whether or not he should be president. He got a lot more attention because of it—compared to other candidates.

A third African American woman in her forties then describes how President Obama's race is productive because it forces the public:

> To step out of their comfort zone, and be open to things that are new to them. I think it helped him in that people were really excited about change, and we were at a point in our society where people were embracing change . . . I do think that people were kinda excited, after the last president, to show progress in terms of where we are as a society.

Across different focus group discussions, a significant number of participants describe how being the first presidential nominee of African descent nominated by a major political party is a valuable asset during a time when the country was primed change. A young white female college student from Virginia explains how she believed: "That a lot of people who voted for him, saw his being black as a good thing. It helped to show how America has changed." Voting for Obama, then, was a way to prove "that if we could have a black president, then we could keep progressing." In a presidential election where change appeared to be the dominant rallying cry, Barack Obama's racial identity helped to distinguish him from other candidates. Several African American participants are adamant in pointing out how voting for President Obama was the most bold statement voters could make regarding change. "What better way to symbolize real change than by electing a black man?" asks one African American man in his late forties who was part of a community focus group in central Ohio. While a number of African Americans across the United States assert the same question (albeit in a variety of forms), only one middle-aged European American woman from Michigan raises the issue. Within her comments, she criticizes President Obama for not really offering anything new except the fact that he is black. Specifically, she adds:

> I think that if he was white, and had the same campaign of change, I don't think that people would have voted for him. There was never anything unique about his campaign. He never stood out on what exactly the issues were. He always tip-toed around them. You never really knew what he stood for because he never said exactly what he stood for. Because then he never would get all the votes ... he just went right in the middle, so you never really knew what he was thinking. But he sounded really good and was someone new.

THE REAL ASSET: COMING ACROSS AS A "WHITE BLACK GUY"

While a significant number of participants believe that Barack Obama's identity as the first competitive presidential candidate of African descent represents a clear asset during the election, others offer a different take on the issue. In particular, they strongly believe that the real asset is that he is an African American man who doesn't fit existing stereotypes. For instance, several participants note that his communication is not reflective of earlier African American presidential candidates. In fact, his communication is more similar to white politicians. In this regard, he is—in the words of a young white female from Massachusetts—"like a white black guy." According to a young white male undergraduate student from Illinois,

> I think what was even more obvious was his communication style was what he sounded like. Unfortunately, this is based on a stereotype but white people listened to him and heard a white person talking. Obviously they saw what they saw, but they heard a white person talking. And black people identified with what he looked like, but white people heard ... maybe they didn't "hear white," but what they heard was "presidential." He sounded like every other presidential candidate that we've had. He was an excellent public speaker. He wasn't too different.

From the perspective of this participant, Obama's mainstream communication mannerisms are seen as a definite asset in that it differentiates him from past African American presidential contenders.

"People talk about Obama like he is an exception of black people," states one young African American woman attending an undergraduate state university in Nebraska. A similar notion is expressed when a young white woman from Indiana explains how President Obama "isn't the 'normal' [using air quotes] black person." A young African American woman from Alabama adds, "He wasn't the stereotypical black guy . . . if you heard that a black guy was running for president, you would think of someone else." A middle-aged white man attending a Michigan community college explains why communicating in a non-stereotypically black manner garners him widespread support:

> As far back as long as I can remember, we as a nation expect—because of our roots—Blacks or African Americans to be of a lesser value. And we think that they are less intelligent when they communicate in certain ways. When you see someone come up like that who is so highly educated and is such a good, smooth talker, everyone wants to grasp this. . . . It's coming at us within a different aspect altogether. When they see this, they like it.

The implicit message within all of these comments is that an African American presidential candidate who exhibits communication behaviors identified as "stereotypically black" will not be evaluated positively. Instead, he will be viewed through a negative filter, or alternatively as a threatening persona. This is the insight seen in the comments of a fifty-something-year-old black woman from Massachusetts who intermittently uses "air quotes" when she shares:

> I don't think that people saw him as that much of a threat—compared to the "typical black man." I think that the black man—the "stereotypical black man"—is always angry and hostile. And for most, he wasn't the "typical black male." He didn't get argumentative when debating McCain, he wasn't interrupting when people were rude—things that people might associate with black culture. In this way, he wasn't a threat to anyone.

Thus far, coming across as a "white black guy" is based on Obama's race and his communication mannerisms. Yet, another variation of this theme is present throughout the transcript data. Many different people of color, most notably African American participants, argue that his biracial identity (as a white and black man) serves as an invaluable asset. One black female undergraduate student attending a HBCU in Alabama makes this point when she shares:

> My personal view is that I think that Obama's biracial background—his mother being white and his grandparents being white—helped him. He really worked that on the campaign trail. I think that that side of him made him more marketable. I think that if he was fully black—if his two parents were solely black or African American—he would not have had the type of appeal that he did. I think that him being biracial had a lot to do with white America's openness

to his candidacy. His racial background was a factor in him getting elected. He repeated it, time and time again. He didn't necessarily repeat that his mother was white and that his grandparents were white . . . he was sure to indicate in some fashion that his mom and grandparents were a clear part of him, and the fact that they were white was always there. It was a point that was constantly hammered. He understood that race was then, and still is today, a factor.

Several African American participants provide anecdotal evidence from Whites that they know who seem to evaluate President Obama differently because he is clearly not "all black." This is the observation of a middle-aged black male from Virginia:

> I actually heard some people saying stuff like that . . . I think that were looking at him differently. Conversations that I had with some of the people I work with—basically all Republicans, they would say, "He's a black guy but he's mixed with white, so that's good. He is educated. He can speak well. And he has some white in him." They give him credit for that—just because he has white in him. My boss would say stuff like that. He's not pure 100 percent black so that works in his favor. He's not Jesse Jackson! He doesn't speak in rhyme.

The idea that, in today's society, being bi-racial has significant market appeal is also seen in the comments from a fifty-something-year-old black woman from Massachusetts. While discussing this issue, she turns to a dark-skinned African American man and asserts:

> If he was as dark as [you], then he would not be president. Period. That's all I have to say. [group laughter . . . several people talking all at once] The reason why I say that is because _____ is clearly racially identifiable. If you are racially ambiguous you have greater appeal . . . you see it in commercials all of the time. When they want to say a certain thing, they hire someone who you can't really figure out what race they are . . . alright? This group is about opinions, and that's mine. I believe that if he was a black man born in Alabama with share-cropper parents . . . NO. Wouldn't happen.

Using the fact that he is part white is a strategy that, from the perspective of several African American participants, seems to garner him support from Whites who would not necessarily support an African American politician. One young African American woman from California makes the following observation:

> I've actually heard other people say that "I think it's cool that he isn't all black." [group laughter]. I think that is why most people, or at least some white people, voted for him . . . because he was mixed and not fully black. They weren't ready for a full-black president, but with Obama they could get someone who was

more white than black, but still be proud that they supported a black president. Honest, and true, I've heard this.

African American participants are also critically self-aware of how biracial people are more highly regarded in their communities as well. An older black woman from Rhode Island describes how historically "If you're a light-skinned black because you are mixed . . . because of internalized racism, you were perceived better by Blacks and Whites." She adds, that "black folks are quick to say that he's black but also think more highly of him because he is part white." Another African American woman—a younger participant from California—comments on how this issue seems to affect Obama's support during the primary.

> In terms of the question of electability, and being biracial, I remember that there was a significant portion of the black community supporting Hillary. And they had to be convinced that he was more electable. And I think that the biracial piece was a key part of bringing them along. The appeal of him being biracial and the appeal of him being able to sit in the board room with white men and feel like he could belong . . . that began to make people think differently about his electability.

PRESIDENT OBAMA: ANOTHER STEP TOWARD A "POST-RACIAL" SOCIETY

As evidence by the public perceptions analyzed in this chapter, the idea that Barack Obama's presidency somehow marks the introduction of a "post-racial" United States is inaccurate and premature. If that is, in fact, the case then any discussions of issues regarding race will not exist. As one African American man from California aptly puts it: "Just because some white people in power have decided that race doesn't matter any longer doesn't make it automatically true for the rest of us." The consensus of over three hundred participants who took part in of my national study is clear: The United States is nowhere near a "post-racial" state; however, President Obama's election represents yet another substantial step toward a time when racial difference will lose its societal significance.

Some of the most powerful insights regarding the historical significance of Obama's election are seen from older participants. The emotion that accompanies some African American participants' descriptions of disbelief, pride, and amazement at times results in tears of joy. (These will be highlighted in the next chapter.) However, a few older Caucasian participants also acknowledge the powerful symbolism of his election. As one Connecticut senior citizen shares,

> I was stationed in the 1960s in Mississippi. And if you were not white—if you were a colored person—you were treated as a second class citizen. I was naïve with that. I came from [the Northeast] and I never knew what prejudice was—like what I saw down there. I even had a friend who was shot at, for no other reason than simply being black. He was at the USO and coming back with a couple of friends and people drove by and shot a couple of times at him. He wasn't hit . . . but . . . I was the leader of the barracks and I knew that that wasn't fair, it wasn't right. So, I said that "we're gonna call the marshal, the deputy police." When they got involved I couldn't believe it. My experience in seeing how that officer treated him was unforgettable. He told him that if he wanted to file a complaint he would have to go down town . . . and, of course, the solider said no. He had just gotten shot at, and knew that going downtown would be dangerous . . . I saw that happen, and then I see today how most people don't care where you came from but focus more on want you can do for us. That shows me that we've come a long way. Thank God for that. It's a good thing.

Like many other participants, this man's comments reflect how the saliency of race has diminished over time. In similar fashion, a majority of participants believe that President Obama's race continues to become less and less important over time.

"I think that for most of the people that I communicate with, and interact with, the issue of race disappeared right after he was elected," offers one fifty-something Middle Eastern American woman in a California focus group. She then adds, "They are now looking at him mostly as a president who is trying to do the best job that he can." Most participants did not describe the role of race disappearing quite as quickly. However, they do agree that the novelty of the situation has worn off considerably. A young Asian American female from Illinois recalls: "At first, it was really important that we finally got our first black president. But now, its kinda normal . . . we see him on the news almost every day." Other participants across the United States agree. A young male college student from Illinois whose parents were born and raised in Syria shares:

> I think that for me, maybe for the first year or so, he was the first black president. There were songs coming out: "My president is black!" [group laughter as he starts to rap the lyrics of the song]. Okay cool. But now in mind, he's just the president. There was all this hype for no reason, but now it is what it is. It's there, but no one really cares.

Similar sets of comments appear from a variety of participants from Connecticut, Massachusetts, Indiana, Ohio, and Virginia. Most agree that Obama might have been inaugurated as "the first black president, but over time, he has become the president who happens to be black"—a quote from a young white male from Michigan.

The most pressing issue for President Obama, according to participants, is not race-related. Instead, it involves his ability to solve the multitude of challenges currently facing the United States A Hispanic woman in her late twenties, who taking part in a focus group in Massachusetts, shares:

> I don't think that race is in the American public's minds right now, at least the general public. I think that people are really concerned about the economy, they are really concerned about problems in the Middle East. I think that most people are thinking of those things instead of the race factor.

For many of the younger participants, race loses its relevance given the current state of affairs. One young Caucasian man from Michigan puts it this way:

> I don't think that race is an issue. Whatever is best for the country is all that really matters. In my opinion, I don't care if the president is black, white, orange, or purple. All I care about it that he gets the job done, that's all that matters.

Based on the transcript data, the general consensus is that Barack Obama's presidency is an important symbol of a changing society in terms of race relations. However, some participants—especially European Americans—are quick to question if all of the attention concerning President Obama's race was hurting or helping the progression toward a "post-racial" society. During a Massachusetts focus group, a white man in his late twenties says:

> I wonder if the hype about his race, in some ways, just continues the racial divide in the United States. Can we accept the fact, recognize the fact, that he is the first black president . . . but then move on?, If we continue to talk about his race, does that set him apart? We have black presidents, we have white presidents . . . not just presidents. When we will get to that point?

Immediately following these comments, a black man in his sixties responds by saying:

> The divide is there. And as long as people are treated differently because of their race, or their color, you are going to have it there. And I think the recognition has been given, you have to see it. I know there are people who tell me that they don't see my race, and I tell them "Then you're not seeing me!" [some group laughter, especially among African American participants]. "That's a part me, that's who I am." So, it's not that I don't want people to see my color, I just don't want them to do great harm to me because of it.

This interracial exchange between two men captures an ever-present tension. On the one hand, individuals advocate that a colorblind approach to race relations is the way to achieve a "post-racial" society. Alternatively, others see a colorblind approach as premature and ultimately a significant barrier to working through existing issues of race. Of particular interest to this issue is the fact that all substantial conversations regarding the tensions between a post-racial and race-relevant approach to race relations occurs within focus groups with all African Americans or all people of color. With only one exception, European American and racially mixed groups fail to engage the topic with any depth.

SUMMARY

This chapter is the first of four that explore how race impacts the public perceptions of President Obama's communication. Specifically, I use this chapter to explore how "race matters" are inherent in what the media—and some in the general public—describe as a "post-racial" United States. As I illustrate through the various comments organized into different thematic points of insight, race has influenced, and continues to influence, perceptions of President Obama and his communication in complex ways. The next two chapters focus on analyzing (and simultaneously challenging) out-group perceptions that regard African American and European American perceptions of Obama as diametrically opposed. My first exploration investigates the widespread belief that President Obama had the unconditional and universal support of all African American voters.

Chapter 7

Black Pride in, and Allegiance to, President Obama

> For African Americans, it is a big deal because he is someone who looks like us.
>
> —Younger African American woman from Massachusetts
>
> Obama should not have to become raceless just because he is president.
>
> —Older African American man from Alabama

A number of political pundits have written books describing, from their perspectives, what President Obama's election means to the U.S. political, social, and cultural landscape (Asim, 2009; Corsi, 2008; Freddoso, 2008) generally, and African American people more specifically (Joseph, 2010; Rush, 2010; Sugrue, 2010). The conclusions drawn within these books widely vary, something that might not be surprising given that each author is writing from his or her particular political, social, or cultural perspective. What is missing from these publications are the voices of everyday U.S. citizens. Consequently, chapter 7 continues to fulfill the objective of this book: To draw from a large national qualitative data set and present a systematic analysis of commonalties and differences in regards to public perceptions of Barack Obama. In particular, the chapter focuses on providing insight into how African American participants describe their perceptions of Barack Obama in terms of a "symbolic relationship." Such an analysis is important in that it goes beyond the statistics found in public polling data that reports almost universal support in the African American community (Todd and Gawiser, 2009). Within this chapter, I begin by providing insight into the particular sources of pride that inform African

Americans' relationship to President Obama. Then, I turn to describe the general public perception that African Americans have a blind allegiance to President Obama. Finally, I conclude the chapter by highlighting the perceptions of a largely invisible group: everyday African Americans who do not support President Obama.

PRESIDENT OBAMA: A DREAM FULFILLED

One of the focus groups that I facilitate is in the home of an African American couple. During the discussion, I notice that a commemorative plate sits on the bookshelf that has a picture of President Obama and Dr. Martin Luther King, Jr. The message on the plate reads: "CELEBRATING OUR BLACK HISTORY (over the picture) . . . A DREAM FULFILLED" (under the picture). This image captures how many African American participants describe their perception of President Obama, as a fulfillment of the dream articulated by Dr. King several decades earlier. Across several different focus groups, African Americans connect President Obama to Dr. King in terms of his communication, leadership, and positive representation of black people. One forty-six-year-old African American from southern Virginia, for instance, says:

> A lot of people compare him to Dr. King. How he commands an audience, for example. He represents the African American community as a strong leader who is really intelligent and can articulate his ideas well. He is someone who we can be proud of.

The emotion that is tied to these feelings of pride is seen in several focus group discussions, especially those comprised solely or primarily of African Americans. One such group in central Ohio includes a middle-aged black woman who is fairly quiet throughout the discussion. However, towards the end of session, I ask the group how other people that they know might respond to the questions that I had asked them. At that point, the woman speaks with deliberate passion and shares the following comments.

> What I think that comes out of all of this, with the people that I know . . . I would say. . . . Being Free. [pause] Freedom. [pause] An open door. [pause] A new beginning. In terms of black people especially. A great freedom that we have as a black race; it's a freedom for other people as well. It lets them see that even though he is black, he is for everyone. That is what his focus is, that's what I hear him saying: That he is for everyone. He is trying to focus on the needs of the people. To me, that is what makes him so awesome. I think that even from the older people, it makes them cry because they know what their

past *was*. And they are feeling like they would never see it . . . or live to see it. Just the struggles that they've lived through . . . I don't know . . . I just think that they are really proud to see a black man as president. Because we are, as a black race, surprised because we never thought that we would see it happen in our lifetimes.

The pride that older African Americans feel is palatable during the focus group discussions, and evidenced by the reverence that permeates their comments about President Obama. Interestingly, the pride of younger African Americans is of a different sort. For instance, one young black woman describes how her twenty-something-year-old brother (someone who she describes as not finishing high school and politically ignorant) is "all hyped" about President Obama:

When he won, being black, it was a big deal. Even my brother was all hyped—and I was like, "You're not into politics!" My brother was like, "Yeah, Obama . . . did you watch the speech?" And I couldn't believe it . . . I said, "When do YOU watch politics?" But growing up in the type of the environment that I grew up in, I definitely noticed the attention he got and how EVERYONE was excited.

According to participants, the pride of African Americans trickles down to younger individuals as well. One young biracial (African American and European American) from Michigan also describes how her brother, a middle school student at the time, and his friends display their pride:

My brother and some of his friends thought it was a big deal. They have to wear IDs in school, and you're not supposed to write on them at all. But, he and his friends . . . all of the black guys wrote on them saying "My president is black." And then they would flip them around so that you could see it. They were supposed to get into trouble, but they never got in trouble. Teachers were afraid to be called racists, so they didn't say anything.

It is difficult to discern whether this message is one of pride, defiance, or a combination of both. However, some comments from a sixty-something-year-old African American man from Massachusetts may provide some insight. During his focus group discussion, he reflects on what President Obama's election means to his granddaughters.

I've been thinking about what my granddaughters would say . . . They are fourteen and eighteen and his being elected significantly changed their world, and their perceptions of the world, and their place in the world. The older one, it literally gave her permission to challenge every person of authority [group laughter]. She has always done what she wanted to do, but now she seems even more entitled to say, "No. You are not right." I think that it gave her the confidence that in fact she could confront her parents, she could confront the people at her school . . . not only could she, but she has the right to do so.

The pride that many African Americans have in President Obama is not limited to the significance of his election as the forty-fourth U.S. president. It also is grounded in the ways in which he conducts himself since becoming president. For instance, participants applaud him for his composure and elegance in a political time where negativity, contention, and criticism are the norm. Consider the comments from one middle-aged black woman from Alabama who focuses on his ability to remain personable:

> Honestly, I don't think that he has changed that much, he is just as eloquent now as he was before. . . . Situations change, he has certain ideals, but now he has also learned what the reality is. You know . . . people are not always going to agree with what he says. Even when he was running, you had those types of people. People who criticized him. But even with that, he remains composed. He still finds time to spend time with this family, walk his girls to school, go on dates with his wife . . . it's not as much as it was before because obviously he has more on his plate now. But honestly, I feel like that he still has that likeability that people are drawn to. He still has that warmth about him.

For some African American participants, his behaviors as president increase their respect and pride. One forty-something-year-old black woman from Massachusetts shares:

> I think that, if anything, I have more respect from him now than I did before. Because as president he has gotten so much criticism, he is always getting critiqued. I mean I know that all presidents get that, but because he is also the first African American president, I think that it is a different situation. He is not only representing America, but he is a representation of black people too. I've always thought—to answer one of your earlier questions—I've always thought that he was a very eloquent speaker. I can't remember that exact first time I initially saw him, but I know that I was so impressed. So, even now I am very impressed. . . . So, I remain impressed by his eloquence.

Like this participant, other African Americans describe that part of their pride is rooted in how President Obama's visibility is able to counter the negative stereotypes that exist for black men. In other words, he represents black people in general, and black men in particular, in positive ways. An African American woman in her twenties, participating in a group in North Carolina, offers the following observations:

Going to an all-white school, I've heard all of the stereotypes before, especially among people who grew up in a community where they couldn't see that black culture is so diverse. They didn't grow up accustomed to understanding how we are different. They only see the rap artists, they only see the athletes, the ones on the news. . . . So, when Obama came into the spotlight, they were like "Oh, there's another kind!" It is important for them to see that not everyone black man fits the stereotype.

My focus in this chapter on African American pride in President Obama is not to diminish the ways in which other participants also articulate a sense of pride in his accomplishments. Instead, it is to help readers distinguish the different types of pride. For instance, several Latino/a participants also describe the intensity that accompanies the support for President Obama in their communities. One twenty-something-year-old Puerto Rican woman from Massachusetts recalls her experiences on Election Day in 2008:

I was working at a polling location—not for either party—but volunteering. A ton of Latinos came in, and I was the person speaking Spanish, and they said "We want to vote for Obama!" Just like that. . . . And I was trying to tell them about everything else (other offices, questions on the ballot, etc.), and they were like "No, we just want to vote for Obama." And there were a lot of older Latina women who just wanted to vote for Obama. They were pretty intense.

For some Latino/a participants, their responses to President Obama's historical election is similar to the comments of the African American woman from Ohio whose quote was included at the beginning of this chapter: It is seen as helping to open the door for other non-white presidential candidates. One focus group in California is held a couple weeks following the 2010 midterm elections. In an all-Latino group, one young Mexican American man shares:

With me being Latino, and him being black, that's also something else that I think that I can relate to. It's cool because his being elected means that we could be next. Who is to say that it would be long before we have a Latino president. It could definitely happen, especially after this [the advances made by Latinos in the midterm elections]. I think that it could happen. His election opened up a lot of opportunities for us.

EMBRACING HIS BLACKNESS AS A POINT OF PRIDE

A particular point of pride specific to African American participants is seen in the ways in which President Obama is perceived as embracing his blackness as a positive aspect of his identity. While this is evident in a variety of different focus group discussions, the words of one young African American man from Indiana seem most illustrative:

> I remember someone actually asking him about how he identified. And it created a challenge for him, because when he tells his story, his narrative is clearly on where he is biracial. He acknowledges, and accepts, and embraces all of the aspects of his culture. But when he answered that question, he actually said, "I'm a black man. I'm treated like a black man." I think that at that moment it was very interesting, because there seems to be a little bit of a disconnect between how he embraces all of the different aspects of his identity and who he is and then versus how other people see him. "People see me as a black man," is what he said. "So, I see myself as a black man." What was most impressive about this is that he said with a sense of pride, not shame.

In a number of focus groups, African American participants compare Barack Obama's self-descriptions with those of golfer Tiger Woods, another well-known person with multiracial lineage. This is a topic of discussion in a focus group of students attending a HBCU in Alabama. Within this session, African American students from across the United States discuss how, unlike President Obama, Tiger Woods fails to get much support from the African American community. In regards to his recent much-publicized troubles with his European American wife, one woman asserts:

> That's an interesting conversation because who could Tiger turn to? Because the African Americans were like "you never claimed us." We weren't open arms ready to embrace him. And the Caucasian community turned their backs on him. . . . He never acknowledged us in that capacity at all. In terms of Barack Obama now, he has always identified as black. I think who you choose as your wife tells a lot about who you are. I think the fact that [Obama] married [Michelle], has a relationship with her that is really open and positive, they have children, things are going well . . . I just feel that he has established and affirmed in his life that African American life can thrive.

The fact that President Obama is married to an African American woman is a topic in several other focus groups—most often these are groups where African Americans are in the majority. Interestingly, but maybe not surprisingly, African American women (of all ages and backgrounds) are the most vocal participants on the topic. For many, his choice to marry a black woman is evidence that he embraces an African American existence. Even more important, according to some, is the specific type of woman that he chose to be his wife. "The fact that he is married to a homegirl—a black woman from the South side of Chicago," points out one middle-aged black woman from Rhode Island. She then quickly adds, "That was a sign that he was a real black man. We read something into that—he's a real brotha!" This "sign" is also something that other African American women across the United States decode. One young African American woman from Maryland who was going to school in Alabama explains:

> I think that it even goes deeper into it than that. It's the type of African American wife that he has. There are different types of ethnicities, hair textures, skin complexions, body types. Usually, the well-educated black men who are highly successful—lawyers, senators, etc.—tend to marry for many different reasons, but they marry those who society general accepts as better. The perfect wife for the perfect African American man would usually be the lighter skinned African American woman with the curly, long straightened hair. Michelle Obama is actually very refreshing because she doesn't look like that stereotypical African American woman who—you know—the "better" African American man would have. The fact that he chose to marry this woman affirms African American relationships.

The first extended discussion of the significance of President Obama's choice for a wife occurs within a focus group discussion of all young women of African descent (African American, Caribbean black, and biracial) held in Massachusetts. With this particular discussion a participant asks: "What if President Obama was married to a white woman, would he have been elected?" Within this group, the question is never discussed with any significant depth. However, whenever the topic is raised in other groups, I would pose the question to participants who always passionately agree that the answer to the question would be "NO!" One recently turned forty-six-year-old black woman from Virginia is adamant when she says:

> I don't think that if he married a white woman he would have been seen as electable. We, as black women, love him so much because he has a black wife. He is a family man. He has this beautiful, smart black woman with him. He has these great daughters. He is the exemplary black man and WE LOVE HIM FOR THAT. We would not love him as much if he had a white wife—Becky with flowing blond hair down to her waist. No, we would not love him as much.

Other African American female participants across the United States seem to be in agreement. This is the case for a young woman in Alabama who shares:

> Honestly, I feel that if he had a white wife, it would have made black females feel like we could never achieve that level of relational success. That successful black men only wanted white woman outside of their race. Not only that, but Michelle has spoken her mind and developed her own style and personality. . . .

> With him having a black wife, and with her not being the stereotypical angry black woman, that shows America a positive image. By looking at her, and looking at Obama, and looking at their children, they have shown that there is not a cookie-cutter image of African Americans. I feel that that is a real positive reflection for us.

The racial significance of President Obama's choice for a spouse arises during in-group conversations among African Americans. However, the topic does appear in a few focus groups where participants are racially and ethnically diverse. In these groups, most non-African Americans do not agree that having a white wife would have impacted the outcome of the election. When several participants call the question "absurd" in one Illinois college student focus group, the only African American woman in the group quickly asserts:

> I believe that! Seriously, I do. As an African American woman, I live with these people every day. I know that if they see a biracial couple, not even Indian and Arab, or whatever. It is just black and white. When they see it: A black successful man with a white woman . . . white successful woman with a black man, they think "Oh, he thinks that he is better than me! He just wants to be with her because she is white!" There is an underlying animosity with that—not that every person thinks that, but it's out there.

Within her comments, this participant argues that a white wife would lose President Obama some support, but also acknowledges the diversity of opinion among African Americans. In other groups, like an all-black male group in California, participants also argue that "a lot of 'progressive' white males wouldn't have voted so progressively if Obama had a white woman on his arm."

For many African American participants, the pride that they have for President Obama is generated, in part, by the positive representation that it provides of African Americans. The positive image of a First Family that is the First [African American] Family is overwhelming for some participants. In a discussion regarding President Obama's successes and failures since taking the office, for instance, one older African American woman in Rhode Island declares his presidency a success: "For me, the victory is his presence. To me, the victory is the picture of him, and Malia, and Sasha, and Mrs. Obama." Despite some recent feelings of extreme frustrations, she goes on to declare, "I just wanted to feel what I felt when I see that picture. The policies are always going to be the policies . . . " A similar set of emotions is evident during another focus group where several African American participants describe how little has changed since President Obama's election. An African American female professor from Massachusetts, a self-described Independent voter, shares:

It wasn't until long after the election and [some students] saw the picture on my computer, and then they said, "Oh, my god, look at the picture on the computer [of the Obama family], we didn't know what your affiliation was!" And I told them, "The reason why I have that picture on my computer isn't necessarily an indication of my affiliation, as much as it is about 'Wow, Michelle Obama looks like me.'" I think about those kinds of things. And her lived experiences which are much more aligned with my personal experiences, and my family's personal experiences . . . and the fact that I can look at their daughters and my daughter . . . my daughter can say, "Oh, they look like me." And what that actually means to her. . . . When he was elected, people in my family shed tears as well. So, they would say, despite the fact the things are basically the same, it is still different. In terms of the day-to-day things, yeah they may be the same. But in terms of the person who is charge, he's black and that's different.

VISCERAL REJECTIONS OF "POST-RACIAL" CLAIMS

When I ask whether the general public views President Obama as a black, white, or "post-racial" president, I receive different reactions from different types of individuals (many of these were described in chapter 6). The responses from African Americans, however, are unilaterally similar in that they reject the notion that his election signals the emergence of a "post-racial" society. In one focus group in California, a young African American man responds the general question by saying: "The very quick and simple way to answer that is how would the police view him driving in a car? Your skin color in America is your race. I don't care if you are 1 percent black, if you are my skin color, then you are black." For many people of color, like one young African American woman from Alabama, not seeing President Obama as black is nonsensical. From her perspective, "Who you are is part of everything that you do. It doesn't make sense, to me, that you wouldn't see his race and only his policies. I don't know, it just doesn't ring true to me." Her comments are in reaction to a white participant who describes her perceptions of President Obama's race as colorblind. Other African American participants, like the woman quoted below, respond to similar claims with equal passion:

> You can't look at him and say that you can't see him as the first black president, unless you are trying to deny that you don't see it. Don't ignore it, don't deny it, appreciate the fact that he is African American. People fought for this to happen. For me, I can't ignore it because people died so that he could be the first black president. He will always be the first black president. You can't say that that isn't true. It is just a fact. (Young African American woman from Indiana)

For many African American participants, refusing to see President Obama as a black man is not a positive perception indicative of anti-racism. Instead of respecting and admiring European Americans who embrace a colorblind approach, they took great offense and question why people don't want to see race. In a racially diverse focus group in Michigan, a young African American man shares:

> I find myself getting offended when I hear people of white descent talking about Obama like they don't see him as black. Maybe it's just me, but I do feel like every time I see Obama I feel proud because I'm black and he's black. I always see a black president. I feel like we always say that we don't—but we see color. WHY? WHY? Even like his swag, or the way that he communicates, I feel like that is the ultimate swag of a positive black man. I see a BLACK president, not that he just happens to be black, he is a black man.

A young African American woman in Illinois communicates a similar message to whites in the focus group in which she participates. When claims are made that there is only one human race, she responds by saying:

> Theoretically it is true that race should not matter, but realistically, it is definitely does. Everybody sees him as a black president. PERIOD. You can play games with all of that, but the truth of the matter is that you see him like that.

Several participants are quick to question the legitimacy of European American participants who refuse to acknowledge that they can, and do, see President Obama as a racial being. The frustration that they feel is palatable as they confront how such perceptions could exist. In an all-African American focus group in Alabama, one black male participant asks a series of rhetorical questions:

> My question is: What do you consider black? If you don't see him as black, then what is he? People can't be nothing, they have to be something. You have to have some type of notion of who they are . . . Obviously, he may not fit into what your personal stereotype of what black is. So, all of a sudden he is not part of anything, he just is . . . That's my personal take on it. You just don't become a piece of furniture or something. It is impossible for an American not to categorize something. So, for someone to all of a sudden say, "He's not this, he's not that." Then what is the difference between him and other people like him. What does he do that others like him don't do? Answer me that! That's my question.

From the perspective of many African American participants, the fact that racism is alive and well only makes them more proud of President Obama's accomplishments. Several talk about the perception that in order to be elected, he had to be "twice as good" as his white competitors. As the first president of African descent, Obama also carries the pressure that comes with that distinction. Part of that pressure, according to one forty-something-year-old black man in Rhode Island, is that any failure reflects on all African Americans.

> I think that he carries so heavy a burden that a lot of people—especially those of us who are African American—are watching him saying "Please don't mess up." It's like when you are watching the news and you think "Oh, God, please don't let this criminal be black!" [group agrees with laughter]. And so . . . we are so proud because he has been able to hold it and keep it going. He has to so that African Americans will also have a chance.

In the eyes of a number of black participants, attempts to characterize the United States as a "post-racial" society is a cloaked attempt to convince the general public that racism no longer exists. While most African American individuals involve in the study agree that the racism of old no longer has the impact that it once did, they are quick to reject claims that President Obama's election proves that the United States has transcended race. One thirty-something-year-old black clergyman in California is clear and concise in his assertions.

> There is no such thing as a post-racial society in America right now. Maybe there will be at some point. Obama is a step, or could be a step, in that direction IF it is put in the right context and geared that way. The other thing is . . . I agree with you all about the different generations viewing Obama differently. But I also think that looking at the larger issue of race, America has never dealt with the whole issue of racism. See we want to talk about race but not talk about racism. The concept of race by its very nature is racist. Race has become so ingrained into society, we often times don't even recognize how pervasive race is. I think that most people don't realize it because it has become so systemic. People don't even see it! [group talking over another] Yes, young people and all people might be interacting with one another, but in terms of the system, nothing has changed. It hasn't changed for Obama, and it [pause] won't [pause] be [pause] changing [pause] any [pause] time [pause] soon.

For these individuals, attempts at creating a "post-racial" society are misguided. The goal should not be on overcoming race; instead it should be on overcoming racism. This interesting distinction emerges from a young African American woman attending a HBCU in Alabama when she says:

> I think that living in a post-racial society shouldn't be anybody's goal. I think that a post-racist society would be the ideal. Post-racist . . . where people wouldn't make judgments that disenfranchise people based on stereotypes

associated with their skin color . . . not acting on stereotypes that negatively impact people. I think that there are still racial, or cultural, differences in society that aren't all bad—that's why a post-racial society shouldn't be the goal. Race isn't the problem, racism is.

OUT-GROUP PERCEPTIONS OF BLACK ALLEGIANCE TO PRESIDENT OBAMA

One of the most interesting aspects of this project is being able to listen to people's different perceptions of President Obama and then comparing and contrasting them with the meta-perceptions that exist. Meta-perceptions refer to the how people think other people think (Cook and Douglas, 1998). Throughout the different focus groups, I am intrigued by the ways in which non-African Americans describe their perceptions how African Americans view President Obama. Several perceptions appear across the data, however, as seen within this section, participants describe them as factual (not perceptual).

One perception of African Americans that appears consistently throughout different focus group discussions is that they—and not President Obama—make a huge deal of his race. A young Middle Eastern American man from California makes this point when he says:

> It's more of the actual black society that makes him look more black because they are so proud of him. But that actually pissed me off a little bit. We are supposed to be equal, and that there is no race . . . we are all the same. But then, there is a guy who is half black who is president, and they are claiming him as the "black knight in shining armor." I mean, really, relax. He's OUR president, not YOUR president.

A young Caucasian woman from Virginia makes a similar point and empathizes how "the African American community is excited because African American parents are telling their kids, for the first time and they feel it is true, that they could be president of the United States." While this participant recognizes the racial significance of President Obama's election, other white participants do not. One woman from Indiana, in particular, seems especially frustrated. Like the young man quoted earlier, she expresses a significant deal of frustration when she says:

> I think that the majority of people actually would see him as just a president, but black people never would let this happen . . . I think that there were a lot of us who wanted to see him as just a president but were told over and over again until

we got it into our heads that he wasn't just a president, he was the first African American president. Why should that even matter?!

"A lot of African Americans were voting for him just because he was black," is another popular perception among non-black participants. According to a sixty-something-year-old white man from Connecticut, race is the single biggest factor in their support:

> A huge percentage of African Americans—including Republican African Americans—voted for him just because he is African American. No question about that. Not all of them—I'm think that Clarence Thomas might have held out. . . . But no, that community was a lock for Obama.

The "fact" that the vast majority of African American support for President Obama is based on his race is called "just plain stupid" by a young white man from Alabama. This perception is challenged in a few focus groups when African Americans describe themselves, or others in their families, as not supportive of Obama. The reaction in several groups is surprise, if not disbelief. Such is the case with one young Mexican American man from California who shares:

> I just want to say that I was surprised when [another participant] said that her father didn't actually vote for Obama. I really thought that all African Americans supported Obama. I really thought that. I thought that black people really like to stick together.

In addition to automatic votes, according to a significant number of participants, President Obama continues to receive the unconditional support from African Americans. One middle-aged white woman from Connecticut compares this support with that which was offered to O. J. Simpson after being charged with the murder of his ex-wife, Nicole Simpson and her male friend, Ronald Goldman.

> When I talk about Obama to my African American friends, there is a much greater sense of unconditional support. It makes me think of the O. J. thing . . . people who I knew who happened to be African American were quick to say, "HE DIDN'T DO IT!" I kept saying, "Shouldn't we let the courts decide?" But it was like, society was pulled apart. . . . There is a quality of that with Obama. I love Obama but I'm careful about what I say about him when I'm around my African American friends. Because if I even mention something not completely positive, they will turn on me.

Several participants do not necessarily take issue with the large number of African Americans that support President Obama; their criticism is specifically for individuals whose allegiance is based on his race. One Caucasian male college student in Indiana states:

> I really had a problem with people who didn't have any idea what he was talking about, didn't have any idea of what he wanted to do with our country. They were just like, "Hey, look some African American is on the ballot, let's vote for him because that's cool."

One woman describes how "a lot of basketball players in [her] high school followed Obama on Twitter and would forward all of his quotes." She adds that "they wouldn't even know what many of the quotes meant, but they would just be following Obama blindly." Another white male from California offers more evidence of African American blind allegiance when he shares what he saw on television.

> On Howard Stein, he had this bit where one of his guys went down to Harlem and was asking folks: "Who are you going to vote for?" And they would all say, "Obama." Then he would describe McCain's policies and asked them if they agreed and were like, "Oh yeah, I'm totally for this . . . " [group laughter and some applause]. And stuff like that. It was really funny, but at the same time, it showed that they were only voting for him because of his race.

THE REALITY: A SPECTRUM OF SUPPORT AMONG AFRICAN AMERICANS

None of the African American participants describe their own support for President Obama as "blind," "unconditional," or based solely on a shared racial identity. However, a few participants do describe how they see that dynamic in friends, family, or acquaintances. In a focus group in Alabama, for example, young African American participants share different observations including:

> For some people, Obama can't do anything wrong. He could be sitting there doing nothing, twiddling his thumbs, and they would still see him as godsend.

> People haven't had someone like him for a long time. And black people have been waiting for someone of his caliber, so anything that comes out of his mouth is gold.

African American college students in Michigan make similar comments. One young black woman states: "My mother is in love with Obama, so she would agree with him no matter what. Like if he killed somebody, she would be like, 'Oh, I bet it was for a good reason.'" In addition to unconditional support, some describe how African Americans would blame any criticism of President Obama on racism. One young black woman from North Carolina offers:

> My parents are Obama's biggest fans. As far as all of the flack that he gets for things, my parents are like, "They need to leave him alone. They are always on his back. He's only been in office so long . . . it's only because he is black."

Several college-aged African American participants, like this woman from North Carolina, make it clear that they do not share (what appears to be) their parents' unconditional support of President Obama. Instead, they describe how their political decisions involved thoughtful decisions. One young black male from Indiana recalls the following interaction with his mother:

> My mom would call me and say "You better go vote. You better go vote. Let's get the first African American in office." And I was like, "What do you think that he stands for, Mom?" And she was like, "People have fought for this day. You need to go ahead and do what's right." And I'm like, "Well, I want to do what's right by me. And what I think might be right for my future children. So, they don't get handed something that their generation can't handle." I would rather vote for that than to vote for somebody just because they are African American. Because at the end of the day, I would rather be well-off than to have a black president. And my friends were just like the same way: "We have to put a black man in office. We have to put a black man in office." And personally, I just couldn't see it. I had to get to the issues. I'm not going to say who I voted for, but it wasn't just because of the person's race.

This participant is one of a number of African Americans who describe how their support for President Obama is the result of a process involving much thought and consideration.

At least one African American participant takes offense to the idea that all black voters automatically support President Obama solely based on race. The young African American man from Michigan acknowledges that a small number might fall into that category, and then goes on to say: "Shoot, the number of blacks that did vote Obama because of race doesn't compare to the number of Whites that voted against him because of it!" A number of other participants explain how being African American doesn't guarantee that other political candidates automatically garner the vast majority of African American voters. One middle-aged black man from Alabama explains why he voted for President Obama, but not past black presidential candidates:

> Every other presidential candidate that I've known in my lifetime, and associated with African Americans, has been Al Sharpton, Jesse Jackson, and

others. They have always been black people for black people. Whereas Barack Obama didn't do that. He wasn't a person who said "I'm here to make life better for black people." He was more like, "My interests are in making the best America possible." And with the demographics of America, that was necessary and important. That is one reason why I voted for him.

Other African American participants make similar distinctions. One young female college student from California explains how the core of her support for President Obama is based on something more specific than just race.

I was raised in a very multicultural school, so there was no expectation about being the stereotypical black kid. So, I was into rock music, I was into rap music, I was into everything. I think that Obama represented a lot of black kids who were not necessarily the stereotype. So, you feel more comfortable voting for what is familiar. I tell you this in all honesty: If he got on stage in a do-rag, and sagging jeans—Oh heck no! I would not vote him at all. He ain't running for nothing. He can't even run my dirty draws to the laundry mat! No. He can't do that. I wouldn't have taken him seriously. To black people, he is not the caricature of that stereotypical black man. We don't want someone to make a fool of us.

As demonstrated within this section, the perception that President Obama has the automatic support of African Americans is a myth. This perception appears to be an extension of the tendency not to acknowledge the diversity within this large racial group. Interestingly, the focus groups include African Americans who do no support President Obama. More often than not, the reason is connected to President Obama's tax policies. One young African American woman from California who is attending college in the South shares:

I know that my dad didn't vote for Obama simply because of the tax policy. He has complained about increasing taxes and the fact that people who earn more money shouldn't have to pay more taxes. I think that he really likes that he is African American, but still didn't vote for him.

Other similar accounts of how African American friends and family members refuse to support President Obama because of specific economic policies appear across different focus groups. In one Rhode Island focus group, a middle-aged African American man describes how political party also is an issue:

I have a friend who is a Republican and black . . . and he just isn't down with Obama. He would say, "I'm a Republican and this is what I believe; I don't agree with what he believes in. Doesn't matter—black, white, red, yellow . . . if you are a Democrat then I'm not voting for you." So, it doesn't matter for him, and he stuck to his guns. He sees the world in terms of two parties.

Within focus group discussions, it is much more likely to hear African Americans describe other African Americans who do not support President Obama versus making the disclosure themselves. However, there are a handful of participants who do make this assertion—often times to the surprise of others. Such is the case for one young man attending a HBCU in Alabama. When he discloses that he had voted for John McCain in the 2008 presidential election, his fellow classmates are shocked and immediately begin asking him different questions. Most interestingly, one woman asks him to describe how it felt being in the minority on campus during the election. One of the more interesting disclosures comes from an African American woman in her late thirties participating in a predominately black focus group in Ohio. At the very end of the focus group, the conversation turns to a discussion regarding the perception that some see President Obama as the anti-Christ. As a pastor, the woman shares:

> From a minister's perspective, this is a conversation that I have had with many of my friends. It was interesting, because when it was time to vote, there were three of us and we had a very heated discussion. While I do not believe that he is the anti-Christ, he does present all of the characteristics of one. . . . What I find is very interesting is that there are people who believe it and you cannot persuade them otherwise. Then they are the people who agree with him on some things, but disagree with him on others. And that is where I was . . . I don't care, I can put this out there: I didn't vote for him. Even in the process of me not voting for him—

At this point, another participant (a black man in his late forties who also is a preacher) interrupts her and shouts, "What!? Take her card! The "card" that he jokingly is referring to is a non-existent form of identification that confirms membership in the African American community. At this point, the entire group begins to talk over one another until the woman asserts herself and says:

> No, I didn't vote for him. But in the process of it all, I listened to him, and found a whole lot that I agreed with. But in all of my processes . . . [group interrupts]. . . . But in that whole process, I prayed and did all of the things that I knew that I was supposed to do. And then I made my vote . . . there were two things that affected my final decision as to why I did not vote for him. It was a personal thing, and it was a moral thing. I was like, "I will not do it. Because if I compromise on those two things, then down the line, I am going to have to

compromise again. And I'm not going to do it." So, from that standpoint, I slept well that night. Even though he won, I was glad that he won. . . . And now he is my president as well.

The number of African American participants who disclose that they do not support President Obama is relatively small. What is more common, however, are those black participants whose enthusiastic support for President Obama has waned somewhat since he took office. Some are critical because they perceive that he has lost his "mojo" after being elected; others are disappointed that he has become entrenched in the negative politics of Washington. The most common source for criticism among African Americans, however, is that he has not done enough for black people. One young African American man from Michigan describes how his family members in Illinois are increasingly critical of President Obama.

> A lot of people in my family are pro-black . . . so they would probably accuse Obama for not being black enough. For not bringing attention to black issues—like why are they closing so many schools in Detroit, or why so many black people getting shot in Chicago. . . . My family would always throw the negative in because they want him to look into more black issues. They are the same way when they accuse Oprah for not being black enough . . .

While this participant focuses specifically on "black issues," African American participants are generally similar to other individuals who express disappointment because they expected more change to happen more quickly. Given all of the hope generated by President Obama's election, the frustration that has emerged from African Americans new to the political process is understandable. Even the most veteran voters—like the forty-something-year-old African American woman from Virginia quoted here—are struggling to balance their criticism of the president with the difficult realities that he faces.

> Well, I'm the type of person who did expect things to change. I was keeping track of all the things he said. Because I was in line at 4:30 in the morning, in the rain . . . me and my son (who was able to vote for the very first time) were in line in the rain. It was dark outside, all early in the morning. But we stood in line for hours to make sure that we voted . . . The thing is that I think that *a lot of people thought that we were electing a king* who is sovereign who could just say something and that would be that. They don't understand. I understand how politics work, but even still, I want to see more results.

Tempering one's high expectations with the realities of the political world is also seen in other focus groups. One young African American man from Georgia who is going to college in Michigan discloses:

I'm one of the biggest fans of Barack . . . I'm always "Barack, Barack, Barack" . . . I support him in everything that he does, almost to a fault . . . I think that my dad brings me back down to earth and reminds me that Barack is—at the end of the day—a politician.

SUMMARY

This chapter explores African American perceptions of Barack Obama. In particular, the comments from African American participants are analyzed, and then compared and contrasted to how non-African Americans perceive their support of the first president of African descent. The next chapter fulfills a similar objective in regards to European American perceptions of President Obama, and the meta-perceptions of non-white participants. In tandem, both of these chapters challenge existing beliefs that foster an overly simplistic approach to understanding the influence of race on perceptions of President Obama. This important point is also illustrated in chapter 9 that focuses on the diversity of opinion that exists to President Obama's communication surrounding the Professor Gates/Sergeant Crowley conflict.

Chapter 8

White Opposition to President Obama

> To me it seems as much of a fad in the white community to dislike Obama as it is in the black community to like Obama.
>
> —Young African American woman attending a HBCU in Alabama

In chapter 7, the focus is on the prevalent perception that African Americans are so proud of President Obama that it results in a blind allegiance to his policies. Within that chapter, I work diligently to establish the "truth" behind this perception while simultaneously offering insight into the diversity among black participants. Chapter 8 follows a similar path. The focus is on the prevalent perception, especially among African Americans, that a significant level of suspicion, fear and criticism of President Obama exists within some European American populations. Toward this objective, I begin with some descriptions of participant comments that illustrate support for this perception. Then I offer several points of analysis that help readers understand the various sources for these public perceptions of President Obama. The chapter concludes by exploring African American perceptions of white suspicion, fear, and criticism of President Obama and acknowledging the substantial support for the president among white voters.

EXCESSIVE CRITICISM OF PRESIDENT OBAMA

"With some Whites, President Obama can't do anything right." This particular quote comes from a middle-aged African American man from Virginia, however, similar comments are heard from black participants from across the United States. Interestingly, this sentiment receives much more attention than the fact that President Obama garnered more support from European American voters than other recent Democratic presidential candidates (Todd and Gawiser, 2009). Across different focus groups, a clear theme among some participants emerges: The passion and intensity of criticism for President Obama seems to be unprecedented.

Given political realities, some criticism of President Obama's policy initiatives is to be expected. However, several white participants describe relatives whose criticism of President Obama appears excessive. For instance, one young white woman from Alabama describes how "incredibly negative" her parents are when it comes to the president. She says, "Every time he is on the news, they are like, 'Oh, I hate everything that he does!' He can do no right in their eyes. All they do is talk about how terrible he is." As illustrated below, several participants point to family critics who focus on his communication.

> I have an aunt who is anti-Obama. She has been really critical of everything that he does. She listens to the weekly addresses and then finds any number of things to be negative about. "He's a horrible communicator. He should have said this and not that." She also critiques how many different people are writing things for him . . . She believes that when so many are writing his speeches that they really don't connect properly. You can hear the different voices in his speeches and that irritates her. (Young white woman from Virginia)

An older white man from Nebraska is also critical of President Obama's rhetoric, which he describes as "fluff":

> [Another participant] talked about the "Yes we can" and "We are the ones that we've been waiting for" messages. And this is when the oceans began to recede and the world began to heal [says sarcastically]. You know I'm old enough to know that this is all just fluff. Just fluff. It doesn't make any sense to me at all. Those kinds of words . . . it's just trying to motivate people. So, for me, it was just a big turn-off to hear that kind of rhetoric. And . . . I don't remember, was it at the acceptance speech at the Democratic National Convention in Denver? They had the big Greek columns, a big whole show. That was a big turn-off for me. The whole thing was ridiculous.

As I demonstrate in chapter 3, many participants' favorable perceptions of President Obama's communication are based on comparisons with other recent U.S. presidents. For many, Obama's skill as a communicator seems especially impressive when compared directly to President Bush (one participant describes Obama as the "anti-Bush"). Yet, at least one participant criticizes President Obama's communication and explicitly describes him as "worse than Bush." Consider the comments from a young white woman from Nebraska who is referencing several examples where the "real Obama" is starting to show.

> I feel like we are seeing the real Obama now. I feel like when you are stressed, when you are going through a really tough time, then you see your true colors . . . I think that we see the true Obama from the remarks that he has said. I know that people mess up sometimes, but I think that those remarks let us know how he really feels. I feel like we are just now seeing the real Obama. I know that he is trying to please some people but then the mess-ups that he does have are important to consider. Like Bush would mispronounce some words, but those are just words. Obama's mess-ups are about people, like the whole "handicap" comment. There are things like that, that to me, are even worse. For me, I would rather have someone mispronounce a word, than insult people or make a rude comment when they are in a position of power. He's worse than Bush.

This set of comments is fairly unique in that the participant is the only person in the study to describe President Bush as a more competent communicator than President Obama. However, other interesting critiques do exist. A twenty-something-year-old white college student in Michigan, for example, offers a unique point of criticism for President Obama who recently gave the commencement speech at a local high school that won a national competition. When others in the community college focus group universally applaud President Obama's ability to inspire the high school graduates, this participant interrupts and says:

> But even coming to [the local high school], even the teachers were saying he's giving the students who already had drive, more drive. The students who didn't have drive, couldn't attend because of their legal background. Anyone who had a misdemeanor or a felony was not able to attend. Even if you graduated, you couldn't walk across the stage because it is illegal for you to be in the same room as the president if you have a felony. A large part of that graduating class that could have benefited from that, couldn't because of it. So, even the teachers are saying, "Hey, it's cool that he did this," but it wasn't effective.

A young white male college student from California offers a simple explanation for the excessive criticism that seems to plague President Obama: "I think that when you just don't like someone, their flaws are going to be magnified." Consequently, the question is not necessarily *if* excessive criticism of the president is going to exist—the question is *why* does it exist? In other words, why do individuals dislike President Obama? Despite the perceptions of many, there is no singular definitive answer to that question.

Negativity Based on Race

According to some participants, issues of race and/or racism are what fuels the excessive criticism of President Obama. This perception is articulated by participants of all racial and ethnic backgrounds; more often than not, younger persons are quick to identify race as a factor in public perceptions of the president. For some, the opposition is grounded in existing racism, especially among persons who are older, less educated, and/or from rural areas or the South. For instance, several participants report that some Whites, even Democrats, did not vote for him "simply because he was black." One young white male from rural Indiana explains how many family members didn't support President Obama: "I come from a very small town, predominately (all) white. A lot of people in my family are pretty ignorant, for lack of a better word. During the election and to this day, they still view him as the black president. And that's not a positive thing, actually it seems to make him a bigger target." According other participants, racism fuels criticisms of President Obama that seem to be more intense than criticisms of other [Democratic] presidents. One forty-something-year-old white woman from southern Ohio shares: "I still think that there is a lot of racism. A lot of people who were finding fault with him were finding fault with him because he is a black man . . . I think that for some people, no matter what he did, people wouldn't have liked it. People wouldn't have liked it because he is black." A young African American woman from Alabama seems especially frustrated by individuals who criticize President Obama unfairly.

> He has taken so much flack because he is the first black president. I often hear the statement, "Obama is the worst president that the United States has ever had." Okay. My question is "Are you saying that because he is black or because it is really what you believe?" Have you not been around when Bush was in office? And how he left the U.S. in the worst economic state ever? But Obama is the worst president that we've ever had. I mean come on now. Really? It seems like a lot of people are viewing him poorly, they are not looking at him and all of the things that he's done. They look at him as black and that he doesn't know what he is doing.

This idea is supported by other participants, including a young white man from Massachusetts who states that "some people are super critical of him, they blame his race for anything bad that is going on." Other participants describe how existing racial perceptions seem to produce an irrational fear regarding President Obama's candidacy. For instance, one young white female from Virginia explains how her older family members express serious concern:

My parents and grandparents, especially my grandpa, he is very traditional. So, to him, his biggest concern when Obama was elected president, he thought that all he was going to do was bring a whole bunch of black guys in the White House. His fear was that the black community would rule the White House, and it would become the "Black House."

The lack of support based on fear described here seems to magnify once President Obama was elected. In a North Carolina focus group a sixty-something-year-old white male express this idea when he states:

All of the big push back went into motion the minute that Obama got elected. This happened for a variety of reasons—number one being race, that is underneath it all. But my Republican friends are the same that they have always been, except now they are a little louder. They are just a little louder . . . I think that they are frightened. I think that they are scared of having a black man as our leader. It is that simple.

The fear of having an African American president is something covertly discussed in a couple of other all-Caucasian focus groups. Most times, the topic is raised by participants in describing the perceptions of family members, friends, or acquaintances. However, in one focus group held in a rural southern Ohio community the issue is explicitly identified when a thirty-something-year-old white man uses the closing moments of the focus group session to share:

The first thing that I thought was that the African Americans, the colored community, was going to take over. More or less, they were going to take over. And I don't know what that would mean, but I got the picture that the next time that I walk in McDonald's or something, I would hear "white boy, you get down and wash the dishes. You go do this. We rule the country now." I don't know if that's happening . . . Is that changing around the South? Is what we've done to them coming back to haunt us? I don't know . . . but that is just a question that I was going to ask: Do you see that happening whenever you go . . . do the Coloreds overrule the Whites? Are they puffing their chests out to say "We are the kings now. We have the man in the Big House"?

A number of participants feel that President Obama was elected simply because he is African American, something that represented a "cultural phenomenon" (using the phrase from a middle-aged Native American man from Michigan). Being a cultural phenomenon, according to some, is the top selling point for voters. This causes some of the general public to remain suspicious of Obama's qualifications. In one Ohio focus group, a young white male describes how his father refers to President Obama as "our token black president who doesn't know what he is doing." Others in the group wonder if this perception is informed by racial prejudice that believes that African Americans are inferior to Caucasian Americans and that President Obama could not be as good as he comes across. This is the sentiment expressed by a thirty-something-year-old European American woman from a Michigan community college who says: "I always thought that he was too good to be true. My friends, and with everyone on campus, they were all like: 'Oh, vote for him, vote for him!' But I couldn't vote for him because I didn't know what he stood for. It all felt fake to me. I don't see any blacks who are *that* smart."

Individuals whose understandings of race make it difficult to see President Obama's qualifications as credible focus their comments on how he is the face—but not the brains—of a movement of advocating for social change. For one middle-aged European American woman from Nebraska, President Obama is wonderful in his role of political puppet: "I thought that he is wonderful: Here's a man who is puppeteered wonderfully. He speaks wonderfully, he's articulate, he talks the talk, and seems to walk the walk. I think that they found the perfect "anointed one" to go out and serve the agenda for the people who were propping him up." This perception appears in a couple of different focus group discussions, including one held in California. In that group, a fifty-something-year-old white female small business owner declares:

> It kind of reminds me of *The Wizard of Oz* and the guy who is operating the big face behind the big drapes. He is just the guy out there and then you have all of these people behind the curtains, moving and telling him what to do. They are the real brains behind the man . . . He was virtually an unknown; his rise was phenomenal. It was off the page—it was a meteoric rise that will go down in history. He was just some guy and then next day he was the president.

The comments included in this section highlight the existing perception that *some* European Americans' criticism of President Obama is a reflection of existing racial ideologies. While most of the participants who are quoted in this section are white, it is important to note that the vast majority of white participants did not believe that racism is the primary cause for Obama criticism. Instead, they argue that what appears as an issue of race is really an issue of politics.

Opposition Based on Politics

Most white focus group participants who are the most vocal in their criticism of President Obama are adamant in declaring that the source of their opposition is political, not racial. One thirty-something-year-old white man describes his contempt in explicit terms. When asked about his perceptions of President Obama's communication, he responds by saying:

> I didn't like him from the beginning. I'm strictly a Republican. I'm a die-hard Republican, so I guess that that might be the military side of me. But I just don't like him . . . I really don't watch anything that has to do with Democratic stuff . . . I can't really even say that I ever saw the guy talk . . . I really don't care to.

The perception of this participant, as well as others like him, is primarily informed by political affiliation. Their ideological perspectives are so closely aligned with the Republican Party that they reportedly "bash" all Democrats regardless of race. Several participants, including one young Jewish woman from Illinois quoted below, describes how family members seem to have an intense hatred of Democrats. This, and not President Obama's race, is at the core of their criticism:

> My god-sister is a conservative Jew who is also Republican. Her reason for disliking Obama is the fact that he is a Democrat. To me, most of the objections that I heard about him were not related to his blackness, or related to his ideas, the objections that I heard were that they were Republicans and they hated Democrats.

This point is made time and time again across the United States. In a focus group in Massachusetts, a white male participant in his late twenties shares how Republican family members "attack [President Obama] because he is a Democrat, not because of his color. They said the same stuff about Clinton, it's just the same type of politics."

While the perceptions of these participants appear to be based primarily on political labels with little careful consideration of President Obama's policies, such is not the case for other individuals. For instance, one middle-aged white woman from California is very vocal about her opposition to President Obama. A small business owner who is increasingly concerned about the economy, she says:

> I want to make it clear. I never voted until this past election. I was never passionate about it until . . . I do remember the first time that I heard that he was on the ballot, because I was raised colorblind and I was actually really glad that we had a black candidate running. And then I did the research and I got really scared. I realized that he had a double message in terms of how he was going to fundamentally change the country. And I realized that it wasn't going to be in a good way. That was my first recollection of him running. The more I learned, the more I didn't like.

Other participants also describe how perceptions of President Obama are not only based on things such as race or politics, but specific policy ideas.

> My grandfather had been in the FBI a long, long time. He grew up as a hard-ass, and he was a hard-ass his entire career, and now he is a die-hard Republican. He sends all these really crazy emails to all of his friends. He did the same thing with Bush. But it seems more crazy with Obama . . . They kinda butt heads on everything. But he is one who does his research. His emails include political facts and tidbits that you wouldn't really hear about in the news—like he takes all of these trips that cost millions of dollars. He passes along the emails so that we know what's going on behind the scenes. (Young white male soldier from Indiana)

The main point here is that, for many participants, political issues (in terms of political affiliation or policy initiatives) trump any racial issues that might exist. In fact, this point is evident in the comments of one thirty-something-year-old man in California who shares exactly why President Obama "sucks":

> My family is all from Texas, they are all hard-core Republican. So, when Obama won I talked to my family in Texas . . . and they are a little bit racist. They were saying: "It's bullshit! He's black and that's the only reason that he won!" And all of this stuff. Then I talk to them two years later and they are like: "It's bullshit. His policies are wrong—all Democrats suck!" So, now they have moved from "black" to "Democrat." So, even a racist Republican family isn't seeing him as black anymore; now he is a Democrat. Me and my family live in California and we see it as him being a Democrat. It has nothing to do with his color; he sucks because he is a Democrat. Democrat policies suck.

Opposition Based on Class Issues

Other participants describe the opposition facing President Obama as ideological. However, instead of focusing on political party affiliations they explain their criticism in terms of specific economic policies. For instance, a small business owner from Connecticut in her sixties is quick to explain her criticism of President Obama: "I am someone who has a business of my own . . . I think that the decisions being made in Washington are affecting me directly. I see Obama as a threat to my business . . . I don't care about race or religion or politics. When I talk to others, the word [black] is never thrown out there. It is all economics to us." Other participants who describe themselves as upper-middle or upper class also offer clarification to their opposition to Obama's presidency. One twenty-something-year-old white man from Michigan explains his stance regarding Obama's tax policies:

> I'm blessed to be born into a family where my father worked extremely hard his entire life. We are—I'm not going to say well-off, but I don't have to worry where my next meal is going to come from. I'm always going to have a roof over my head. I have parents who care. And we are going to get punished for it, because we worked hard? Yeah, tax the rich to give to the poor. Well, you know what? We've done this before. It's failed then, and its gonna fail again. Who was it? Herbert Hoover fought poverty, and you know what happened? Poverty won. Things don't work like that. I apologize because I'm getting worked up here and getting off topic. But, at the same time, that is the way that I was raised. What you earn is what you get to earn. Now, okay 10 percent of our population is real rich. Another part of it doesn't want to do a damn thing. Pardon my language, I do apologize. So, we are going to take money from the rich folks and then pay for the rest of society and then we are going to take some money out and give you money for this, for that . . . It's just one of those things . . . I don't know . . . I'm kinda pissed about it all to be honest.

Other participants express similar concerns about President Obama's policies regarding economic issues. Several are quick to explain how his liberal—socialist—policies are the reason for the vocal criticism. One sixty-something-year-old white man from North Carolina articulates how that issue is more relevant than others.

> I was just trying to think back when recently I've heard any real mention or hint to him being black, white, or anything like that. I've heard "Damn Democrats." I've heard of the "Damn Liberals" and the "Damn Socialists." All of those labels are code for big government. I don't really think that the criticisms are there because he is a black president. I think that there is a perception of him as a president, who has the same issues that any other Democratic president would have . . . Even when you look at him on television, frankly he looks like anybody else up there. He has a nice white shirt on and a tie. The key issue here is economic.

Another Caucasian male (in his fifties) in a different focus group in the same North Carolina city supports this idea. Within his comments, he defends individuals criticism—including conservative Republicans and Tea Party members—as non-racist.

> I run around with a lot of right-wing Republicans. I think that the objection is—I don't think that it is based on race at all. I think that it is based on a deep-seated belief of what the proper role of government is. They are always calling Obama a socialist. "Look who we have in office now. What is he going to do to us now?" It is a totally different view, economically, in terms of how government should operate. A couple of times, I attended a Tea Party rally down in southern North Carolina . . . They were railing against the government being too big and

giving too many benefits to people. It is hard to get to the bottom of this, and I don't really think that any one will. I think that most of it is an emotional backlash to the economy and the fact that they haven't done as well as they should.

According to this participant, public fear of President Obama isn't based on racial divisions. Instead, they are primarily steeped in economic concerns. An older white woman from California demonstrates her agreement with this perspective when she asserts:

He really is a socialist! When he said that he was going to fundamentally change the country, I think that everyone assumed that it was going to be in a good way. And then they didn't bother to look to see exactly what type of changes he really wanted. Re-distribution of the wealth. The creation of this group who wants the government cheese but don't want to work for themselves. Wiping out the middle class. THAT'S the perception that I'm getting where this man is going to . . . or would like to go.

Most participants appear open to consider that white opposition to President Obama is stimulated by political and economic differences. However, many Obama supporters—of all personal, social, and cultural backgrounds—question the role that racism plays alongside of these other issues. For some, President Obama's race appears to magnify public criticism. One middle-aged African American male from Alabama suggests: "I think that most older, conservative Republicans don't like Barack Obama because he is trying to mess with their money. They already don't like his policies, so the fact that he is black, just makes it more intense. He's trying to change things, and they don't like it." Several participants suggest that some Whites remain racially prejudiced to the point where they will not support a president of African-descent. Yet, in order to avoid accusations of racism, they use non-racial reasons to explain their non-support. This idea is articulated by a thirty-something-year-old white male from Illinois who says:

My mom would never say this to me or her friends, but she wouldn't vote for a black president. She wouldn't say it to me because she knows that we would get into an argument. But instead she says, "He's helping the lower class too much." She would flip it to another issue. She is always like that, even before he was elected.

The next section explores the idea that white opposition to President Obama is racialized in implicit ways. In particular, it focuses on how certain segments of the public position him as the "Other" in seemingly non-racist (yet equally powerful) terms.

ALTERNATIVE CODES FOR "HE ISN'T LIKE US"

According to focus group participants, most Americans who think in racially prejudicial ways learn to avoid explicitly racist comments especially when it comes to public figures. As such, participants are quick to point out that opposition to President Obama based on racial difference is often times situated in more acceptable, non-racial terms. In the words of one young black man from Alabama, "Most of the hate generated against him is based on race. They can't say they don't like him because he is black, so they say it in different ways." A young white male participant from Illinois echoes this sentiment when he says:

> Obviously a lot of people would not be willing to admit that they didn't vote for him because he is black. That is a social taboo; that is not appropriate to say in most social circles. So, how many people might justify—and I'm not saying that this is the case here—but I'm sure that there are plenty of people who justify not voting for him, not liking him based on issues . . . and in reality, if he was white, those issues wouldn't have been a deciding factor.

For some focus group participants, the impact of race is undeniable especially since no other plausible explanation exists to explain the extent of the opposition. A twenty-something-year-old white male Alabama college student comes to this conclusion in terms of his own family members.

> My mother, before the election, was pretty far liberal. And she still is. She is pro-welfare, pro-taxes, pro-social services, but she is not pro-Obama . . . which is something that I just don't get. I don't understand if you are "pro" all of his policies, but you are not "pro" the person . . . My grandfather was really, really, really pro-Clinton, but is also anti-Obama. Again, I don't understand. I look at all of the policies that they like, but they don't like the person. There's not many conclusions to draw except that it is because of his race. Why else would they feel that way? These people are largely the same on the issues, but you don't like him? What's the reason? They won't say that it is because he is black, but how many other reasons are there?

According to a forty-something-year-old black male from Rhode Island, opposition to President Obama is "racially based" and "coded in very subtle ways." These codes are enacted to communicate one message: He is not like us so we cannot trust him. In order to solidify the difference, individuals go to great lengths to portray him as an "Other." One white male college student in North Carolina explains:

> I feel that people are making really loooooong strides just to separate him from others. They call him a Socialist, or a Communist, and they to separate him from

the rest of us without talking about race . . . but that's what they really mean. He isn't like us. He gets a lot of criticism, I know that all presidents get unwarranted criticism, but it just seems like he is getting a lot more than others. People are making far stretches just to isolate him. They can't say, "We don't like him because he is an African American president." Everybody tries to hide whatever racist ideas that they have . . . whether they are good at it or not. They do it in other ways. Obviously, Muslims are the enemy, so let's make him Muslim. We don't like Socialism, so let's make him a Socialist. Or a foreigner.

This point is made time and time again throughout the different focus group discussions. In Massachusetts, for example, a fifty-something-year-old black woman comments on how accusations that President Obama is secretly a Muslin continue to exist. Her take on this is: "I don't think that people think he is Muslim at all. I think that that is a strategy for people to think negatively of him."

Supporters identify a number of labels that critics use to cast President Obama as "Other." As demonstrated in the quote from the last paragraph, this includes being a Muslim, a Socialist, or an unpatriotic foreigner. One twenty-something-year-old man who is serving in the military at the time of his Indiana focus group, President Obama's difference is evident on multiple levels:

What about his religious views? He's the first non-Christian, non-Catholic president. He has the distinction of being the first non-Christian president that we have ever had. What about that? I think that that is more important than his race. His race is just one piece of the puzzle, there are so many things about him and race is just one small piece of that puzzle. He is just so different than any other president that we've had on so many levels.

By far, however, the most extreme characterization of President Obama as "Other" is perpetuated by those who describe him as the anti-Christ. This perception is first articulated by a thirty-something-year-old white woman in one of my very first focus groups in Michigan: "I also have an aunt who literally believes that he is the anti-Christ. Because of the way that he presents himself, in her mind, that's too good to be true. No one human and godly could act that way, he must be the anti-Christ." While some may believe that this perception is an isolated one, at least one participant describes it as common within her West Virginia hometown.

There was a lot of talk about that where I'm from. I remember that being the topic of a lot of conversations in my high school. When he was running, people seemed to repeat what their parents were saying—they had the whole . . . you know how people mesh things up biblically, between what is happening now and is in the Bible. People were making assumptions, and crazy conclusions. It got you thinking, "Wow, he really is charismatic . . . and perfect . . . he came out of nowhere . . . and he is really young." All of these people were following him all of a sudden. And how many young politicians just appear just like that? It made you think. (Twenty-something-year-old white woman attending college in Virginia)

BLACK PERCEPTIONS OF WHITE OPPOSITION TO PRESIDENT OBAMA

For the vast majority of African American participants, issues of race are the cause of (what they describe) as excessive criticism of President Obama. In several mixed race focus groups, the issue of race is discussed with a certain amount of hesitancy. For instance, in an Illinois group where she is one of two African Americans, a young woman states: "Nobody wants to bring up race in this discussion, but the fact of the matter is that it is still a big deal." However, in all-black focus groups, discussions of race appear more honest and free-flowing. For example, many of the in-depth comments featured in the previous chapter occur during focus groups which are exclusively or predominately African American. In this context, one of the most powerful narratives is shared by a young black woman attending college in Alabama:

> My dad spent most of his time in southern California, and he will tell me certain things that happened to him and my uncles. Being profiled, and discriminated against . . . When Obama won he was so excited! Then some of the Republican pundits started really tearing into him, especially with the whole universal healthcare issue. That just dogged him out. My father is a medical doctor and he has a lot of patients who he does the best he can with, with whatever insurance they have, but he was really bothered by it all. He watches all of this stuff—he's a very strong guy—but it bothers him. One day, I was sitting with him watching all of this go down on television, and I could tell that he was bothered by it all. He just looked at me and said, "_____, they just think that he's a nigger in a suit." Like he made his way, through adversity through the time period that it was. My father was just flabbergasted that the people who had the power to change things would do that to "one of their own." That was too much for him. . . . he could not get over it.

While African American participants criticize a variety of Caucasians for their fanatic opposition to President Obama, their most impassioned counterattacks are saved for members of the Tea Party. One middle-aged black man from California describes the movement as "operating like the old Klu Klux Klan—just taken to another level" during an all-African American focus group. Other participants quickly add their criticism including an assertion that "the Tea Party came to exist because of the first African American president." This comment is greeted by a chorus of agreement within the group. An older (seventy-something-year-old) black man provides a counter argument encouraging the group to see the economic dynamics in messages from Libertarians or Tea Party members. According to his perspective, "When they say that they don't feel any racism among themselves, I think that they are being as honest as they can be. They are concerned about keeping their money. They don't racialize it consciously." His comments are met with some acknowledged agreement. However, a forty-something-year-old man continues to assert comparisons between the KKK and the present-day Tea Party.

> I get what you are saying, but this is the same thing that happened in the South when black people got the right to vote (pounding table with every word). Rich white people got together with poor white people and convinced them that the "Negroes" were going to take what little you've got. And they believed it. Even though they would have been better off if they pooled with the black folks . . . Economically they would have been a lot better off. And now the media is doing the same thing with the Tea Party movement. It's the same thing, only a much higher scale.

Others in the group support this comparison, but also recognize that Tea Party members are not all the same. "I know that it is not everyone in the Tea Party [who is racist], but they are there and giving off lots of racist messages. It is probably the least educated of them, and also the most vocal," concludes one black male participant.

White opposition to President Obama, especially that which exists in certain groups in certain settings, is such a serious concern that a number of African American participants express fear for the president's safety. This is pointed out by one twenty-something-year-old black college student from Illinois:

> Honestly, I sometimes am afraid if someone is going to murder him or not. In my community, we have a lot of fear when black people are in power, because when people are fearful of black leaders, they murder them. So, I used to always think in my mind that I pray that Obama doesn't get killed. Because he is the first black president, he is making changes. He is a great person, but some people don't think that.

According to African American participants, the fear existed during the presidential campaign and was magnified after he was elected. A fifty-something-year-old black woman shares: "In my family, everyone loved Obama . . . Everyone's fear was that Obama would be assassinated. They pointed to the fact that we have a white vice president, so they would say 'Oh he is going to be killed, so then a white man would be president. Just like all other times.'" The most intense fear among African Americans is evident in southern focus group discussions. One older white man from North Carolina explains how some of the fear is based on what "rural, uneducated whites might do." However, he also adds that he fears

> Those radical Republicans whose agenda is to try and defeat everything that he does . . . Really, the radical Republicans in our state are frightened because we have a black president in office. I wonder what type of climate that produces.

The climate that this man from North Carolina refers to is felt by some African American participants. Within two different focus groups at a HBCU campus in Alabama, individuals discuss the genuine fear that was felt on campus before, during, and after President Obama's election. Several instances, including a bomb threat, prompted the university's administrators to caution students:

> We were in the South at the time of the election, that's was scary. Remember that at the time of the election, this school had a bomb threat. That was actually kind of scary. We were told to be careful on Election Day, not to wear Obama shirts, or anything like that because people could target us. We didn't know what the reaction was going to be. And since we are in a predominately white area, and as you could see on the electoral map, we were pretty much the only area that voted for Obama. Everywhere else in this area voted for McCain. So, it was like, wearing an Obama shirt got you that ridicule. And you didn't know if they were carrying a shotgun, you don't know what they are capable of, you didn't know what their reaction was going to be . . . Even afterwards, you heard reports that there were even more hate crimes after the election.

The comments from these students describing their genuine fear of white southern violence are shared in serious, thoughtful, and reflective tones. For instance, one young woman discloses: "We were scared of the backlash of it. It was unfortunate because I couldn't celebrate because I was intimidated by the hate crimes that could have happened." Both focus groups include descriptions of several racially motivated incidents including police intimidation, vandalism of Obama's campaign office, and verbal assaults in public places. For many students, especially those who were from the North, these occurrences are quite frightening.

> Someone drove through our campus with a Confederate flag on the back of their truck. A lot of us are from up North, so we were really excited about a black president, but being in the South, many of us were scared about what might happen. With two HBCUs in the area, the white community . . . this was still a

scary thing. The school was getting bomb threats and we were told to be careful where we went . . . You aren't used to that, you aren't prepared for that because that was the 1960s, not 2008.

The hostile climate immediately following President Obama's election impacts the everyday lives of these students. For instance, they typically seek out opportunities for any off-campus activities; however, this changed after the election. One woman explains:

My boyfriend and I were out at the store after the election—the day after the election. And we just got stared down. And I'm used to getting stared at down here, but it was like . . . I mean with a hatred. I mean conversations would just cease when we walked by. We were like, "Holy crap! We have to get back to campus!" And that is something that I never normally say! [group laughter] Because we hardly ever want to be here. But it was ridiculous. We were here and hearing stories about people being shouted at as they walked to their cars. Stuff being thrown at people's cars as they drove by. So, we decided to spend the day on campus.

More often than not, discussions of race in racially diverse focus groups lack the intensity and depth of similar discussions in racially homogeneous groups. Again, most discussions appear to address issues related to race in largely cautious ways. One of the exceptions to this pattern occurs in the first group with college students at a Michigan state university. Within this focus group, a balance of African Americans and Caucasian Americans engages in a discussion regarding white opposition. It begins when a white male participant shares:

My family is primarily conservative, I'm the only liberal in my family. So, they HATE everything that Obama does only because he is a Democrat. I think that if it would be a Republican president doing the exact same stuff, they would be totally fine. But, just because he is a Democrat, they totally hate him.

While other white participants share similar perceptions, a few African American students in the group trade glances of suspicion. Unlike other focus groups, however, one young African American male speaks up after white participants' comments. In an interesting moment of cross-racial transparency, he shares:

This is all really interesting to me . . . Your parents [referring to the white male quoted earlier] are so against Obama because he is Democratic. And, in my mind, I was like, "Yeah. And probably because he is black." I really hate that I think like that but I'm pretty sure that a lot of black people feel that way.

Especially for hard-core Republicans who are like, "Okay, he's a Democrat AND he's black! Come on now!"

An African American woman quickly adds, "I think that that's true. We always think that white people are against us, all the time." The African American man continues:

> And as black people we have to get past that, but it is still heavy on our minds. Especially for people who are so against Obama, I always feel that it's because he's black. We know that every white person who doesn't like Obama, it's not because he's black. But I don't know what it is about our culture but we believe that. So earlier when you said that your parents don't like Obama because he is a Democrat, I even said to [an African American woman sitting next to him] "It's because he's black." And she was like, "Yeah, I know." It is just so interesting that sometimes black people—we—have a harder time getting over race than white people.

WHITE SUPPORT FOR PRESIDENT OBAMA

The focus of this chapter is on participant comments regarding the excessive criticism of President Obama among certain groups within the white community. Part of my decision to include such a chapter in this book is based on the forcefulness that accompanied comments from participants in describing their perceptions of this segment of the general public. Other chapters highlight the support that President Obama has among all racial and ethnic groups, including European Americans. According to focus group participants, the rationale behind this support is as diverse as the reasons for opposition.

"Some of my friends voted for Obama because it was 'trendy,'" one twenty-something-year-old white man from Massachusetts shares. The perception exists that some European Americans, like some African Americans, support President Obama without much critical thinking. As described by a thirty-something-year-old white man from Illinois, the media sell Obama as the popular choice—something that was attractive to people of all backgrounds: "There were some conservative people who voted for Obama . . . they did it strictly for novelty purposes. They put very little critical thinking into their decision. First black president. And he was portrayed as the hip, youthful decision, the youthful choice."

Other participants suggest that some support from European Americans is generated by a desire to prove that they are not personally racist and that the United States has moved beyond its racist past.

> I think that part of the reason why the U.S. elected Obama is because they wanted to prove everyone wrong. Do you think that they really wanted Obama or did they want to avoid being considered racist? I think that part of people's decision was that "We have to prove everyone wrong and show them that we support a black man for president." We are not racist, we can have a black man for president. (Young Latina from Massachusetts)

This perception is evident in other focus group discussions as well. For instance, in one Illinois focus group, some participants argue that white support of President Obama is an indication of a "post-racial" society. A Mexican American young woman asserts:

> I would actually argue that the U.S. is incredibly racist. It is a different racism than in the 1960s and the civil rights movement . . . We live in a racist society who likes to believe that we are colorblind . . . Instead of addressing race issues, we rather say "Look we've elected a black president. There is no way that I'm racist, I voted for a president who isn't white."

The idea here is that the support that President Obama receives from some European Americans is not genuine, but motivated by a desire to appear as "post-racial"—something that is described as "trendy."

Several European American participants take issue with perceptions that their support for President Obama is less than genuine. In an Illinois focus group, a young man provides some insight as to why individuals may embrace a colorblind approach to discussions of race.

> Can I jump in here? I want to clarify something that I was saying earlier. I had some more time to think about it in my head. I think that people who identify as white are more likely to say or believe that they are not racialized. People do not perceive whiteness as a race. Being Caucasian is a race. Maybe it's guilt . . . there are a lot things. In society—especially those of us who are younger—we have this ideal that we are colorblind, that race doesn't matter. That's the wrong perspective to take any way. But beyond that, we have been primed . . . we want to ignore race in a lot of ways.

He goes on to explain how when he was young, his parents would reprimand him when he asked about racial differences or described people with racial labels. The lesson learned is simple: Noticing a person's color means that you are racist. From this perspective, the solution to avoid racism, then, is to do whatever possible to not notice a person's race.

The reality is that, just like people of all backgrounds, whites' opposition, support, and/or apathy toward President Obama is not the result of any one factor. One white man in his late twenties makes this point explicit during a Massachusetts focus group.

I have other friends who are adamant that Obama stands for everything that this country should be. But then again, they are not as politically engaged. Then they are others who have done their homework. They look at the speeches, they look at his books, and they know the issues, and they are convinced hook, line, and sinker. But not everyone is thinking so critically.

One of my goals for this book is to counter existing perceptions that promote stereotypical generations among different cultural groups. For instance, I take considerable caution in this chapter to dig deeper into dominant perceptions that excessive criticism of President Obama is solely fueled by racism. A young Caucasian woman from Alabama also is adamant about making this point:

> I have something to say about the whole racial thing. My grandfather is eighty-nine and my grandmother from my mother's side is eighty-seven. My grandmother is from Ohio, but my grandfather was born and raised in a small town in Alabama. I mean he had to walk on dirt roads and really didn't have a store in the town, they had to eat everything that they got off of the farm. I think that the reason that I see Obama the way that I do (which is colorless and just a person) is because of my grandfather. Even though Paw Paw was born and raised in a time where segregation was the norm, he is not like that. Neither is my grandmother. I don't like when people make assumptions about us just because we are from the South. Yes, there are some really crappy people here, but those kind of people are everywhere. I think that Alabama gets stigmatized.

It is also important to note that not all African Americans reject the idea that being colorblind is a farce. Some understand it as way that Whites protect themselves from being labeled racist. Others, however, believe that being "post-racial" is admirable. When I ask one young black woman from Alabama about her reaction to those who declare that they are colorblind, her response is:

> I would say, "Bravo" actually. I think that it is nice that there are actually people who think that way, because then that means that race is a non-issue for those people. But in reality, I know that that is not popular thought. For me, when people say that they don't see him as a black person it takes me back to my childhood before I saw race. Seriously, that's a great thing. I wish that there were more people like that.

Another black woman from the same focus group adds that:

> I think that one of the things that is going to be important as we move forward is that looking at both sides . . . whenever you have a lack of contact with people from other groups, a lot of fear and unreasonable viewpoints can take hold. I didn't see his election as my way of getting back at white people. It was more like, "Praise God, we've come together and I'm happy that we have come that

far to actually elect a black man." That is indicative of us, as a country, going in the right direction. I think that generally we need more honest conversations where Whites are being honest and we are not bashing them over the heads. And vice versa.

SUMMARY

This chapter on perceptions of white opposition to President Obama parallels the previous chapter on black allegiance and unconditional support. Within both chapters, I provide descriptions of racialized perceptions of President Obama with significant effort to dig deeper beyond generalizations that seemed to be promoted by most media outlets. While these two chapters individually address issues of race, collectively they also reflect how the lack of substantial interracial interactions can lead to significant misperceptions. Facilitating opportunities for people of all cultural backgrounds to come together and discuss different issues in productive ways is a crucial means toward greater cultural understanding. Even if individuals do not reach agreement on all issues, being exposed to different perspectives through quality interpersonal interactions can only work to reduce cultural misperceptions.

Chapter 9

Gates/Crowley Conflict and the "Beer Summit"

When it comes to race issues, it's a no-win situation for Obama.

—White male traditionally aged college student from Alabama

Within each of the forty-two focus groups, I ask participants to "describe specific examples when they think that President Obama's communication is especially effective or ineffective, and appropriate or inappropriate." The very first example provided in the very first focus group involves his communication surrounding the Gates/Crowley conflict that ultimately led to the "Beer Summit." In fact, this topic is discussed within thirty-five of the forty-two focus groups. Some of these discussions are held in groups where participants share a common identity based on age, race/ethnicity, gender, or socioeconomic status. Other groups are mixed with people of various groups. The result of this aspect of data collection is participant insight that reflects both comments derived from both in-group and intergroup conversations. As such, public perceptions of President Obama's communication around the Gates/Crowley conflict provides an excellent case study to demonstrate the complex ways in which diverse lived experiences inform particular perspectives on issues related to race, politics, and power.

THE SITUATION: WHAT HAPPENED

Cooper (2010a) provides a detailed essay comparing and contrasting the competing views of what happened during the incident between Professor Gates and Sergeant Crowley. While these perceptual differences certainly deserve critical attention, they are not the focus of this chapter. Instead, I focus in on how the general public perceives President Obama's reaction to the conflict. Accordingly, I turn to *The New York Times*—the national paper of record—to provide the following details about the Prof. Gates/ Sgt. Crowley conflict. On July 16, 2009, Professor Henry Louis Gates, a prominent African American scholar, returns to his home in Cambridge, Massachusetts after spending a week filming a documentary in China (Zezima, 2009). Upon arrival at his Harvard Square home of eighteen years, Professor Gates discovers that his front door is jammed and enlists the driver that had picked him up at the airport for assistance (Van Natta and Goodnough, 2009). After securing entrance to his home, Professor Gates is confronted by Sgt. Jim Crowley of the Cambridge Police Department who is responding to a neighbor's call about a possible break-in. Reports of the exchange between Professor Gates and Sgt. Crowley vary depending on the source, however, most concur that: (1) Professor Gates believes that he is the victim of racial profiling and would be treated differently if he wasn't African American, and (2) Sergeant Crowley believes that Professor Gates was disrespectful, uncooperative, and threatening (Robbins, 2009). The interaction ends when Sergeant Crowley arrested Professor Gates for "loud and tumultuous behavior in a public space" (Seelye, 2009). After being held in police custody for four hours, disorderly conduct charges against Professor Gates are dropped.

News of Professor Gates's arrest does not become public until July 20 when *The Harvard Crimson* posts a story on its website (Van Natta and Goodnough, 2009). Two days later, President Obama is involved in a primetime news conference where he is discussing the pending healthcare bill when he is asked by a reporter to comment on news that Professor Gates has been arrested and what it says about race relations in the United States (Cooper, 2009). President Obama's response is:

> Now, I don't know, not having been there and not seeing all the facts, what role race played in that, but I think it's fair to say, number one, any of us would be pretty angry; number two, that the Cambridge police acted stupidly in arresting somebody when there was already proof that they were in their own home; and, number three, what I think we know, separate and apart from this incident, is that there is a long history in this country of African Americans and Latinos being stopped by law enforcement disproportionately. And that's just a fact . . . [The incident] is a sign of how race remains a factor in this society. (Seelye, 2009)

A great deal of public criticism regarding President Obama's comments follows, something that is credited for a significant drop in his approval ratings especially among working-class whites (Guy, 2010). Soon thereafter, President Obama acknowledges that his comments have contributed to intensifying the situation. Within a subsequent news conference, he attempts to defuse the situation by acknowledging that both men had some responsibility in the conflict:

> I continue to believe, based on what I have heard, that there was an overreaction in pulling Professor Gates out of his home to the station. I also continue to believe, based on what I've heard, that Professor Gates probably overreacted as well. My sense is that you've got two good people in a circumstance in which neither of them were able to resolve the incident in the way that it should have been resolved. ("I could have calibrated those words differently," 2009)

President Obama reports that he has talked to both Professor Gates and Sgt. Crowley via phone and invited them to the White House to have a beer and talk things over. After ten days of a news media blitz—including thousands of different news stories about race and the forthcoming "Beer Summit"—both men join President Obama and Vice-President Biden for a brief meeting, closed to the media, at the White House on July 30, 2009 (Cooper and Goodnough, 2009).

In no uncertain terms, the media surrounding President Obama's involvement in the conflict between Professor Gates and Sgt. Crowley help to stimulate national discussions regarding race, racism, and race relations in the United States. Several rhetorical analyses and political commentaries of the series of events exist (e.g., Cooper, 2010a; Patterson, 2001). However, to my knowledge, no scholarly analyses exist that use public comments of everyday people across the United States to provide thematic insights into public perceptions of events. This chapter focuses on understanding how people from diverse backgrounds—based on age, race and ethnicity, gender, regionality, and political affiliation—have similar and different views on President Obama's involvement in this conflict.

THEMATIC INSIGHTS: FOUR POINTS OF INQUIRY

A careful analysis of focus group transcripts produces four points of inquiry that provide insight into how U.S. citizens from diverse backgrounds perceive President Obama's reactions to the Gates/Crowley conflict. The remainder of this chapter describes each of these topical insights through the voices of different study participants.

"Police Acted Stupidly": Honest, but Inappropriate Response

By and large, participants from diverse backgrounds and across various U.S. regions describe President Obama's initial response to the incident involving Professor Gates and Officer Crowley as inappropriate. As explained in this section, the reasons behind this dominant perception vary.

Many participants describe President Obama's involvement in the situation as inappropriate for a president. One older white male in North Carolina puts it most simply, "I think that he should have stayed out of it." This perception is shared by most participants across the United States, including a twenty-something-year-old black male attending a historically black university in the South who shares:

> I don't know. It just seemed like it went way too far. Maybe my problem with him was because I've never seen a president get so involved in a situation like that. Maybe that was my problem with that. It just seemed so out of place for a president of the United States.

Another participant—a young white male college student from southern Ohio—is more critical when he says, "It wasn't any of his business, so it was a stupid move on his part." He later adds that "the reporter was also out of line for asking it—it didn't have anything to do with the government." His recommendation is that "Obama should have just blown off the question." Other participants across the United States, like an older African American woman from Boston, also comments on how Obama "is being asked questions that other presidents would have never been asked." Several participants feel as if the media is baiting the president on racial issues—something that previous presidents (given their racial identities) were able to avoid. The solution, according to the woman from Boston, is simple: "He needs to stop answering those questions . . . he is setting himself up by trying to answer them." While she interprets President Obama's intentions as genuine, others see his responses to such questions as a desire to gain popularity. This sentiment is evident in the comments from a young European American male from Alabama who says: "I think that something like that was probably really ineffective because it shows that he is some celebrity president focusing on these small events that give him more media coverage. He wants to be a popular president without focusing on the important things."

Not all participants believe that President Obama's initial comments are inappropriate based on his position. For them, being a president—especially the first president of African descent—does not preclude him from commenting on the situation. Instead they describe his comments as inappropriate based on word choice. One fifty-something-year-old European

American woman in North Carolina uses the word "terrible" to describe the situation: "It was terrible! Terrible! The word, 'stupidly,' should never have been used. Somebody who is so eloquent should have found another word. That was an open door asking for trouble." Other white participants, like those involved in a focus group of rural volunteer firefighters in southern Ohio, agree. One man shares:

> So, there again, calling him stupid wasn't the best thing to do. His choice of words wasn't probably the right thing: You know that stupid is as stupid does ... You don't want to tell him, a professional in his field, that he was stupid. He was just doing his job to the best of his ability. Yes, maybe he did do something wrong, but Obama could have handled it a different way. Calling him stupid wasn't the best thing. But I've been called worse than that while on the job!

An Asian American female participant from a college student focus group in Nebraska also agrees. She, like others, focuses on Obama's choice of words.

> I wonder if he hadn't used the word, stupid, would there have been a "Beer Summit" or a week of news devoted to it at all! You caught him in a moment where he didn't exactly use the perfect word choice, but is that why people voted for him? I'm sure if he used the world "irrational," "inappropriate," it wouldn't have been a big deal at all.

Other participants recognize Obama's unfortunate choice of words, but also focus criticism on the inappropriateness of his comments given their perception that he lacked sufficient information. This is most evident among European American male focus group participants. For instance, one white male in his seventies from North Carolina group shares that:

> Words are really important, and the selection of words is extremely important. In my opinion, Obama made a gross mistake in jumping to a conclusion before he had the facts. When I was in engineering school many, many years ago in Detroit, the president of my school was asked a question about a controversial situation in Detroit. And he said, "I'm sorry. I can't comment on that, I don't have the facts. I don't know enough about it to make an intelligent conclusion." I think that Obama violated that principle. He did not have enough facts.

His comments appear neutral, however, other comments critique the president for taking the side of Professor Gates, who is described by several participants as "one of Obama's friends" and is known to "always mouth off." A young white male in Boston—who voted for President Obama—expresses his disappointment:

I was very, very disappointed when it first came out and he instantly took the side without knowing all of the information. And then he went about critiquing it the way that he did. I felt that it undermined his role . . . again the fact that he got involved in this small-level incident. It is a mistaken identity in a breaking-and-entering. I couldn't believe that it had gotten to the president's level . . . the fact that it got to that level and he commented on it the way that he did, I thought was inappropriate.

Finally, participants describe President Obama's initial comments about the incident between Professor Gates and Officer Crowley as inappropriate given the precedent that it can set. One thirty-something white man in Ohio addresses this concern by asking: "Is that how he is going to solve every problem in the world? Inviting them to the White House for a beer or glass a wine? Are you setting a precedent? If next week something happens around here is he going to do the same?" Similar sentiments are heard from around the United States. Another white male participant in Boston echoes this concern and extends it by questioning how President Obama is using his time:

I am in my forties and I think that is was terrible. If he's getting involved in all of these little disputes, he can't solve every little problem around the country as far as something between a police officer and a resident. He can't spend his time doing that . . . there was a greater message there, I know, but still the president can't get involved in stuff like that.

This critique is also offered by another forty-something-year-old man—this one an African American army officer born and raised in Alabama and currently stationed in Virginia. Unlike his white male counterparts, this participant acknowledges the reality of racial profiling in his own life; however, he questions the time and money spent on the issue.

So, do you think that Obama will come to my house and help mediate an issue between me and my neighbor? Will he come to Virginia Beach and help me deal with the police officer when I'm racially profiled? . . . He made a bad move. That should have been handled in the police department, like it was, and he shouldn't have had anything to do with it. Then it would have been done and over with. But he had to get up down there, waste taxpayer's money to bring people to the White House lawn, and have beer to talk about something that could have been handled with a phone call.

The Role of Race: Racist, Racial, or Personal Issue?

A substantial number of African American participants across different focus groups describe President Obama's initial reaction as being "from the gut" (Oakland, CA) "heartfelt" (Providence, RI) and "very natural and honest" (Huntsville, AL). The sentiment behind these descriptions is that many African Americans appreciate President's Obama comments given the problem of racial profiling in the United States. One forty-something-year-old African American woman in Virginia shares, "For me, he was real. He described exactly what I felt about the cop. [group laughter]. I happen to appreciate that—and other people I know appreciated that. We appreciate the lack of pretension." Another African American woman, part of a group of traditionally aged Indiana college students, is more adamant about her feelings toward Obama's honest response.

> That's what you want from your president. You want honesty. Do you want him to lie? He could have said something about how the police used his discretion, but the fact of the matter is that the police officer did act stupidly! . . . Yes, he could have said it better. But my thing is that he can say whatever he wants as long as it's the truth. That's how I feel. I'd rather have the truth than have to search through all of these politically correct statements and not really know how he feels about the situation.

The "truth," according to most African American participants (of all ages and backgrounds), is that racial profiling is a huge problem that is largely accepted in U.S. society. Interestingly, only a handful of European American participants acknowledge the truthfulness of President Obama's initial comments. One is a participant from an all-white focus group in Connecticut—a woman in her fifties who, in her own words, is a "mother of black children." She shares that "I think that he reacted the way that a vast majority of black men would have reacted. He was saying what was on most everybody's mind." She goes on to conclude her comments by adding "It was probably very honest, but again, I'm not sure if it was necessarily appropriate."

The perception that President Obama's initial comments are honest, but inappropriate is echoed by some African American participants. However, the strongest perception is that Obama shouldn't have to apologize for something that occurs so frequently. In one mixed-race group in Alabama, some white participants argue that Professor Gates makes the issue a racial one, a misperception that Obama supports. A thirty-something-year-old African American female military veteran in the group is quick to disagree:

> Well, I'm sorry, [but] I see it all of the time. When the incident happened, it was too typical. You have a black homeowner and a white neighbor calling the police because they think that someone is breaking in. So, then you have a white police officer confronting him . . . I would have probably done the same exact thing and gotten arrested too . . . why is it that the cop automatically has to jump up and confront him like that? I think that Obama saying that the cop acted stupid, I'm sorry I agree with him 100 percent. Because if it would have been a white person,

would he have acted the same way? If it was a white person, the cops would have never been called. But you had to call the cops on a black man!

The European American participants in this particular focus group appear unconvinced of this argument and contend that a black police officer would confront a white homeowner in the same situation.

Interestingly, a similar disagreement emerges in an all-white focus group of traditionally-aged college students in southern Ohio. Consider the following transcript excerpt which begins when one white male (WM#1) attempts to describe the situation as "racial" but not "racist" and is questioned by others, including several white females (WF).

> WM#1: Going along with what she said, I believe that it is a racial thing but not necessarily a racist thing.
> WF#1: But President Obama is the person who brought it back to the race issue. I understand that he has a reason to be proud that he is the first African American to be president. But as the president, I feel that he shouldn't be dividing people into groups.
> WF#2: But it was a racial issue.
> WF#1: No, it wasn't. If any person who was breaking into a house at night . . .
> WM#1: It was during day, wasn't it?
> WF#1: Well, during the day, at night, whatever. If someone is breaking into a house, getting into a residence, it is going to look like someone is trying to rob it. Whether they are white, black, purple, yellow, green—it is going to look like they are going to rob you. It is not a race issue.
> WM#2: He claims that he is being profiled, if not by the cop than by the person who called it in. And the person who called it in was actually a minority too, she was Hispanic. So . . .
> WF#2: She was a neighbor. I feel like if the neighbor felt that he was breaking into the residence, then there is no racial issue there. At all.
> WM#2: The fact is that he didn't get charged with breaking into his own house. He got charged with making trouble with the cop. So, he made it a race issue, but he would have gotten out of it with no trouble at all if he wouldn't have gotten all riled up and started trouble with the police officer. It is not a race thing . . . it is a. . . . if someone is breaking into this house, the police are going to check it out. Then they find out, "Oh, this guy lives here fine." But he decided to get excited and probably started yelling at the police officer and that's when he probably got arrested. He didn't get in trouble for breaking into his own house, he got in trouble for something that any white person, or Hispanic person, would get in trouble for if they were doing that.
> WF#1: That's what I was saying . . . he automatically turned it into: "This cop is judging me because of my race." And then President Obama reacts to it with no information that was factual. He just jumps to a conclusion and says

something that shouldn't have been said . . . I think that he did it because other people expected him to.

WM#2: I don't think that we know the motive of the person who called in . . . they might have racially profiled the man based on his appearance—

WF#1: But they just said that the person was a neighbor who was a minority—

WM#2: They can still racially profile . . .

WF#1: I know, but I just don't think . . .

WF#3: The whole point is that none of us can know if it was racial or not. How can we say that it was racial or not? How would we know? And maybe that's the problem with what Obama said—how could he know? I don't know, maybe he had some obligation to defend the minority perspective.

WM#2: I don't know . . . as the first African American president, a lot of people might be quick to say that racism is over. And maybe he feels like it is important for him to highlight examples that demonstrate how that is not true.

This particular exchange begins with questions regarding the role of race within the conflict between Professor Gates and Officer Crowley, something that is not a topic of discussion within most focus groups. When addressing issues of race and the "Beer Summit," most participants involved in this national research study concentrate their comments on how President Obama's racial identity—and the expectations that come with it—affect the situation.

Not surprisingly, the topic of race is engaged in different ways within different focus groups. Many participants who are involved in all-European American focus groups appear hesitant to discuss the issue of race. This leads several groups, in the words of one forty-year-old white male from Connecticut, to describe President Obama's race as "the elephant in the room." In comparison, many African American participants are quick to point out that—as an African American president—Obama's racial identity leads many to assume that he will address racial issues while in office. According to one young African American female college student from a mixed-race focus group in Chicago, "Nobody wants to bring up race in this discussion, but the fact of the matter is that it is still a big deal . . . it makes white people think that Obama is only going to work on 'ethnic problems.'" Another African American woman (forty-two-year-old from Virginia) participating in an all-black focus group passionately talks about how many people had similar expectations:

> I think that in the beginning that expectation was huge. Once he was elected, all of the white people thought that he was going to do all this stuff for black people, and that he was just going to be the president of the black people. And I think that the black people thought that too! [entire group laughs in agreement]. And that's why they are mad now! "That's right! That's right! He's OUR president!"

Many participants agree that most of these racialized expectations have diminished somewhat over time. However, several participants share their perceptions that certain expectations about how Obama should address racial issues continue to linger in the minds of the U.S. public. This point is best captured within the comments from an older black male from Boston who says:

> I think that we need to remember that [his initial gut reaction] was not political . . . I don't know if it was inappropriate because whether we like it or not, he is the first black president and he is going to be asked a lot of questions that have to do with race. And he can't avoid all of them. Now, politically speaking, it doesn't make any sense at all. But given the context, and given who he is, I don't know if he can avoid all those types of questions. Perceptions, I think, will be that he is trying to avoid something that is blatantly obvious to everyone else: He's a black man. He can't act like he's not.

Another black man—several generations and states away—adds his concern on how many people expect President Obama to become "raceless" as he does his job.

> I think that he has put race on the radar more so than any other president . . . With instances like [The "Beer Summit"], he is still being subjected to questions about race . . . He shouldn't have to become race-less just because he is president. I think that that was a good idea, because it showed that he was human. Everybody thinks about the president as high and mighty, and someone who you don't think that you could relate to. And I like the fact that President Obama is somebody who everyday regular people can relate to. He is moving in and moving out of politics and regular people issues.

This particular set of comments must be understood in the context in which they are shared. This young man is part of a large (thirteen member) focus group comprised of African American college students attending a HBCU in the South. Within this communicative setting, his reference to "everyday regular people" refers specifically to people that he knows from his particular community. Accordingly, his comments reflect an appreciation for President Obama's efforts not to lose relevance with African American communities that helped to elect him.

Expectations from the African American community, according to some participants, work to apply pressure on President Obama. For instance, one thirty-something-year-old black man from North Carolina shares:

> I liked that he got involved, but I think that the media blew it out of proportion. However, there is a small part of me, coming from an African American

perspective, I'm sure that he has seen a lot of pressure from the African American community to deal with these type of issues. Partly because Gates is a prominent African American professor and so, from that perspective, he had a lot of pressure. Being the president, being an African American president . . . this was a chance to address not necessarily racism, but at least try and bring about a dialogue regarding that . . . To not do it, he would have been criticized by the African American community. They might have shunned him, or looked down on him, if he didn't get involved.

This perception is shared by a southern white female business leader in her sixties in the same focus group. Her experiences with different civil rights issues—and as a mother—prompt a similar sentiment.

If he hadn't done anything, it might have looked like, he was trying to distance himself from all of that. Almost like he was above all of that now, because he is president it wouldn't happen to him anymore. . . . I think that he needs to address it, because we have had case after case in this very County when African Americans have been stopped in their cars for nothing. These have been students who aren't doing a thing. Mothers that I know have to be very careful about how they coach their children. I think that it may have been a situation that may have offered a chance for him to do what he has done in the past—explaining so that we can understand better.

Her understanding, however, is not the norm when it comes to the expectations of most European American participants. This is evident in the extended discussion shared earlier where some participants argue that race has little, if any, relevancy in the Gates/Crowley conflict. Interestingly, other participants also express a certain level of disdain when (in their perceptions) President Obama highlights the role of race in commenting about the situation. This is apparent within the comments of a young white conservative woman from southern Virginia who says:

Yeah, that was a particular time when his rhetoric didn't really work, because he had the baggage that came with the Obama administration's attempt to sell him as the post-racial president. That runs him into problems when he has to deal with issues that involve race. He said that it was "stupid" for the officer to do that, or whatever. But that was counter to his usual post-racial rhetoric. So, that was a big contradiction that he was going to have to deal with, and that he is going to have to deal with in the future.

Her comments reflect an existing perception among many European Americans who embrace President Obama as a leader that transcends traditional racial divisions: Race is no longer a big deal in the United States. The expectations that come with this perspective diverge with those from others who believe that racism exists and must be addressed. The result for Obama, as one young white male college student from Indiana describes, is a "no-win situation." Another participant—a middle-aged European American woman from New England—also acknowledges this tension: "He really can't win whatever he does. No matter what . . . People are always trying to find some reason to criticize him and focus on what he hasn't done . . . He has to deal with the negative energy no matter what he does. It seems like it comes from all sides."

The fact that President Obama's racial identity presents a unique challenge for his attempts to "do good work" is also discussed in an all-African American focus group held in Oakland, California. Within this particular setting, one thirty-something-year-old man describes the challenge specifically in terms of communication terms when he says:

> He really is in a very difficult situation . . . what do you do? What can you do? . . . There's no middle ground. And if he does take the middle ground people STILL criticize him for it. Where does he go? What does he do? Where's a safe communication space? I don't think that he has one. There is no safe way to communicate!

This particular participant points to what he describes as a "media conspiracy" to discredit the first African American president. Other participants across different focus groups also raise issues regarding the role that the media played in creating a "media spectacle." More substantial treatment of public perceptions regarding the media is the focus of chapters 10 and 11.

Spin Control, Hidden Agenda, and/or Reaching for Higher Ground?

As I explicate in the initial section of this chapter, the vast majority of participants perceive Obama's initial comments regarding the conflict between Professor Gates and Officer Crowley as inappropriate. However, more participants describe his decision to invite both parties to The White House to talk over the situation as a competent means to diminish the growing criticism over his earlier remarks. Within different focus groups, his attempt to have both parties come together and "talk it out like men" is called "smart," "unique," and "effective." Others call the decision "unusual" or "arrogant."

The vast majority of participants who offer their perceptions of the White House gathering believe it reflects a strategic move by Obama to quell the media frenzy that had occurred after his initial comments. This perception appears frequently among participants from a variety of diverse backgrounds and regional locations. For instance, a forty-year-old multiracial American man in Rhode Island bluntly says: "The 'Beer Summit' was about spin control and having an opportunity to have an off-the-record conversation about issues that really affect the country . . . we know that President Obama had to do something." A similar perception is provided by a European American man in his sixties residing in Connecticut who questions why he is involved in the situation at all:

> There are lots of other things that should be getting his attention . . . that isn't necessarily in his job description . . . I think that he had to cover his butt, because when the whole thing started he opened his mouth without knowing all of the facts. And he wanted to get involved, help to fix the mistake he made.

For others, getting both individuals to agree to sit down and talk about the situation is a tremendous coup for Obama. An older African American woman in Alabama states:

> With everything that was going on and how everybody was putting their own two cents into it, I think that what he did was right. Having them to sit down and talk it out . . . I thought that how he brought both of them together and sat them down to talk was good. The officer could explain how he felt, Skip Gates could explain how he felt, then they could clear the air. I think that that was a great idea, we need to do more of that.

Other participants across the country agree and describe the situation as ideal: "Sometimes the best way to solve a conflict is through face-to-face interaction. Texting, calling each other, or letting the media do it for you, is not the best way to go," concludes one twenty-year-old white male from Nebraska. Another young person—this one a white female from California—agrees and adds that "the last thing [the situation] needed was a bunch of uptight men in suits sitting around negotiating." For many, getting people involved in a conflict to sit down and process the disagreement is perceived as extremely positive especially when the conflict involves racial issues as a white male senior citizen from North Carolina articulates: "I think when people have differences it is very important for them to sit down and talk about it. It is easy to dislike people that you don't know, it is quite easy to like people that you do know. So, I think that sitting down and talking about it is very important."

The fact that the discussion is closed to the media enhances people's perception of Obama's effectiveness in addressing the situation. In that regard, he is able to reduce the media's ability to spin the conflict in riveting, yet unproductive, ways. As a Latino male participant from Boston offers: "It was effective, to a degree, because it got a lot of the news media—FOX, NBC, ABC,

CNN—to stop talking about it . . . It was the end of the conflict, and I think that that was the ultimate objective." A Jewish American forty-something-year-old man in Rhode Island also makes this point when he says:

> I think that the point that he got the two main parties where it started together was significant . . . Because as long as that happened, then we at least know at those two parties who were directly involved came together and hopefully came to some agreement about it. Both sides learned something, and whatever they learned was for them. And we are left, along with the media, to create our own story.

For several participants, getting involved in this dispute affords President Obama a unique opportunity to focus the nation's attention to a racial issue that deserves to be addressed. According to one participant—a traditionally aged white male college student in Alabama—the whole situation allows the pubic to talk about an important issue: "The [initial conflict] situation was just misunderstood. I would think that Obama would want to use that as a platform to address larger issues that are happening a lot. Hopefully he would try to make some improvements or at least try and open up some dialogue." This point is echoed by many African American participants who describe countless conversations within a variety of contexts where the situation is discussed in terms of its personal, social, cultural, and racial relevance. As the first U.S. president of African descent, several of these individuals regard Obama's engagement on this issue as evidence of his desire to address race. In this regard, his commitment to bringing diverse people together to discuss the issue is—in the words of an older African American woman from Providence, RI—"Just plain smart. For me, it is him trying to reach for the higher ground. It was unique and unusual, and he was trying to live by the principles that he extols."

However, not all participants believe that President Obama's efforts are altruistic. Several, including a few outspoken critics, see it as a "pitiful attempt to try and secure more TV time" (Older white male Libertarian living in Nebraska). A younger European American woman in Michigan agrees, and questions Obama's motivation as well:

> Just the thought of having them come out to the White House to have a beer . . . I feel that that communicates to the public, "I'm just sooooo relaxed and cool, so I'm gonna hash this out and fix this . . ." Him, getting into the middle of that, I feel that wasn't a good decision. It was just so public-oriented: "Like me, this is what I'm gonna do—see how great I am with this." Some of the things that he does, instances like that, communicates to me how arrogant he is. I think that he just bombs it every time. It doesn't send a good message. It's almost like he's trying to do things differently, trying to get us to see where he is coming

from, but as a political figure, it comes across as arrogant a lot of the times . . . He's got an agenda. You have to assume that he has an agenda for everything, so what's your agenda when you have that cop and your friend coming out at the White House to have a beer?

The Significance of Having a Beer

One of the most fascinating features of this research project is the ways in which focus group discussions reflect diverse perspectives that work to inform larger dis/agreements. Consider, for example, the following extended excerpt from a predominately white focus group held in northern Alabama where four college students (two black females, one white male, and one white female) discuss Obama's decision to invite both Professor Gates and Officer Crowley to The White House to sit down and share a beer.

> BF#1: I don't have an issue with the beer part of it, big deal they had a beer. But I don't know if it was appropriate for him to even call those two people together. He's not their personal therapist . . . mediator.
> WM: But I think that that was his attempt to say, "Listen. I've said something wrong, let me do what I can to make it right." Maybe he was trying to prove that he wasn't taking either side, but trying to help them come to some resolution.
> WF: I think that he just could have retracted that statement. Because he already sorta has this reputation that he focuses on stuff that really isn't that important. So, to take that much time to get people together and talk it through . . . it's a personal issue. Yes, it could be symbolic, but talking it out with those two individuals doesn't really do much on the larger scale. I don't think that that was a good idea.
> WM: But if I wrong somebody, I'm going to say, "Okay, let me buy you a beer." It's almost like an admission of guilt in a way. . . . They are all sitting at this little table—that was the image in the media—like they are having this great conversation, maybe even having some dialogue.
> BF#2: But what I'm saying is: how is it so wrong that he did something different? He did something different—something no other president has ever done. Like [WM] said, he sat down with two men and tried to be the mediator. To me, I thought that it was good that he did something different than any other president. That way, I think that he did do some good.
> WF: I like that he had them over for a beer instead of trying to do something more formal, like using a proper process and a mediation hearing. By having a beer, it was like he made more of a joke about it, and put it in more proper perspective. It was like the American way, let me buy you a beer so we can talk it out.

Interestingly, this one short excerpt depicts several of the issues that are raised by participants across multiple focus groups. Specifically, it points to another facet of Obama's efforts to get Professor Gates and Officer Crowley together that is widely discussed amongst different focus groups: The prominent role that beer played in the meeting. A few participants criticize President Obama's inclusion of alcohol as inappropriate given the problematic issues surrounding underage drinking and alcoholism. Others describe Obama's decision to highlight alcohol early on in setting up the meeting as "unprofessional." For example, a thirty-something white male participant from Ohio explains that "once they got there, they could have popped open a cold one and talked the situation over. But putting it out there they he has invited them to talk it out over a beer wasn't smart."

Yet, these criticisms pale in comparison to the number of participants who see the inclusion of beer as an important feature of the informal meeting. For many individuals, inviting both men to share a beer as they discuss the conflict creates an atmosphere that is casual and personal. A young white woman from California shares:

> That is exactly what I would want to happen if I had a fight with someone . . . why don't we all just get a beer and talk it out? Again, I think that it personalized himself, to help them get over it. . . . I mean he didn't get a mediator and have to give someone a pardon, or anything like that. It was very casual, and informal . . . "Come meet my friend Joe, and we can have a beer together."

For another younger white man, part of a focus group in Boston, the fact that Obama held the meeting "over some beers" fosters a less stressful means to foster dialogue where personal accountability could emerge and become more important than any racial differences:

> I thought that [the meeting] was unique. It was not expected to say the least. But, I thought that it was a good way, because it took race off the table and made it a couple of guys sitting around having a beer. I think that is what he was going for. I know that it is a stereotypical American male thing. But at the same time, I think that it made it more effective for him; it put less pressure on the situation. You didn't have a formal hearing or a formal press conference . . . This way the battle lines weren't drawn; he didn't have other people go and find out what had happened. I'm gonna have you come over here, take a tour of the White House, and we can find out what really happened. That way both gentlemen can know the consequences of both of their actions, on a personal level.

The perception that Obama uses the inclusion of beer to ease racial tension and stress the commonality of all men is articulated in numerous focus groups across the United States. As expressed in the following quote from a twenty-something-year-old white man in California, Obama's invitation to "pop open a cold one" is also seen as an indication that he is "one of us:" "I think what he tried to communicate when he invited them to the White House was that he was the average guy. Having a beer together? He was concerned with the everyday person—whoever that is. That was part of his strategy to be like the average person." It might not come as a surprise that other traditionally aged college students also find the symbolism of "sharing a beer" as a positive. One Mexican American female college student shares that by having a beer with them, it shows that President Obama "cares about the little problems of everyday citizens—not just the bigger problems of the country." A twenty-something-year-old black male attending college in Michigan describes how beer helped to create commonalty:

> I think that is why he had the beer, because everybody—white, black, green—drinks. So, as a black man, you always have to be conscious of racial situations. Because he is the president, he probably thought: "Okay, I'm a black man. I'm president and it is a white-black situation. How can I handle it?" It's touchy because people say we always see race. . . . I think that it did a great job, putting that beer right there saying "Here's our commonality."

Interestingly, using beer as a representation of the "common man" is also discussed in focus groups of older participants. For instance, a forty-something-year-old African American male pastor in Central Ohio states that:

> With him saying "Let's come together and have a beer," that's him saying "I'm a common person." There are so many people around the United States who will come home from work and have a beer. It is like a regular, normal type of thing. That is him again to take the opportunity and try to express some mass appeal, regardless of political party.

Similar sentiments are expressed by a diverse array of focus group participants. This includes a fifty-something-year-old Middle Eastern American woman from California who shares: "I think that having a beer made it more relaxed. Not too serious. That's my opinion. It made him more casual, more like one of us." Another participant, a thirty-something-year-old white man from a rural southern Ohio community, confirms this perception:

> The language that he put it in—a cold beer—was good. That is what was in the paper, people saw language that they understood and read the article. We can identify with that. He invited a couple of guys over to pop open a cold one. That's the way that we understand it. It's not just what you do, it's how you talk to us. The politicians have their mumbo-jumbo, and Obama can speak our language.

SUMMARY

This chapter draws from public perceptions of the conflict between Professor Henry Louis (Skip) Gates and Officer James (Jim) Crowley and offers an analysis of how diverse individuals regard President Obama's effectiveness in engaging in race-related issues. Using this series of events as a case study provides a valuable opportunity to explore how various segments of the U.S. population think and feel about race in the United States.

In particular, the chapter demonstrates the diversity of perspectives within and between different cultural groups. Most agree that President Obama's initial comments regarding the Gates/Crowley conflict were "inappropriate" for a variety of reasons. However, African Americans are quick to point out the "truth" of his comments and how it reflects his ability to highlight the subtle ways in which racism continues to be an issue in the United States. Those persons who embrace President Obama as our first post-racial president find his comments to be problematic and racially divisive. In this regard, the chapter serves as an insightful means to complete a section on "Race Matters in a 'Post-Racial' Society." Given that participants also criticize the role that the media play in making the "Beer Summit" an event worthy of international news coverage, it serves as an excellent transition to the next section of the book: The Media Machine.

Part IV

The Media Machine

Chapter 10

Media Influences

> My family is really intense about politics, but they are really ignorant most of the time. [group laughter] They don't even know really anything about politics at all. They just know what they see on TV.
>
> —Young African American man from Michigan

As I stated in chapter 1, this book presents the findings of a national study designed to explore public perceptions of Barack Obama's communication. From the very beginning, I anticipated that this general topic could not necessarily be examined without also addressing—directly or indirectly—issues of race within the United States. However, what I did not anticipate are the ways in which focus group participants would describe the influence that the media had on their own, and others, perceptions. Comments regarding the media, to some extent, are present in every focus group. I include references to media influences throughout the entire book. Given the power of the media in shaping public perceptions chapter 10, as well as chapter 11, focus on the topic. This decision is consistent with a discovery-oriented qualitative research, which seeks to give voice to topics participants deem as important (as opposed to solely focusing on the researcher's pre-determined agenda items).

The pure volume of references to the media require that I address the issue within this book. Most of the participants' comments include subtle references to how the media influence public perceptions of President Obama. However, a smaller number of individuals are much more direct and critical of the role of the media. Regarding this, one thirty-something-year-old African American man from California makes the following assertion: "The whole book should be about the media." He goes on to say:

> My question is: Is this a book about people's perceptions or how the media portrays President Obama? I wanted to ask you this because there's a certain aspect of how the media portrays communication versus how he actually is in terms of communicating. So, my question to you is how are you going to take into consideration the fact that President Obama says something and the media takes one sentence out of the entire speech and focuses on the negative aspects or tone . . . versus the people who actually listen to the entire speech and look at it as an entire package (versus a sound bite) . . . how are going to account for that?

This chapter works to address the issue that this man, and others, raise throughout the focus group discussions. In short, it examines media influences on public perceptions and attempts to describe—through the various insights of focus group participants—the power of contemporary media.

THE POWER OF THE MEDIA

Within my introductory comments for this chapter, I make the statement that most focus group participants in this study do not explicitly name the media as an influential source in their perceptions. Most, in fact, offer their opinions with no direct reference to the role that the media play in shaping them. Some participants comment on this pattern, and point out that the public's lack of recognition of media influence is what gives the media so much power. For example, one forty-something-year-old African American woman from Alabama states:

> I believe that the majority of the United States is ignorant. People are basically educated by the media. As [another participant] was saying, the media takes opinions and creates facts. And they only tell you what they want you to know. In regards to news broadcasting, they basically tell you what's important. So, people don't have their own opinions any more. They are walking around with the mindset of what the media is portraying to them. So, basically you've been asking us about what media's perceptions do we feel are true. Honestly, it's TV, it's radio, it's the Internet . . . People don't even recognize it.

An older African American man from California makes a similar point when he says: "The average person doesn't even realize that they're getting biased news. They think that the news is the news. The average rural person doesn't recognize that what they are listening to is biased."

Interestingly, several participants seem to gain additional insight into media influences during their focus group discussions. Often times, this occurs as individuals are reflecting on their own perceptions. For instance, one Mexican American male college student from Illinois recognizes the power of the media in a politically oriented commercial he just saw:

> There was actually this political commercial that I saw this morning that was saying how the government wants to put taxes on certain types of drinks and foods. And the woman was really angry, saying "Don't tell me what I should drink! Don't tell me what I should eat! Politicians shouldn't be telling me what to do!" I actually found that funny. Of course I agree with her points, but now I'm thinking that I really didn't know what was behind it. It's crazy how TV can just throw things at you like that.

Another example of increased awareness is seen with a Caucasian woman in her forties who is participating in a community focus group discussion in North Carolina. For this participant, an interaction with a neighbor while walking her dog causes some critical reflection of media influences:

> One time, one of my neighbors said something about Obama—it was pretty offensive. I can't remember if it was a racist comment or just something really hateful. I was just taken aback, and said "I don't feel that way. I'm sorry, I just don't agree with that." We didn't talk about it. And the next day, he came over to me and said, "I am really sorry about what I said yesterday. My wife would kill me if she heard me say that." So, it is really interesting . . . what I've learned is that the media makes people out to be more hateful that they really are. If we could find more ways to come together and talk, outside of how the media portrays it, we would have a lot more in agreement than we think. Because right now, we are afraid to talk. We are afraid to talk because the media polarizes us.

BIAS IN THE MEDIA

Another major theme that emerges from my analysis of media influences is media bias. In part, the power of the media is seen through the ways in which it is able to communicate the news through commentary that impacts the perceptions of the general public. In other words, many participants demonstrate an understanding that the media functions as a filter in terms of what it selects to present as news. "In general, we get piece-meal information from the media—and all of it is not true. That is what bothers me," states a sixty-something-year-old white male from North Carolina. In terms of President Obama and other political leaders, participants acknowledge that the media play a central role in public perceptions. According to one European American man from Illinois,

> Bias is the definition of politics and the media. It controls how Obama can communicate. Whenever you have to express yourself, you're put into a box because your words will be minced, or fragmented. Your words can take on a totally different meaning when people do that—they can alter the original meaning to their liking.

Participants are quick to identify the biased slant of specific television channels. One traditionally aged black female student from Michigan is clear and concise when she states: "FOX News is more Republican and CNN is more Democratic. MSNBC is for black people." The slant of these, and other, channels is acknowledged by other participants as well. In North Carolina, for instance, a young white woman responds to my question about how the general public perceives President Obama by pointing to the role of the media.

> If you watch FOX News, then he is black. He is the black president, and there is a lot of negative stuff that comes with that. But if you watch MSNBC, then he is the president who just happens to be black. And there are lots of positives with that. And if you watch BET, then he is *the first black president* and there is a lot of pride because of that accomplishment.

Similar to that which is contained in this quote, individuals across the United States acknowledge media bias and describe various ways in which reliance on one particular media source can work to reinforce one (limited) view of President Obama. According to a forty-something-year-old black woman in California: "That is why I am such an advocate for NOT watching the same news program over and over again. NOT reading the same newspaper over and over again. Even though FOX News is a sworn enemy to everything that is good in politics, go ahead and watch it every now and then. You need to see different perspectives." The focus of her criticism is FOX News, a particular media source that attracts a lot of attention with participants from all parts of the United States.

While a variety of individuals understand that the media is not neutral, FOX News is targeted as the most biased of all networks. From the perspective of one young white male from Illinois, they are in another category when it comes to presenting the news with a biased slant: "That's the FOX News effect—they have more spin than the top factory!" A few participants, in more politically conservative focus groups, disagree and describe FOX News as one of the only networks that aren't controlled by the liberal media moguls. In one Illinois focus group, an African American woman in her sixties explains how she appreciates the insight from FOX News programming:

> I listen to all of those right-wing talk shows like Glenn Beck, Sean Hannity, and Rush Limbaugh. I don't agree with everything that they say, but some of the things that they are saying about him are true. That is why a lot of Blacks aren't voting for him next time . . . He hasn't done anything that he said he was going to do. . . . Some of his policies are close to socialism. I don't know if he is a Marxist, but some of his ideas are.

In a Michigan community college focus group, a young white man (who identifies as an Independent voter) openly criticizes some of President Obama's tax policies. In particular, he focuses on specific tax incentives that benefit the undeserving. In addition to higher taxes for the wealthy, he targets an Obama initiative for Muslim business owners, something that he learned about on FOX News.

> I watch FOX News to learn about things that other channels won't cover. Like the thing on FOX News about the Muslim tax that might come into effect . . . There's a radical group that is actually pushing for taxes that if you are not Muslim, then you will get taxed. Muslim business owners, because of all of the taxes that they've paid in their own country, could come here and not pay any taxes. Obama pushed for it, and if he had his way, it would become law.

Interestingly, this young person does not fit the norm of a typical FOX News viewer as focus group participants describe them; that distinction is held for older U.S. Americans, especially those from rural areas.

According to one forty-something-year-old black man from California, senior citizens are the primary viewers for FOX News. In his view, "that's all they know about Obama. It's like senior citizens are mouthpieces for FOX News. They repeat everything that they hear." While this participant's comments are general and broad, a substantial number of other individuals have anecdotal evidence to support the claim. For instance, one young male college student from North Carolina shares how his grandparents' criticism for President Obama stems from their viewing habits.

> My grandparents only listen to FOX News and think that he is terrible. They try and tell me, "The news said this, and the news said that." And I say, "Hey, Grandpa, why don't you try and watch a different news station?" You just can't take one medium and make that your gospel. You have to do your own research, and look into different avenues. And that's something that they don't do. They look at one side of it, and think that that's the news, then they make all of their assumptions based on that.

A similar example is provided by a young Jewish woman from Illinois who uses her friend's grandparents as an example of how FOX News influences public perceptions.

> I know people who only watch FOX News, so their views would be totally different than others. Obviously, if you only watch FOX News and you are Republican, your views are going to be one way. And the people who actually watch it believe that it is fair and balanced. We are educated so we know that no media is actually fair and balanced. I think that people who watch news

that come with a certain bias will view it because they have that bias. And that reinforces that bias . . . My friends have grandparents that only watch FOX news, and to them, anything that FOX News says is GOLD. They tell the Truth, and there is no other truth. What FOX News says, goes.

While senior citizens are most often portrayed as "FOX News followers," other participants offer examples of how the channel's influence goes beyond that particular demographic group. Several individuals describe how young Republican groups on their campuses, older business men that they interact with on a daily basis, and family members of all ages also are huge fans of FOX News. One Costa Rican American forty-something-year-old woman from Rhode Island shares with the group how she lost a close relationship due to disagreements about Barack Obama. In her mind, FOX News is a major cause in their relational troubles.

I actually lost a friend over Obama and the election. She started to watch FOX News regularly. I always knew that she was a little bit conservative, but you know, not all that conservative. But after listening to all of these shows, she really changed . . . It really is poison because she would come out with some of the most weirdest things. Obama is going to ruin the country, he's going to do this, he's going to do that. It was like he was the anti-Christ. And she isn't even religious! But I had this woman who I had known for fifteen years and I couldn't believe it . . . who is this? It was just so different from what I had thought. She and I were just so different when it came to different issues. We haven't spoken since . . . Because I was thinking that if she listens to that, what does she think about Latinos and those issues—who also are dehumanized by the talk radio folks and FOX News?

MEDIA AS BIG BUSINESS

During several focus group discussions, participants critique the media's role in the creation of what is considered "news." Some participants are highly critical of this practice, while others describe it as to be expected given that the "media is big business" (a phrase used by a middle-aged white man from Connecticut). Within this perspective, the primary function of the media is not to inform the public but make money. Viewing the media through this more critical lens allows participants to understand the reasons behind certain media coverage. For instance, chapter 9 focuses on what has become known as the "Beer Summit," something that one forty-something-year-old African American man from central Ohio describes as a "media spectacle." He comments:

The fact that is was called the "Beer Summit," the media did that . . . The media called it that because part of what they do is put things in ways that "sell" with the public. Using language like that allows them to make sure that it becomes bigger and allows them to carry it further and further and further . . . which allows them to make more money. This was a way to get more mileage out of the whole situation. It wouldn't sell if it was just a meeting between people.

Another African American male (of similar age) in the same focus group adds: "The media is a double-edged sword. You can use it but it uses you too. They reduce everything that is said down to sound bites, and half-truths." He goes on to say, "The media likes to stroke the fire because that is what gets the general public to read the newspapers, watch the TV programs, or read the blogs. They are not trying to spin it completely for the truth. The bottom line is that they want for it to sell."

A wide variety of participants, across different focus group discussions, describe how increased technology has put pressure on the media. In the words of one twenty-something-year-old from Nebraska, "the media is under intense pressure to create stories that sell in a 24/7 news cycle." Some participants criticize the media for focusing on the negative, but other participants are quick to point out that, for the general public, negativity is what sells. This is the point of an older African American woman from Alabama when she says:

> I think that we have become a society that focuses on negative things . . . it kind of made me think of before we began we were talking about how in small towns, news is different than news in big cities. Anything that is out of the ordinary, anything that is different, and anything that makes the news, that is what driving things now. When it gets on the news, it is shown over, and over, and over again. It is on YouTube, it's on all of these things. I think that because of technology and the appetite of the people—whatever sells—there's always something that has to be news. We are looking for anything that can make news.

In their attempts to make money, the media is criticized by some participants as ignoring important events and focusing instead on insignificant things. Ironically, according to one young African American man from Illinois, the media's selective coverage is then used as evidence to critique President Obama.

> You have people who might say, "We gave you this chance . . . we were open to a black man as president . . . and look what happened." You have all these guys like Bill O'Reilly and Rush Limbaugh . . . They show him playing basketball, meeting with different famous people, and going to a baseball game. Then they

ask "Why is Obama going to a baseball game with the country in such a mess?" They don't show all of the other stuff that he is doing. People will accept a lie over the truth, it's human nature, especially if it matches what they want to hear. When Bush was doing all of these things, like talking about weapons of mass destruction. No matter what, they believed that "truth." That caused thousands of troops to die . . . but here is Obama trying to help the entire world, but here they are bashing him. So, it just goes to show you that people have their priorities mixed up. They need to check themselves.

As I describe later in this chapter, some participants—most notably African American participants—argue that the media is involved in a conspiracy to denigrate President Obama and derail any policies during his presidency. During one community focus group of black participants in California, discussion of a media conspiracy based on race took center stage. However, an older black male in his seventies encourages the group to understand that the core issue is one of economics—not race.

I don't think that any of what we've been discussing has the relevance that we think it has. The message is being controlled by multinational corporations. They were happy with Bush. They were happy with him borrowing and spending, and all of his involvement in the bad housing situation. When Obama came in . . . if you noticed, they actually took what they needed before Bush even got out of office. They took whatever they wanted to keep themselves in business. But Obama and the Democrats were about putting some brakes on all of this. They wanted oversight, restrictions, checks and balances . . . Who felt the effect of this? Big business. As ethnic people, I hear us not being able to understand how the media moguls control things . . . and that bothers me. We need to understand the depth of how these multinational corporations are controlling things. This gives me pause, because I think . . . I think that it is a shell game. We are not really understanding what the real issues are. I think that our preoccupation with race keeps us from the real issues.

A similar dynamic plays out in another Californian focus group in another city. Based on her experiences growing up under a dictatorship, a Middle Eastern American woman in her fifties explains to others how the media can be used by those in power.

I love democracy, that's why I'm living in this country. But I also see the abuse in democracy, especially how the media is controlled by those in power . . . The owners of these networks are very rich people and they would be very much hurt if the ideas of Obama come into law. They are very rich people who don't want him to succeed, so they use what they have to see that he doesn't.

Regardless of the notion that the media represents "big business" designed to maximize profits, the vast majority of participants do agree that the media plays a highly influential role in terms of public perceptions. What is happening to Obama, according to them, is no different than other high profile celebrities. As one African American male senior citizen from Virginia says: "I think that is something that happens to everybody who lives in the public eye. The TV is always on, we have a 24/7 new cycle. The mics are always live. You have to be really, really mindful that you are always on . . . " This fact, coupled with the idea that "Obama is a lightening rod," creates a reality that has become dangerous for those who aren't careful:

> But that's how dangerous it becomes when people take your words, add some political commentary, and then create something that is much bigger than it ever intended to be. When things are played out in the media in certain ways . . . the political commentary left him little option. Clearly, President Obama is a lightening rod, so everywhere he goes, every word he speaks is going to be used to create drama. (multiracial American man, in his forties, living in Rhode Island)

Many participants recognize the changing dynamics of a media-driven reality, and a few are surprised that Obama isn't more careful given his past media savvy. This is the point articulated by a sixty-something-year-old white woman in a North Carolina focus group when she discusses President Obama's use of "stupidly" in the Gates/Crowley conflict:

> We live in a whole different world media-wise. I think that he is probably one of the most brilliant people that we've had in that office. I heard that remark and my impulse was to dive under the table because I knew what was coming. I thought, "Whoa! Is FOX News going to pick up on this?! And here we go!" People have got to understand that in this day and time, we are so tied up with media, it's a different time and we have to communicate differently. He, of all people, ought to know that. Not only because of where he comes from, but because he is intelligent enough to know that.

MEDIA CONSPIRACY

The argument that the increased negativity in the media is based on what sells is not embraced by everyone involved in the study. Some participants—most notably African Americans—argue that the criticism toward President Obama seems especially volatile. One black male undergraduate student at a HBCU in Alabama notes that "the media seem to be coming at Obama especially hard." "The population, in my mind, has been turned against him by the media. I really firmly believe that," states one African American woman from North Carolina. The strongest media criticism comes from an all-black male focus group in Oakland, California. Some participants in the group characterize the media's contempt for Obama as racially motivated: "The media is trying to do anything that they can, use any little opportunity that they have, to tear him down—to make him look ineffective—to make him look like he doesn't know what he is talking about. That's the stereotype that they have of black men." Not everyone in the group agrees with this assertion; however, many do believe that race plays a role in how the media is covering President Obama's first term. One man—a thirty-something member of the clergy—states:

> I have to agree with that. I see that he is being put on a different path than he wants to be. It seems like he is constantly at odds with the media. There's one way that he really wants to go, but is forced to deal with these issues. Same thing with Jeremiah Wright . . . you don't want to talk about a media conspiracy but I think that that has some truth to it. You see all of these issues that he has to deal with . . . these are things that the other forty-three presidents never had to deal with.

In terms of a media conspiracy, some participants argue that the media seem to be working diligently to keep President Obama "off message." These individuals believe that the media is constantly focusing on personal attacks or insignificant issues, something that keeps President Obama in "reaction mode" (middle-aged African American man from Virginia). This sentiment is heard from a couple of different participants including a fifty-something-year-old African American woman from Rhode Island who says:

> I don't think that the public doesn't understand, I think that people don't even hear his message. If you look at the media, they block out his message. All you get are all of the attacks . . . most of the media is right wing anyway. That's how I feel. Thank God that he goes to these town halls, because the media really doesn't know what the people think . . . They are always concluding [in a mainstream announcer voice] "The American people . . ." I hate these programs . . . the media is controlled by the right. And it is true that they are really disrespectful of him as president. If he were to commit even a quarter of the mistakes that Bush had committed. They talk about the economy but they don't remember that it was going downhill for years—we were almost in the abyss. Thank God for Obama we have moved in the right direction. But who put us in the abyss? People don't remember that. My problem is with the media. We don't get his message because it is blocked. You know?

According to other participants, the media's tendency to set the agenda for the general public has been largely successful. In a community focus group in North Carolina, a forty-something-year-old white man shares:

> I hear a lot of complaining from people in my circles who are really disappointed because they wanted to see more things happen more quickly. The media helped create the impression that things should be different. But I'm like, "We survived this!" It's kinda like that guy who landed the plane on the Hudson River. People complain that it wasn't a smooth landing and shouldn't have happened there . . . But be thankful that you didn't die!

A Costa Rican American woman, in her forties, also makes this point to other participants in another community focus group in Rhode Island. She speaks with significant passion when she states: "The media system is set up to criticize him. They have to bring him down, because they can't just report on the issues. They are trying to set up him so that he can't succeed. And even though he won, I don't think that they will let him succeed with all of these great ideas he had."

One subtle, but powerful, way that the media works to derail Obama's presidency, according to participants, is through the language that they use to describe his policies. An older white woman from North Carolina argues that:

> The media controls the metaphors. The example that I've heard is that the politicians have talked about taxation in terms of relief. Taxation by definition is bad, so you want to get relief from something that is erroneous or bad. Instead of talking about it in terms of what you pay to be in a free society—and have all of the benefits that we have. That is where I would love to see Obama, and whoever is writing his speeches, start to use different metaphors. They would help people get past all of these catch phrases about socialization or redistribution of wealth, or even middle class.

Participants in other focus groups also comment on this point. One seventy-something-year-old African American man in California gives an example where President Obama attempts to create a metaphor to help the public understand the current recession. "He came out with this thing about running the car off of the road, and being in a ditch, putting it in drive versus reverse, and that kinda thing. He was using a metaphor that everyone could understand, but it didn't take for whatever reason," he states. Other participants were quick to point out how the metaphor was never embraced by the media; instead they continued to talk about the advances in the economy as failing to meet the high expectations of the general public. Not all participants place the blame on President Obama's inability to communicate his successes to the media. At least one participant, a young Latina from Massachusetts, finds fault in President Obama's team.

> I thought that during the campaign, he and his campaign was really quick about and disciplined about responding to different comments—whether positive or

negative. But I think that his administration has done a poor job at communicating to the United States, the American people, on different issues—such as the health care plan. What it included, what they really meant by it, and what the objective really was. They were communicating very clearly early on, but they stumbled eventually. And a lot of Americans were left scratching their head wondering what this healthcare program was really about. And how is it going to benefit us. I think that they actually addressed that after it had passed. I know that his organization, Organizing for America, released a statement that had information calling the health care reform, "The Patient Bill of Rights." And whether you agree with that statement or not, the language contained in it—the way it was described was really good. I know that the Republicans called his plan, "Obamacare" and that really stuck with the press. And his administration never really challenged that consistently.

"THE FIRST WIRED PRESIDENT"

Barack Obama's use of the social media during and after his election is also a popular topic of discussion among participants. Interestingly, a significant number of individuals—more often than not college students in their young twenties—report that they are friends with President Obama on Facebook, follow him on Twitter, or receive email messages or text messages from him on a regular basis. One young black woman from North Carolina describes him in the following way:

> He is really the first president to really use email . . . I know that he uses his cell phone a lot and different kinds of social media . . . I think that is a different way to get your message out to the masses, especially young people . . . I think that he was the first president to get permission to keep his own Blackberry—and not have everyone go through someone else to get to him. He's the first wired president!

President Obama's use of various social media is heralded by focus group participants as unique, innovative, and especially effective. In a racially diverse focus group of college students, faculty, and staff at a state university in Alabama, a white woman in her fifties (WF#1) initiates a discussion of President Obama's social media efforts.

> WF#1: The focus of your study is on communication competence and during the campaign he showed how competent he was by going on-line. He was the first president who utilized the Internet, Twitter, Facebook—he used all of those things to communicate with people. He did that in ways that no other president did before.

WF#2: People feel more connected to him because of it.

WM: Kind of like how FDR used fireside chats to communicate with the public. It made people feel closer to him. People are always saying how President Obama speaks in an intellectual manner, but by doing things like using Twitter, he is really reaching out to the average person who may not understand everything in his speech, but you can understand what's in a short Twitter message. He makes it very understandable and open.

BF: And that's the thing about his campaign. I have never donated to a campaign before, but his campaign was like, " Can you donate five dollars?" " Yeah, I can donate five dollars!" You know? He made everyone feel like they had a part in it. Five dollars is not a lot and people are open to that. No, I can't go to a $1,200 dinner but I can send five dollars. I think that he reached so many people, the working class people, through the Internet, email, and Facebook.

This one brief exchange highlights how President Obama's campaign efforts utilize social media to reach out to voters, communicate updates and messages to supporters, and mobilize everyday people to invest financially in his campaign. Yet, according to focus group participants, the important aspect of Obama's use of social media is his ability to establish personal connections with the general public.

Across focus group discussions, individuals laud Obama's use of social media to connect with the U.S. public in meaningful ways. Some discuss how receiving information directly from him make a favorable impression. According to a young white female college student from California,

President Obama made pretty big waves when he put his campaign on Facebook. People were making all these changes to their profiles, putting the " Campaign" symbol and other pictures on their wall. I think that no other president as done that. Using that social network, he made such a huge impact. He personalized himself, and made himself open to those people who usually don't follow politics so much. It got him connected to us. Instead of having to go and look it up ourselves, he sent us information directly. Signing on to Facebook, I would see Barack Obama's face on my page, and then click to see everything that was going on.

Another participant, a young black Caribbean American woman from Massachusetts, discusses how her mom became more engaged in politics due to personalized email messages from President Obama.

My mom is an immigrant who is just in love with Obama . . . She has never been really politically active, but she is constantly talking about Obama. She gets loads of emails from Obama, which I think are really effective. He sends emails to you and they say your name, and they are signed by Barack Obama. It will be a letter talking about what is going on in the White House. She will forward them to me and say, " I really think that you should read this."

For many participants, receiving political information from President Obama is viewed as more accessible and personable, compared to other politicians. For instance, one young white male from Alabama shares:

> I used to listen to his weekly radio address on NPR with the Bush administration. But then you go to Obama, I still listen to it but I feel like I get more information from what is being sent out all the time, every day. I have his Twitter info on my phone, so I do feel more connected, feel more like he is your personal president. It is a more personal thing.

As articulated by a young black woman from Massachusetts, the personal connection is just as, if not more important, than communicating information on political issues.

> I think that one thing that he mastered is the fact that all communication doesn't have to be political. Like some messages could be about the confines in the Oval Office, or something like that. He talks about his wife, his family, and all of that makes him more relatable to a lot of people. It's not always about politics—we feel as if we know him outside of just politics.

A young African American woman from Michigan provides a specific example how personal emails from President Obama, as well as his wife Michelle, are instrumental in creating a sense of immediacy and accessibility with the public.

> One time Michelle Obama sent a request for people to send Obama little notes for his birthday. And I guess that so many people sent notes saying that he was doing a great job. And I think she made up a package of all of the messages . . . it's just like, you know, what other president did that? How many messages were sent to previous presidents saying that you're doing a great job? Granted we are now in a time where technology allows us to do that . . . Twitter, Blackberry, etc., they are all huge. But no matter what age you are, you have no excuse not to get involved and be active in politics. You can do it any number of ways. Just follow him on Twitter and you will know what is going on. You will have some idea of what he is doing.

Other participant comments also indicate the public's positive reception of President Obama's use of social media. The following excerpt is from a focus group of students from a Virginia university. Within their discussion, these three young women—one white American (WF), one Middle Eastern American (MEF), and one African American (AAF)—acknowledge that President Obama is not personally engaging the public via social media but still describe how the efforts facilitate a more personalized relationship with him.

WF: I follow Obama on Twitter. I know that it is probably done by someone from his campaign. I sense a change in his communication style since he became president. Following him on Twitter is like I'm able to capture a daily snapshot of what he is doing, like I was able to do during his campaign. It is almost like a campaigning strategy. The rhetoric that I hear when he is on TV now, or being interviewed, he is talking about policy. But the Twitter is more personal; I think that it is a way that some people have stayed with Obama. The importance of social media has really changed things.

AAF: I think that that is one of the reasons why he was able to win over so many young people. I don't think that there has been a president before who used Twitter, Facebook, and all of that other stuff to communicate. It creates a personal connection with people.

MEF: We were talking about it in one of my classes. He communicates with younger people through social media. We are so informed about everything, and we felt as if we knew more about what was going on. And that's why so many of us voted. That's why people's grandmothers who had never voted, got out on a rainy election day and voted . . . because they felt that they were so informed and knew what was going on.

WF: And even beyond the whole information thing, there is the relationship dynamic. You feel . . . I know that during the campaign, you usually feel so separated from the politicians that are running. But when you have a medium such as Twitter, you get all of his thoughts and things that they are working on. The way that his Twitter account is set up, it seems like he is talking directly to you about things that he is working on right now.

TARGETING YOUNG VOTERS THROUGH MULTIMEDIA CHANNELS

This chapter highlights participants' comments that herald President Obama's use of various media to reach out to the general public. In particular, they discuss how his use of multimedia channels—news programs, pop culture radio and television programs, Twitter, Facebook, websites, and YouTube—are especially effective in connecting with those individuals with the most experience with new forms of technologies: Young people. As many of the young (eighteen to twenty-five years of age) participants involved in the study discuss, President Obama's efforts are instrumental in motivating them to get involved with politics for the very first time in their lives. Part of President Obama's attraction, as captured by the comments from a young white community college student from Michigan, is his youthful demeanor:

More people of our generation—the demographic of people between eighteen and probably thirty years old . . . I see that our age group is more willing to listen to someone his age and accept what he is saying and consider it as true . . . He is more appealing to our age group. We would probably listen to him more, and his communication would hit us more relevantly than a different person, especially an older person.

Many college students across the United States also discuss how Barack Obama's persona seems to make him more at ease with the younger generation. One young white male from California says: "He seems more 'with it' than other past presidents were. Yeah. I think that that also goes with him being accessible with the everyday people." Traditionally aged college student participants also comment on how President Obama's youthful personality "appealed to the youth a lot more than other politicians." This quote comes from a white female student from Ohio who also states, "He was different. He spoke to my generation like we mattered more than older people." According to one white female college student from Virginia, all of these things combine to make following him an easy choice:

> I think that it was really easy for everyone our age to jump on the Obama bandwagon because everything that we saw in the media was so pro-Obama. You got so many messages from him—he was everywhere. You saw all these celebrities come out for him, and they all encouraged us to vote in the election and vote for him specifically. The focus was on getting young people involved. It was like they were talking directly to us.

Twenty-something-year-old participants all describe President Obama's use of multimedia channels as effective in reaching out to young voters. As I demonstrate in earlier chapters, these efforts work to get individuals—especially younger voters and those traditionally disenfranchised—involved in the political process in unprecedented ways. This is most evident within the comments of those participants whose first opportunity to vote was the 2008 election, like one young white woman from Virginia: "As someone who was voting in their first election, I remember how intense it was. We watched everything on TV. We were turned into CNN 24/7, our entire suite was watching." Throughout the different focus group discussions, college students describe how their campuses were transformed into "mini-political centers." Many recall how waiting for election results spontaneously became community-wide celebrations. One African American woman recounts how the support of young people on her private college campus transcends differences based on race and income.

> I was in a hall where myself and one another African American girl live, the two of us with all of these rich white people . . . And the night that he won

literally everyone was running up and down the hall. And again there were just two of us. Most of the people running up and down the hall were white. And, um, that night a bunch of girls got together in a room and were watching the returns. Literally, we got the entire dorm into one room . . . very stuffed, very cluttered. Everyone was watching it together and very excited. It was definitely a community-wide thing. It was not just limited to the African American community.

Throughout the focus groups, traditionally aged college students are not the only ones to comment on President Obama's use of the media to connect with younger voters. A number of older participants also share their perceptions of this topic. Several speak specifically about the optimism and enthusiasm of young people, and how they gain inspiration from it. In one North Carolina focus group with people of all ages, an older white woman talks directly to several students in the group:

Listening to you all is so inspiring and uplifting. It's so exciting to see you all so excited about President Obama. And I think that it is phenomenal to have this kind of person, who is a politician that can communicate in the way that he does. I think that it is exciting that that was your first presidential election. My first was to vote for John F. Kennedy and many of us experienced the same excitement back then.

Other older participants also discuss young people's reactions to Barack Obama's election. In a Rhode Island focus group of community members, a forty-something-year-old Jewish man comments:

You know what's amazing? The students. On election night I saw hundreds of students pour into the streets and start cheering. They met others . . . I don't know it was like they were just drawn to the [State] Capitol . . . and then they all started singing "The Star Spangled Banner". All together. It was amazing. These are twenty-somethings who aren't nationalists. They are crying, weeping on the Capitol steps. And this wasn't planned, there was no schedule for that. It just happened. People just did it because they believed in President Obama. And they want the president to do all of the things that he believes in.

Not all participants describe President Obama's use of multimedia technology to reach out to young voters in positive terms. Several older participants, in fact, critique it as a purely strategic move. One fifty-something-year-old white woman from Alabama describes President Obama's efforts as "going after the younger generation." She adds, "You might love it or hate it, but it has reached people that others haven't before." Another white woman of similar age but from California suggests that his strategy to appeal to younger voters is due to their lack of experience with politics: "He is smart to go after younger voters with his message. The more seasoned people know better and they aren't going to be fooled. So, he thinks that he is going to step back from this group, and start to focus his efforts on this group. And this is how I am going to reach them—through the media." A similar sentiment is articulated by a forty-something-year-old Caucasian man in a focus group of community members from southern Virginia.

> I think that his campaigning strategy was really smart. To target young people—I feel that that is what he did. I feel that there are a big portion of voters are young who have a whole lifetime ahead of them. They are coming out of college and getting jobs, and he wants them to be in line for us. His strategy in targeting them was very smart. These are children of the baby boomers; they are going to be voting for some time. They aren't easier to persuade, but they don't have all of the baggage that their parents have.

Other participants see President Obama's strategy to direct his message to younger voters as a "mixed bag." A middle-aged black male participant from northern California captures this point when he says:

> Youth who were never involved in the political process because they weren't old enough, or they weren't interested, got involved when Obama came on the scene. He was talking to them, much like Kennedy's message forty years earlier. Obama's message resonated with people who had never been involved politically before. They are the ones that never wanted to deal with politics before because of the bullshit of both parties—or even Independents. Then Obama came along and got people's attention. They thought that, after he was elected, Obama was going to come in and change the world, and change American politics, and change the whole system. That hasn't happened, so now a lot of them are disillusioned and didn't go out to vote last Tuesday.

Within this excerpt, "last Tuesday" refers to the 2010 midterm elections which are a frequent topic of discussion given that the majority of focus groups for this study are facilitated during the fall of 2010.

The perception that President Obama's focus on reaching out to younger voters might backfire, like which some participants describe as happening in the 2010 midterm elections, is evident in a few focus group discussions. One sixty-something-year-old white man in North Carolina echoes the sentiment of the participant quoted earlier in terms of how high expectations among younger voters are working against President Obama.

> With as many young people who participated with his election, they were new to politics. They didn't know what they were expecting to happen. They had

these grand illusions and all of the promises that he made. But they also did not know history. People who have observed past presidents and have seen things happen before, they didn't go into it with the same sort of expectations. They have quickly become disillusioned.

These comments are provided prior to the mid-term elections, however, are delivered with concerns regarding low voter turnout that seems to have come to fruition. The catch-22 for President Obama's success with engaging younger voters via the media is that their lack of political experience translates into quick frustration with the bureaucratic nature of government. President Obama's communication with young voters must include explanations of the process; if not, then he will not be successful.

> Young people voted for Obama, but then they couldn't understand the political process. People were like, "Okay I voted, but are you saying that my vote doesn't go to Obama directly but through some Electoral College?" What is that? People couldn't understand the process, and I feel like that discouraged people from voting again. Obama was a different type of candidate and his message was so simple and meaningful. "Yes we can." We've heard those different types of slogans before but this time, it was something different. He was a really unique candidate. All of the people who he had ran against, they all had a background that worked against them. He was new and he had the endorsements of some of the heavy hitters, like the Kennedys, Oprah, and people who other people looked up to. He was all over YouTube, everywhere you turned there was an endorsement for Obama. And in the end, people thought "Okay, my vote may not mean a lot, but I have to at least try to make a difference. My one vote might actually matter." If Obama can just get that message out to people for state and local elections, then I feel that this country would progress. He is going up for re-election, and if we can't show people that his ideas were implemented and affected the local level, he won't get re-elected. Clearly, there needs to be an explanation of what the federal government can do, and what the local government can do. (Thirty-year-old African American woman from Alabama)

SUMMARY

Chapter 10 is designed to summarize some of the key themes that emerge from participants in terms of how public perceptions of President Obama are inextricably tied to images communicated via mass media channels. The first half of the chapter utilizes participants' comments to discuss the power of the media and how different understandings of its role impact the particular ways that people perceive President Obama. The opposite is also true: people's perceptions of President Obama appear to influence how they evaluate various mass media outlets. The second half of the chapter focuses in on how participants describe and evaluate the emergence of social media as a means to reach younger voters—an important but seemingly unreliable voting block. Chapter 11 continues my exploration of Barack Obama's use of multimedia to engage different segments of the general public. Specifically, it explicates participants' perception that he is the very first "celebrity president" in the United States.

Chapter 11

The Celebrity President

> Is he a celebrity or a president? It's like watching the ultimate reality television show.
>
> —Twenty-something-year-old Caucasian man from California

As I explain in chapter 2, good qualitative research is discovery-oriented in that it seeks insight into a topical area in ways that resist pre-determined agendas. All of the chapters in this book represent topics that emerged as major themes during my analysis of the focus group transcripts; in this regard the focus of these chapters were not decided upon before data collection. Many of the chapters cover topics that were expected; however, chapter 11 represents a subject area that was totally unexpected. No specific questions regarding the media are included in the Topical Protocol. Within each of the focus group discussions, participants raise and discuss the influential role that the media play in public perceptions of President Obama and his communication style.

Most often comments describing President Obama as a celebrity president emerge during questions that ask participants how the general public perceives President Obama. These questions are asked to explore if President Obama is perceived as a black president, a biracial president, or simply as a president. Most of the responses to these questions initially focus on the saliency of race in public perceptions. However, a significant number of participants are adamant that their perceptions of Barack Obama are more closely aligned with other issues. As reported in earlier chapters, some individuals describe how they see him primarily in terms of his politics (e.g., "Democratic president," "Liberal president," "Socialist president"). For these persons, race is less relevant than political affiliation and ideology. This chapter focuses on another aspect of Barack Obama's presidency, one that an unexpected number of participants describe as more compelling that his race, politics, or age: The fact that President Obama is first celebrity president in the history of the United States.

BARACK OBAMA: THE MEDIA CELEBRITY

Participants from focus groups across the United States engage in discussions about Barack Obama's celebrity status. The first reference to this perception occurs within the second focus group discussion at a Michigan university campus, when a young white male says: "I just have to say that Obama has a celebrity-type persona. If you look on TV, you would see the younger generation supporting Obama. A lot of celebrities were all about Obama . . . Everybody thinks that he is like a star." When this particular comment is shared, it does not provoke much discussion. Instead, the discussion quickly moves to other topics. However, other focus groups spend considerable time discussing how President Obama "definitely had a huge presence in the media" (Latino graduate student from Massachusetts). Across a variety of groups, participants discuss how Barack Obama's presidential campaign benefited greatly from a type of media exposure that was unprecedented. Best-selling books, appearances on traditional and untraditional news programs, cameos in various popular culture forms (e.g., music, animated shows, cartoons, radio), promotional messages through the Internet and other social media forms are all cited as examples of President Obama's proliferation across the media.

Several participants describe President Obama's use of various media as strategic. For some, like a young African American woman from California, his willingness to use nontraditional media venues is a welcome change:

> He does things differently. He was on *Saturday Night Live*. I heard him on the radio—I think it was KISS-FM. You hear his voice and you want to listen. You want to know what he is saying. In the past presidents haven't done that before. He is reaching so many more people. In the past, presidents would never do that. So for me, that is how he reaches people. I think that that is a very positive change.

As I demonstrate in the previous chapter, many participants perceive President Obama's use of non-traditional media channels as an effective means to reach and make connections with segments of the population that historically have been politically apathetic. A twenty-something-year-old Latin American woman in Massachusetts explains how he is able to connect with her mother—despite language barriers:

My mom also likes *The Ellen DeGeneres Show* so when he came on that show and started dancing with his little moves, she loved that. The images that she sees on the surface, they are all really appealing to her. And because of that she makes sure that she watches the news and keeps up with him. Even though she may not understand it completely [due to English being her second language], she makes an effort to watch and keep up with it.

According to some participants, Obama's celebrity status is achieved through his association with other celebrities who are viewed in a positive light. A young Middle Eastern American man from California makes this point when he discusses rap superstar Jay-Z:

I think that he associated himself with people like Jay-Z . . . [group laughter]. He hangs out with people like him, and Jay-Z is someone who I really like. He is the type of person who hangs out with people like him, and goes to basketball games and stuff like that. That kind of stuff makes you feel like he is close to you. It makes him seem like he is our age. I know that he isn't but it seems like that. He has been on MTV, and other shows like that. It seems like he is very aware of pop culture—stuff that I'm interested in. But he is president . . . so I think that he may be able to represent me better than some other folks. He is someone that I haven't really seen in the office before.

Other young people discuss how President Obama's association with, and knowledge of, rap music helps demonstrate his standing in the community as "real" and "authentic." As established with the quotes included earlier, this seems most evident among young African American and Latino participants. Such is the case for a young black woman from Massachusetts:

I definitely think that he tries to appeal to various audiences. I don't remember which speech it was, but he mentioned Weezy. And I was like, "okay, he referred to a rapper!" Wow! He was basically not only appealing to the higher education, or higher class people. He used Weezy to appeal to the audience that actually listens to that type of music. What was interesting is that once he did that, people understood the reference. And he really connected with us.

A black Puerto Rican student from Alabama also discusses how his perceptions of President Obama are initially formed through his love of rap music.

I first actually heard of him through a rapper whose name is Common. He had a CD with a song that had a line that said Barack, Uniter of the People. Usually when I hear songs and I don't know who they are talking about, I will go and research them. Common is from Chicago and so I researched Barack in Chicago. But that was the very first time that I heard of him and knowing what he was doing in Chicago—working in inner-city urban areas. I didn't really hear too much more about him, but then when I heard about him again as a president candidate, I remember relating that to that first connection. I think that it was really good that his message, or his impact, even got rappers to talk about him. I think that shows how much he has influenced people, he's communicating out of a genre that most politicians don't know about, or can't utilize like Barack. I think that that was really good.

Not all participants connect with President Obama through the media attention that he receives through his association with rap artists. Other individuals discuss reading this autobiography, seeing him on popular television shows, or watching various clips found on the Internet—especially those on YouTube.com that attract millions of viewers. For many of these participants, these media outlets allow them to connect with President Obama in a variety of ways. For one young white male from California, the connection is through the ways in which he deals with questions about his past drug use:

The first time I heard him, my roommate googled him and said, "Look, this guy is going to be our president!" And then I saw one of the interviews of him on YouTube where they asked him, "Mr. Obama, have you ever smoke marijuana?" And it was like, "Yeah." "But did you inhale?" "Well, that's the idea, right?" I really didn't have a strong impression, but I just thought that it was kinda cool that he said it in a way that admitted it . . . but not really putting like it was above the rest of us (like most politicians do). Most walk a thin line . . . but it was kinda cool.

From this perspective, individuals acknowledge that President Obama's media persona is highly likeable. This is the case for many participants, including people who did not necessarily agree with his politics. A forty-something-year-old white female community college student from Michigan, for example, shares:

My first exposure to him was when he went on *The Jay Leno Show*, I think it was when he had just announced that he was running for president. He was really likeable, funny, outgoing, and I really liked him. Then I thought, "Oh my goodness, I hope that he isn't a Democrat." [group laughter] And he turned out that he was, so I was like, "Damn." But he was very likeable, warm. He came across really good on TV.

Most of the participants that I have quoted thus far don't explicitly describe President Obama as a "celebrity president." Their perceptions are that he effectively uses the media to reach out and connect with the U.S. public. More often than not, descriptions of President Obama as a celebrity implicitly criticize the media hype that he seeks out to promote himself. The more President Obama appears within various media forms, the more criticism he receives regarding his celebrity status. Participants criticize him for, what they perceive as strategic attempts to be associated with other celebrities. One twenty-something-year-old Caucasian woman from California criticizes how President Obama's "desire to be famous" is ridiculous and specifically comments on how he appears "all over the media," including rap songs: "I mean he is even in rap songs now! When has there ever been a president in a rap song before? 'My president is black. My lambo's blue and I'll be goddamn if my rims ain't too!' What the heck is that about?" Interestingly, a few participants even suggest that President Obama is more interested in becoming famous than being president. This was the sentiment when one young white man from Nebraska argues that Barack Obama "wanted to become president so that he would be a celebrity."

President Obama's association with famous celebrities also raises suspicions regarding his allegiance to different individuals and groups. A number of participants question his relationships with celebrities who might encourage him to support certain causes, policies, and other initiatives. One young white man from Indiana discuss how his Internet research reveals that President Obama is part of a secret society of masterminds interested in establishing a new world order:

> I heard that he is part of the . . . you know what the Illuminati is? Have you ever heard of Proverbs 18:21? To sum it up, if you enjoy the words, then you get to eat from the truth. The Illuminatis are a group of people who are very, very wealthy and want to take over by getting power in the world's banks. A lot of people think that he is part of the Illuminatis . . . him and Jay-Z . . . You should look it up! It's all over the Internet. You know on the dollar bill where there is a pyramid and the eye. The eye represents a bunch of stuff . . . His relationships with all of those celebrities isn't as innocent as you might think.

THE OPRAH EFFECT: PRESIDENT OBAMA AS THE POPULAR CHOICE

Of all of the celebrity associations with President Obama, his relationship with Oprah Winfrey receives the most commentary from participants. When I ask about their first exposure to Barack Obama, the number of individuals that discuss his appearance on *The Oprah Winfrey Show* rivals those that remember seeing him speak at the 2004 Democratic National Convention. The following comments from a forty-something-year-old Caucasian woman from Connecticut mirror those shared from others across the United States: "I didn't know much about him, I first heard about him from Oprah. So, I knew that Oprah was backing him, and then through family contacting me, I learned more about him myself." Within this particular focus group of individuals from lower-economic communities, every other woman in the room also has a similar story about their first exposure to President Obama. Participants in other focus groups, especially those which are facilitated among college educated participants, seem hesitant to self-disclosure a similar occurrence. One thirty-four-year-old white woman from Massachusetts shares: "This is kinda embarrassing but he was on Oprah one day—as a senator. And Oprah was asking him if he could see himself as president one day. He was well spoken, well articulated, and you could see Oprah really pushing for him. For one, he would change history, but two, she also agreed with him on different stuff."

In addition to introducing Barack Obama to millions of viewers, participants also describe how Oprah Winfrey generated tremendous support for his candidacy through praise for him. One young African American man from Michigan discusses the influence that she has on her audience, who also spreads the word to others: "I've heard that he had Oprah on his side, and White women LOOOOOOVE Oprah. So, whatever Oprah says to do, they do. So you have rich white people who watch Oprah and then they got their husbands to vote for Obama to make them happy, so then, BAM! He was elected." Another participant (middle-aged white woman from Connecticut) extends this idea when she says: "I think that that was one of the main reasons why he got it over Hillary. In the sense that women who were going to be voting were influenced by Oprah." In focus groups across the United States, individuals speak about how Oprah Winfrey uses her media power to get Barack Obama elected. One fifty-something-year-old Middle Eastern woman from California boldly states "If you have Oprah on your side, you're set!"

Many of the participants' comments regarding Oprah Winfrey are more descriptive rather than evaluative. However, a number of individuals are quite critical in assessing the role that celebrities had in garnering support for Obama from novice, largely uninformed voters. In one of the most interesting quotes of the entire project, one twenty-something-year-old Caucasian woman from Illinois describes how celebrities like Oprah Winfrey promote Barack Obama like a product: "People see Obama as this celebrity figure. Because Oprah put a stamp of approval on him, everybody got on board . . . she got us to fall in love with him, sorta like one of her books or favorite things. It was a trend, but now the trend is fading out."

Within this perspective, participants argue that celebrities use their social status to make Obama the "popular choice" among voters, especially young and novice voters. According to one white male student from a state university in Michigan:

> I have to say that Obama has a celebrity-type persona. If you look on TV, you would see the younger generation supporting Obama. A lot of celebrities were all about Obama. You would see it on TV, on MTV, on YouTube, all over. Whatever our age group would watch, everything was Obama, Obama, Obama. Everybody thought that he was like a star. . . . More celebrities liked him. There are some people out there, if a celebrity likes something, then they are going to like it too. He was younger—obviously compared to McCain, who is obviously really old. Obama was definitely the candidate who was more popular with young voters.

Participants criticize President Obama and his celebrity friends for making the presidential election a "popularity contest."

> From the beginning, they made all of this seem like it was just a popularity contest . . . so he doesn't have much merit. He just won because he was more popular. Even in pop culture itself, many celebrities were "team Obama" themselves. So, that just adds to the idea that that is all that he had behind him. He was just a more popular candidate . . . he had big names, like Oprah Winfrey, supporting him.

The criticisms are harsher in other focus groups. In Illinois, for example, a young Caucasian female college student is visibly angry about how Obama uses celebrities to win an election against a more qualified candidate. In particular, she says:

> I don't know. He is very much the celebrity president. I don't know. I very much did not want him elected. He's a joke. He was so disgusting from the very beginning. There was so much celebrity involvement. And that's how he got elected. Famous people gave him money and told everyone to vote for him. It's disgusting.

A number of participants discuss how Obama's popularity as our first celebrity president is working against him. Several talk about how his social status takes focus away from his policy initiatives and weakened his credibility with more serious-minded members of the U.S. public. One middle-aged white man from Massachusetts describes his popularity as a "double-edged sword":

> Insofar as getting him an elected, being viewed as a celebrity was definitely a plus. But as far as him being an actual president, I would say that it is a double-edged sword where he is getting the benefit of having a large, pop culture following. But at the same time, he is being critiqued as much as a celebrity. So, if he goes somewhere, or if anything happens . . . if he takes one step out of line, he—like most presidents—it's covered. For him, it's a little bit heightened.

Whether it be because of race, or the tough financial times that we are going through right, of all of the media hype that he created, the spotlight is on this man. And people are being much more critical of him.

Another participant (an older white woman from North Carolina) comments on how his social prestige seems to create a certain level of "cockiness." Specifically she says: "Given all of his popularity, I almost think that he thinks that he is above everyone else now." According to others, this leads President Obama to communicate in ways that are inappropriate. One young African American male college student from Michigan cites this false sense of popularity as the reason why President Obama has misjudged the public's acceptance of his reaction to different events. "I think that sometimes, because he is a celebrity president, he can get too comfortable—like saying "jack-ass" [in describing Kanye West's behavior] or "stupid" [in describing Officer Crowley's actions].

Supporters of President Obama did not perceive these "slips of the tongue" as evidence of his arrogance. Instead, participants describe how such instances prove that he is human and not perfect. In one Michigan community college focus group where Republican participants are especially critical of President Obama, a twenty-something-year-old African American woman offers:

> I don't think that a few instances show that he's ineffective. That shows that he is human, and not perfect. People—even people who don't like him—have him on a pedestal but they shouldn't. He's human. Those instances show that he is human, he's not going to be perfect every single time in his communication style. Nobody is, no matter who you are.

Other participants describe how, given the intense media scrutiny, President Obama's imperfections are going to be seen by others. One young white man from Michigan discusses how people's perceptions of Obama as their political "knight in shining armor" promote certain unrealistic expectations:

> He can't put that block up continuously. He's gotta be a real person. He's gotta be a real person once in a while. And, yes, for him to be saying ass on television—kids are going to hear it, and yeah, they are gonna notice it and maybe say ass all day long. But its tough with that type of exposure. He can't be the knight in shining armor continuously forever.

According to these participants, President Obama's ability to be seen as human (mistakes and all) only adds to his credentials as a political leader who was "real." As such, his commitment to make a difference in their lives of everyday citizens is viewed with a significant amount of admiration and respect. One Caucasian woman in her fifties praises President Obama's efforts in a world where he is constantly under "a media microscope." Within her community focus group held in rural southern Ohio, she says: "He can't do anything out of the pubic eye. He has people following him around all of the time. No privacy. Secret service following him and his family around all of the time. Who wants that world? I have a lot of respect for him." The idea that President Obama's life has become a media spectacle—with every thought, action, and interaction recorded for public consumption—lead some participants to describe it as "the ultimate reality TV show." This particular phrase came from a young white male from California; the concept is the focus of the next section.

PRESIDENT OBAMA IN THE MEDIA: THE ULTIMATE REALITY TV SHOW

> Question: Has there ever been anyone who is surrounded by media and followed for everything that he's done . . . has there ever been so much light shone on anybody, and then they remain the same? I don't think that there has ever been anyone who has sacrificed so much to accomplish something—any president—and stayed the same.

This quote is taken from the comments of a black man in his 40s who was participating in a focus group of African American religious leaders. His comments perceive the media scrutiny of President Obama's life as indicative of the times that we live in. Other members of the focus group also describe the media presence as an overwhelming challenge. A middle-aged woman shares:

> It is unfortunate for him that he represents the country 24/7, and they are watching him 24/7. So, whatever you say and whenever you say it, they are going to take it as if you are saying it as the president, not that you are saying it as Barack Obama an American citizen. You are always the president. That is a very difficult thing to do, especially for someone who sees himself as a normal everyday person who loves everybody. Now you realize that you are a president 24/7.

These two excerpts describe the media coverage of President Obama as relatively neutral. However, other focus group participants perceive the media attention related to the fact that he is an African American president.

> Everybody has him under a negative microscope and everything that he does is blown up. I remember the first time that he played in a basketball game, and

it was all over all of the news. The president having a beer, all over the news. The president fist-bumping, all over the news. But people never commented on Bush or Clinton like that. They weren't under a microscope like he is . . . it's all because of his race.

Other African American participants also point to racial issues as a factor in the media's negative coverage of President Obama. One African American male in his forties describes a shift in media attention to others in a California community focus group:

> The media is not trying to do it that way. They are not trying to make this positive. They did at first because it was big news, FIRST BLACK PRESIDENT. But now that is not news anymore. Now that we have a nigger up here in the White House, and we need to vilify him and put a microscope over everything he does every day and magnify by three times every time he does something—even those things that aren't newsworthy. So what—he called Kanye West an asshole? That isn't even news! Why is that even on the TV? If he wasn't black, he wouldn't even have been on the TV! The media wouldn't even care.

The role of race notwithstanding, most participants are in agreement that the media coverage is fueled by the public's desire to get an up close and personal view of President Obama. According to one young African American woman from North Carolina, "He's different than all other presidents because the media delve into every aspect of his life, whether if it is him going on a date with his wife, what he had to eat, where he went, etc. We want to know all of these things—like what team he is rooting for in the Super Bowl, or whatever." Part of the equation of the media's coverage of President Obama is related to his popularity among certain segments of the U.S. public and the perception that he is more accessible than past presidents. One white male college student from Indiana explains:

> I think that he is more socially open than any other president that I've seen in my lifetime . . . The way that is open to the public. Letting people into the New Year's Eve Party at the White House. Simple things like shooting basketball with Howard from the Magic at the NBA Championships. It is like he is one of the guys . . . It's just a totally different look than any other president that I've seen in my lifetime. I like it, though. I like it, but it's just different.

As I allude to earlier, the notion that President Obama has opened his life to the U.S. people has lead to comparisons of the public's obsession with reality-based television programming. In addition to a couple of direct references, participants describe how their media consumption of President Obama's life parallel the ways in which they watch other programs. For instance, one young Caucasian woman from Nebraska recalls how she made sure to watch when President Obama went on FOX news: "I watched the interview that he had on FOX News. It was like a big TV event. I wanted to see that because it was such big news . . . This happened last spring, I think. I was really curious about it, so I watched it. And the conflict between Obama and the FOX newscaster didn't disappoint." Similar to other reality TV programming, the media seem to focus on conflict and drama because those are the very things that attract the most viewers. For some participants, like a middle-aged man born and raised in Hawaii (participating in a North Carolina community focus group), this creates media spectacles that people "couldn't get enough of":

> People love drama! That was very evident at the State of the Union. Remember that? You have Judge Alito acting a fool in front of the camera . . . his facial expressions were ridiculous! Then you have the Congressman who called President Obama a liar. You have a Supreme Court Justice and members of Congress caught on camera disrespecting the president. And everyone loves watching it.

Other participants also discuss the ridiculous nature of media outlets which are determined to create drama out of the most mundane happenings within President Obama's life. In an Indiana focus group of college students, one white man laments:

> You can't turn on the TV nowadays and NOT see something about President Obama. At least once a night, every day, you see Obama. Something about Obama. And it doesn't make sense. They followed him to Taco Bell and there were millions of people outside watching him walk in to the restaurant. Or even during one interview when a fly was flying about and he swatted it and killed it. The cameraman panned down and showed the dead fly lying there. For two weeks, that was one of the biggest things on the news: He killed a fly. [group laughter] He got some criticism from PETA because he killed a fly. He can't pass gas and not get some criticism from someone. The media is covering him 24/7. All presidents have had that to some extent, but it just seems more blown out of proportion with him. Being the first African American president, being the one who put into action so many changes so quickly, he can't do anything without media attention. For one week, he refused to wear an American flag pin on his label, and he got all of this criticism. Now if George W. Bush had done that, it wouldn't have been a big deal at all. But with Obama, it was. The minute that he does something it is all over the media.

Like with other celebrities, President Obama's presence in the media has fostered the development of parasocial relationships, a term that refers to one-sided relationships where one person knows a great deal about the other person, but the other person does not (Horton and Wohl, 1956). Most often, parasocial relationships develop between celebrities and their fans. Across different focus group discussions, participants—most often African Americans and younger persons—describe President Obama as if he is a father-figure, friend, or member of the family. This is evident as several participants refer to him on a first name basis (e.g., "I support Barack and all that he does"). One older black woman from Rhode Island describes President Obama's willingness to share his life with the public as "magic." In particular, she says: "I think that he and his family allow—and this part is magic—us to enter into their lives in various ways. And that way we get to know him and feel like we are part of his family." The existence of these types of parasocial relationships facilitates a close identification with President Obama, and also lead to a desire to defend him as if he was a family member or close personal friend.

> I was just gonna say that we get to know him—through his talk show appearances and being everywhere in the media—on a different level. Like once, I don't remember what show he was on, but someone asked him what was on his iPod. And there were a broad range of things that he listened to, and that person was really surprised. I was shocked. He said, "Yeah, Jay-Z . . ." And I was like, "Oh, okay. Wow." Because I had my own stereotypes about what he would be listening to. He is so open to us and I get really defensive when other people criticize him without even getting to know him.

In an all-African American focus group in California, several men discuss the ways in which Obama relates to other black men just through being himself in various contexts. Their ability to relate to President Obama in very personal ways leads a female participant in her forties to recognize that the role that media plays in all of this.

> I think that most people in popular culture, we know about them through the media. I'm a former reporter, some disclosure here . . . As a former reporter, I was guest lecturing at a college. This was shortly after Princess Diana died, and I was talking about the paparazzi and how they chased her down and pretty much caused her death. The students were talking about how much they couldn't stand the media and how overzealous they are. They talked about the tragedy, what a beautiful person Princess Diana was and how much she did for the community. So, I asked them, "How do you know that?" You know that because the media told you that. You don't have a personal relationship with her. You don't know her. What people know about Barack Obama has come through the media.

Despite the realness of the images that we see, a few participants warn others that all representations of President Obama must be understood as a mass-mediated entity. Just like other forms of reality-based television programming, individuals must be aware of the power that the media has in the process of making news. A middle-aged Jewish American man from Rhode Island makes this point when he says: "Think about it: The media takes certain things about President Obama and that's what they cover. If you think about it they are creating their own reality about what he's doing." His comments are offered during a discussion about how the media focuses on the personal events in Obama's life and ignores all of his efforts to promote important policy changes. Most of the participants in his focus group are supporters of the president; unsurprisingly, they agree with his assessments. One fifty-something black woman shares: "My problem also is with the media. I think that people don't even hear all of the good things that he is doing because they are focusing on all these other idiotic things. Why? Why is the media doing this?" During a discussion among college students attending a HBCU in Alabama, participants also focus in on criticizing how media coverage has taken attention away from all of Obama's accomplishments. One participant shares:

> One criticism of Obama is that he hasn't communicated well enough to the general public. As we have talked about in class, we were literally on the road to a depression . . . because of things that happened before he was elected. With GM, he recently has been harping that the bail-out bill could actually work. And people are more conscious of that now, more so than they were before. But there are a lot more things that he's done before, but he has talked about that.

Following this comment, a man in the group interrupts and states: "But people have said that he has, but the media hasn't talked about it. They want to talk about other things—the celebrity thing, all of the different mistakes that he has made." At this point, several participants begin talking over one another. Although their particular comments are not discernable, the essence of their perceptions is clear: As supporters of the president, they wanted him to make greater efforts to communicating about all of the good things that he is doing.

Discussions regarding the media's role in sharing President Obama's life are drastically different among non-supporters. In fact, they have a very different take on the extensive media coverage of Barack Obama's life. They believe, like the young European American woman from Nebraska quoted here, that the liberal media is depicting him in overwhelmingly positive ways: "Some of the media is always painting this picture-perfect version of Obama. But I see that as the . . . I don't want to say fake public persona. But is it real? I want to see the real President Obama. The media doesn't give us that, they portray him as the perfect person." From this perspective, President Obama seeks out all of the media attention because it helps him gain celebrity status. The result, according to some participants, is an overexposure in the media that negatively impacts his abilities to function as an effective leader.

OVEREXPOSED: BARACK OBAMA'S OWN DOING

In discussions of the media's influence on public perceptions of Barack Obama, there is a genuine disagreement in terms of which factors are most to blame for his celebrity status. Some participants argue his youthful personality and charisma trigger a public desire. Others focus on issues of race, most often that the media attention is fueled since race is a hot topic that sells in the media. This section presents a third perspective: The perception that Barack Obama's celebrity status is his own doing—a strategy to gain popularity and win the White House. In an exchange from a group of college students from California, several participants (four white males and one white female) also describe how it also helped with a major award.

> WM#1: Going back on Obama being a celebrity, think about the Nobel Peace Prize that he got. He got the award for his communication—words that he said. At the time when he got the award, he had *announced* the troops' withdrawal, but he was actually building up the troops at the time. All he said was "We will withdraw." And I was thinking back on that, if Bush would have said that at that time, or McCain said it if he was elected, I doubt that he would have gotten the Nobel Peace Prize. Obama—the black U.S. president—was the hottest thing in the world at the time. I definitely think that that celebrity status helped to get him that award. I don't know if people agree with that or not . . .
>
> WM#2: I do. I do. I think that it helped. I think that the majority of the country has their opinions based off of the fact that they hate Bush. You know? So, they were up for just about anything. In the beginning, I think that all supported Obama. So the Nobel Peace Prize was given to him, and now he has been screwing up, so people that voted for him are re-thinking it. We are so quick to switch sides . . . we love to kick people when they are down. We love to see negative things about so-called celebrities . . .
>
> WM#3: I agree that people like to kick folks when they are down . . .
>
> WF: When he consciously made the decision to become a celebrity, all of the tabloid magazines that he is in . . . He did that, he talked to all of these magazines. They just don't put you on the cover. You talk to them and then they ask "Do you want to be on the cover?" And then they talk to you. I work for a magazine so I have to read them all the friggin' time. But, he's in there. And his wife and kids are in there, right alongside Brad Pitt. You would think that Obama would want a separation.
>
> WM#1: Well, going back to what you said about him making a conscious effort to be a celebrity . . . he is trying to figure out his target audience. You know last time they were pushing that "Get out to vote" thing . . . get young

people out to vote. Well, what do young people watch? What do they read? Tabloid TV, magazines, late night TV, *South Park*. He's been a character on *South Park*. Think about his appearance on *Saturday Night Live*! In previous elections, it was the older crowd voting, it wasn't the fresh, young crowd. Now since they are trying to get the younger people out to vote, being a celebrity has actually helped him in a sense . . . but it has also made him lose a little bit of credibility outside the United States.

WM#4: Don't the voters say that? I think that goes with the misinformed stuff. They just don't know everything that is going on. So, they vote for the celebrity . . . they don't think that they can be informed just yet. It is kind of like religion, people are always saying that they can't be religious because they're too young. "I have to wait some so that I can have all of these experiences and then make a decision." That way you can really understand what you are practicing, and not just practicing what your parents told you to practice, or believe. Until then, you just follow the crowd.

This one excerpt contains a great deal of insight regarding the public's perception of President Obama, the celebrity. First, participants describe Obama as choosing to become a celebrity, and how his race assists in this objective. Second, the exchange highlights the utility of celebrity status in maintaining the media's attention, but also acknowledges the fickle nature of a public that loves drama. Third, and last, the comments offered here describe President Obama's celebrity status as a strategy to target novice viewers, most notably those influenced by popular culture.

Not all participants perceive President Obama's media presence in negative ways. Some individuals do agree that he is overexposed, but blames that on the media's intrusive coverage, not on President Obama's attempts to reach the masses. One young Middle Eastern American man from California comments:

> I don't necessarily think that it is a bad thing. I feel like that wasn't his focus—to be a "celebrity" [using air quotes around this term]. I think that, as president, he wants to meet the masses in a different way. Through the channels of radio, of television, or talk shows . . . he wants to be involved in things that Americans do on a daily basis. I don't feel like that is a bad thing, if anything that's a good thing. He is trying to step out there, but not with the intention that he wants to be a celebrity . . . He is trying to be a leader, but a leader who reaches the public in different ways.

In this regard, participants describe Obama's ability to utilize a variety of media platforms to reach different segments of the population as laudable and effective. A young black woman from Illinois describes his efforts as "amazing:"

> I actually think that the reason why young people and minorities went out to vote was because of the way that he used his communication. He engaged people through different media. Not everyone is going to watch PBS or CNN,

or listen to NPR. I mean he actually went on *Ellen*, he went on *Saturday Night Live*, he went on all of these talk shows. I even heard him on *The Steve Harvey Morning Show*. He actually used Twitter and Facebook because that is how the youth communicate. He saw that and used it to his benefit. That was amazing.

While these, and other, participants appreciate President Obama's efforts, most agree that the extent of his media presence has a negative effect on the public's desire for information. According to one young white male college student from Indiana,

You can't turn on the TV nowadays and NOT see something about President Obama. It wasn't always that way. Like with President Bush and President Clinton, they would be on TV, but there were huge gaps of time when you wouldn't see them at all. But now, at least once a night, every day, you see Obama—something about Obama. And it just doesn't make sense.

Supporters across the United States offer comments that depict a public that has fizzled in its excitement over Barack Obama's historic election. One young black woman from Massachusetts shares how "the buzz isn't there anymore . . . the hype is gone." Several participants, like the one quoted here, describe how their attention has waned to the degree where seeing President Obama is a point of frustration.

When he was running for office and first elected, every time he came on TV, I made sure that I watched. Every single time. Now, I'm like, "Okay, he's on . . . " But now I get frustrated—just like every other president—because he is interrupting my show! [group laughter]. (Forty-six-year-old African American woman living in southern Virginia)

These comments are provided in a context where this particular person perceives President Obama's communication skills as "the best of any president." As such it illustrates the public's resistance to overexposed "celebrities" regardless of their communication competence. A similar sentiment is illustrated through the experiences of a white female teaching assistant from a Nebraska state university:

I have a story from the classroom that I would like to share. I was teaching a communication class where we watched a Barack Obama video in terms of speech delivery. I was setting up the video and explaining to the class all of the things that they should be looking for—remember it was specifically for different aspects of speech and delivery. And when I asked if there were any questions, a hand went up in the back of the room. "Does it HAVE to be HIM?' ANYBODY but HIM." That's just something that stuck with me. The way that he didn't call him "the president," "Obama," but just "HIM." In the classroom

I've definitely stopped showing Barack Obama video clips. I'm not sure why there is so much resistance. I don't know if he is because of political differences or just the fact that everyone has been inundated with Obama.

Other participants are much more critical of President Obama's efforts to gain celebrity status and dominate the media. One young white man from Nebraska calls Obama "the faux rock star whose star has fizzled out." According to him, President Obama seems like "he is desperately trying to remain relevant in a media system that no longer cares as much." Similar comments are shared in a California focus group of college students, where one young white woman shares:

> That's another thing about him—he is almost out there too much. He seems desperate. He is going on all of these talk shows and doing things that are inappropriate. I don't necessarily want to say inappropriate for our leader but it crosses that line: Are you a leader or are you trying to be a celebrity? You know? You lose a little bit of respect for him, at least for me it does. You know? To go on *The View* . . . REALLY?

The perception, according to some participants, is that President Obama has his "priorities mixed up." This is the point made by a white male college student attending a university in southern Ohio who shares the following:

> Well, my parents really discuss how Obama goes on midnight TV, or makes his basketball bracket, or whatever . . . he is spending all of his time doing things that normal people do, instead of spending his time working as the president. So, it would definitely be that they are a different generation than us, but they definitely see him doing all of these meaningless things as a waste of his time. He shouldn't be doing all of that; he should be working on presidential issues.

Other participants share comments that mirror this concern. One middle-aged white woman from California, for example, asks:

> Why is he wasting his time with Ryan Seacrest? And all of these late night shows? We never saw presidents before on all of these shows . . . they actually make fun of him for it. It's become a joke. Someone's daughters came on one of talk shows, and they said if you ever want to know what the president is doing, listen to Ryan Seacrest. It was a total jab for publicizing himself like that, putting himself out there like that. Why are you wasting your time as president doing all of this?

The message from this segment of the population is clear and aptly summarized by a young white male from California: "Don't be a celebrity, be our leader. What you are doing is cool, but we don't need that right now."

An interesting meta-perception of Obama's celebrity status appears in a couple of different focus group discussions. In particular, participants describe how friends and family members in other countries regard President Obama. Their perceptions of international perspectives are that his celebrity status is viewed through an increasingly critical lens. One thirty-something white man from California shares an experience when he was in China:

> I had a tour guide and they are not really supposed to talk politics. But he was in our hotel room, and he started asking questions, and he started to open up. And he brought up the question: Is Obama a president in your country, or a celebrity? It depends on who you ask. I don't know a lot of people who get big time national press when you're a smoker and your wife asks you to quit. I remember that was really big when the election first started. They view it as a joke. But the joke is on us.

This set of comments triggers a discussion where participants acknowledge that much of the international community sees President Obama's celebrity status as saying more about U.S. culture than the president himself. A Middle Eastern American young man uses the word "celebrity obsessed":

> A few of my buddies from London have mentioned before, when it comes to Obama, they feel that our country is the country that is celebrity obsessed. We have celebrity and authority backwards as such. They would say that people make a big deal about Obama—whether why he is in office, or why they agree or disagree with him . . . no matter what people say, it is something that has nothing to do with politics.

In this context, the criticism of President Obama as the first celebrity president is shifted from Barack Obama or the media and onto the American public.

SUMMARY

This chapter highlights a public perception that one of the most unique things about Barack Obama is his celebrity status. As such it is designed to extend the insights of chapter 10 which describes participants' perceptions of the role that the media play in President Obama's election and work in the Oval Office. The insights in this chapter are important in that they illustrate how the public generally perceives President Obama's media presence in similar ways (e.g., a sense of overexposure similar to other celebrities), yet view the reasons for, and effectiveness of, this heightened media presence in different ways.

Part V

Conclusion

Chapter 12

Critical Reflections and Concluding Thoughts

Barack Obama has been described as "a highly ambiguous blank slate on which popular fantasy could be projected" (Mitchell, 2009, p. 126) and "the ultimate Rorschach that will unite us all as Americans in crisis" (Radhakrishnan, 2009, p. 153). In this way he is often read as a cipher (Maira, 2009, p. 14) who can be perceived as any and everything aligned with the perceptions of the public. According to Harris (2010), in order to be elected, "Obama presented himself as a non-threatening everyperson with an understanding of the needs of a diverse American society and world" (p. 69). These sentiments capture the essence of the diverse thematic findings described throughout this book. As such, it makes a valuable contribution to the growing literature on Barack Obama, and joins other resources as academia experiences an Obama bump in scholarship (Ng, 2010b). This final chapter is designed to summarize the key findings of the 2010 national study and offer a series of critical reflections and concluding thoughts.

Differences in perceptions regarding Barack Obama generally, and his communication style by extension, are commonly represented across various U.S. media outlets. For instance, individuals can get contrasting opinions through television stations, newspapers, radio programs, and various Internet venues. Interestingly, I was able to access the great diversity of such perceptions while collecting data through *USA Today*'s "Opinionline" feature whereby they publish excerpts of various newspapers' editorials often times illustrating just how wide the perceptions of President Obama are (e.g., "Obama plan: 'Pitiful' or 'compelling?,'" 2011).

Interestingly, Barack Obama's election as the forty-fourth U.S. president has been described in ways that mirror the diversity of public perceptions featured in this book. As I wrote in chapter 1, most often it is heralded as "historic" on a number of levels: "The election of the once-improbable candidate has challenged conventional thinking about American politics and suggests that the contours of the American political map may have changed permanently" (Ng, 2010b, p. 267). However, other political experts (e.g., Kenski et al., 2010) describe Barack Obama's election as predictable and unsurprising given the low ratings of an unpopular president, economic conditions, and an electorate that had more Democrats than Republicans. This set of circumstances, couple with an opponent that was viewed as "too old," "out of touch," and an extension of President Bush and a vice-presidential candidate that was viewed as unprepared for the presidency, made an Obama victory undeniable.

BARACK OBAMA AS COMMUNICATOR

The primary focus of this book is to offer insight into the perceptions that the general public has of President Obama's communication. As demonstrated through the national study that I conducted in the second half of 2010, the vast majority of participants portray Barack Obama as a masterful communicator whose style is motivational, inspiring, and engaging. Compared to other politicians generally and recent presidents specifically, his personable and relatable style is seen as a breath of fresh air. His ability to communicate effectively, in part, creates unrealistically high expectations, a reality that results in a shift in communication style when negotiating a political system rife with divisive bipartisan politics. Despite this dominant perception, however, a vocal minority perceives his communication through a highly critical lens. Interestingly, some non-supporters believe that President Obama is a masterful communicator, but one who has uses his oratory skills to deceive the public. All of the perceptions of participants are, consciously or unconsciously, informed by existing standards of what is considered the norm for "presidential communication"—standards of what is considered appropriate and effective for a U.S. president. President Obama's responses to a number of specific events including the BP oil spill, Kanye West's outburst at the MTV Music Video Awards, and the controversial proposal to build a mosque near Ground Zero illustrate how he is simultaneously being held to existing standards and contributing to extensions of these very standards.

Many of the participants' descriptions of Barack Obama's communication thematized in this book could have been predicted given publications that have appeared over the past couple of years. Specifically, scholars have written about the positive effects of his high levels of his communication competence (e.g., Italie, 2010; MacGillis, 2009; Remnick, 2010; Sweet and McCue-Enser, 2010) *or* criticized his communication as being strategically all style and little substance in order to maximize the emotional appeal of his messages (e.g., Corsi, 2008; Freddoso, 2008; Mattera, 2010; Rush, 2010; Spicer, 2010). Few, if any, scholars have succeeded in demonstrating how public perceptions are embedded in both of these communication realities. The in-depth analysis of the diverse public perceptions contained in a large qualitative data set reported here works to bridge the gap between the extreme representations that seem to be featured in most media outlets. Instead, I sought to demonstrate how public perceptions exist *within*—and most importantly—*between* the extremes of a continuum that is not fully represented in most public opinion polls.

Listening without evaluation to the ideas, opinions, and perspectives of individuals from diverse backgrounds is invaluable in understanding the how's and why's behind diverse perceptions of President Obama's communication. For example, a young Caucasian male from Alabama teaches me about "Wiio's Law," a communication approach that provides insight into the topic. During a diverse focus group discussion on a state university campus, he shares:

> I have a comment about the communication stuff. I'm a firm believer in Wiio's Law. The more communication that you have, the more likely you are to fail. Wiio was a Swedish man who said that communication is always flawed, and only by accident does it ever succeed. Since President Obama is actively communicating, he is trying to communicate with all of these people, so of course he is going to fail more and more—especially because as president he has a larger and larger audience. If he does get it across to more and more people, it's wonderful. If he does that then he does it more than any other president.

Before this participant's comments, I had never heard of "Wiio's Law" so I immediately asked him to clarify the spelling of his name and basic ideas so that I could do some further research once the focus group concluded.

Wiio's (1978) pessimistic take on communication competency includes a number of "principles" articulated as tongue-in-cheek maxims. In the context of public perceptions of President Obama's communication they offer some considerable insight as to the growing criticism of a leader commonly recognized as a "masterful communicator." Three principles appear to have significant relevance: (1) If communication can fail, it will, (2) If a message can be understood in different ways, it will be understood in just that way which does the most harm, and (3) The more communication there is, the more difficult it is for communication to succeed. Taken collectively, Wiio's axioms help us to understand how President Obama's communication—in a mass-mediated technologically advanced age where his words instantly reach larger and more diverse audiences than ever before—is bound to fail. As a communication professor, I would like to think that competent communication skills can be developed so that we succeed more than just "by accident." However, the major lesson here is clear: Competent communication is extremely difficult, and without significant effort, thought, and preparation, we typically have more failures than successes.

For many participants, perceptions of President Obama's communication are informed by both intersections of gender and race. In fact, during the 2008 presidential campaign the communication styles of Barack Obama and John McCain were an important point of distinction. In one editorial, Carter (2008) writes:

> Now that the actual presidential campaign is under way, we have the traditionally "masculine"' style, embodied by John McCain, emphasizing experience, toughness, feistiness, stubbornness, grit, exclusivity, etc., and the newly emergent "feminine" managerial style practiced by Obama and emphasizing communication, consensus, collegiality and inclusivity." (p. A18)

For many, Barack Obama's gendered communication can be considered as embracing a nontraditional, non-essentialized form of maleness (Connell, 2005; Katz, 2006). This reality differentiates him from other presidential candidates (both Hillary Clinton and John McCain), but also opens him up for criticism especially after the election.

Barack Obama's gendered communication style is discussed by numerous participants across a variety of focus groups. In fact, several make reference to different publications that discuss the possible consequences—both positive and negative—of an individual whose communication style is markedly more feminine than previous presidents (see Cooper, 2010b for a summary). "Obama may prove to be our first male president who pays a political price for acting too much like a woman," wrote one columnist (Parker, 2010, p. A17). Most study participants, like the columnists referred to here, focus exclusively on the gendered dimensions of President Obama's communication. However, a small but significant number of African American participants discuss how public perceptions of President Obama are informed through intersections of both gender and race. In particular, their comments acknowledge the existence of dominant stereotypes of African American men and how these present a challenge for the first African American male president.

Cooper (2010a; 2010b) writes extensively on this issue and provides some insight as why "race worked for Obama in a way that gender did not work for Hillary Clinton" (Logan, 2010, pp. 256–257). He proposes that, in the general public's eyes, African American men are put into one of two categories: (1) the threatening Bad Black Man or (2) the fully assimilated Good Black

Man. According to Cooper, the Bad Black Man is most commonly seen with images of criminals on the local news, black conscious political leaders, and popular public icons like athletes and rappers. In order to be perceived as an acceptable presidential candidate, Barack Obama had to avoid perceptions that he fit into this stereotype. Scholars have discussed how he is able to avoid attempts to connect him with other "bad black men" like Al Sharpton, Jesse Jackson, Rev. Jeremiah Wright, Minister Louis Farrakhan, and Detroit Mayor Kwame Kilpatrick (Kenski et al., 2010; Steele, 2008) as well as those who are part of the rap and professional worlds (Joseph, 2011).

Cooper (2010a; 2010b) describes the Good Black Man as one who is assimilated to white America. This image is most seen with the conservative religious spokesman, the token member of the corporate world, and political leaders who are adamant that we have reached a "post-racial" reality. According to Cooper and others (e.g., Isaksen, 2011), Barack Obama's feminine style is necessary because he has to avoid the angry black male stereotype that is associated with the Bad Black Man. The challenge, however, is seen in the fact that he has to be feminine to avoid the negative stereotype, but not too feminine because that would be viewed as "weak" and "unpresidential." As seen in chapter 5, President Obama is criticized for not communicating in a more forceful manner. Political talk show host, Bill Maher's comments criticizing President Obama's response to the BP oil spill is telling in this regard. Specifically, he calls for a more aggressive response but, in doing so, reveals the implicit connection to the Bad Black Man persona: "You know, this is where I want a real black president. I want him in a meeting with the BP CEOs, you know, where he lifts up his shirt where you can see the gun in his pants" (as quoted in "Our News," 2010, p. 97).

To date, President Obama has seemed to successfully negotiate the two extremes of the Good Black Man / Bad Black Man dichotomy (Isaksen, 2011). Some suggest that this aspect of his communication is largely strategic in the ways in which his campaign presents him as an ordinary family man who is race-conscious but not race-obsessed. His ability to promote this image through the media—and do so with great frequency—is largely successful.

> To the extent that non-black people found him alarming at first, their brain's amygdalae would have been on high alert, vigilant for danger. But they kept encountering him in the least alarming, most reassuring series of nonevents. He never lost his temper. He never appeared hostile. . . . Frequent exposure to an otherwise fear-inducing stimulus in a safe environment allows people to relax. And they evidently did. (Fiske, Bergsieker, and Williams, 2009, p. 97)

Cooper (2010b) argues that President Obama's communication reflects a constant balancing act between appearing feminine but not too feminine.

I might argue that he is successful in negotiating an androgynous communication style where both masculine and feminine communication traits (or at least what society describes as "masculine" and "feminine") are adapted to the needs of the situation (House, Dallinger, and Kilgallen, 1998; Pearson and Davilla, 2001). As such, he demonstrates a communication competence that meets the challenges inherent to public perceptions that are gendered and racialized.

RACE MATTERS

According to Christopher Edley, "Race isn't rocket science . . . it's harder" (as quoted in Remnick, 2010, p. 467). Consequently, four chapters of this book are dedicated to exploring race matters. More specifically, I explore shared participant perceptions on the role of race in public perceptions of President Obama. While some embrace current realities that come with a "post-racial" reality, most describe how race has influenced, and continues to influence, perceptions of President Obama and his communication in complex ways. In particular, participants' responses are analyzed to reveal the complex ways in which African American and European American perceptions resist generalizations (e.g., black voters support President Obama just because he was black, white critics of President Obama are racist) that exist in various public sectors. Using the conflict between Professor Henry Louis (Skip) Gates and Officer James (Jim) Crowley that ultimately led to the infamous "Beer Summit," I demonstrate how public perceptions may be racialized in some ways but extend far beyond overly simplistic black-white comparisons. In the end, I found that facilitating opportunities for people of all cultural backgrounds to come together and discuss different issues can be a productive means toward promoting greater cultural understanding. Even if individuals do not reach agreement on all issues, being exposed to different perspectives through quality interpersonal interactions can only work to reduce cultural misperceptions.

In the United States, race is a hot-button issue that gains immediate news attention. Not surprisingly, the media promoted the racial dynamics of the election. During the campaign, Jones (2010) argued that Barack Obama's biracial heritage "embodied the promises and challenges of integration in a racially troubled society" (p. 131). Interestingly, scholars have analyzed his communication regarding his racial identity. His self-descriptions as a black man are reinforced through multiple signifiers (Moffitt, 2010; Winfield, 1997). However, he continues to emphasize his biracial ancestry—being the son of a white woman from Kansas and a father from Kenya—but never identifies as a biracial person (Jones, 2010). Some argue that close relations with white family members allow him to locate his identity within a white world (Rowe, 2010).

Given all of this, most agree that Obama's campaign attempted to downplay the racial dynamics of the race. According to Joseph (2010),

> Obama's campaign, from the start, implied that his candidacy transcended race. He sought to appeal to white Americans by stressing commonalities over difference, unity over division, and the potential for racial rapprochement over racial war. Regardless of his efforts, however, from the beginning, race formed the underlying focus of the intense fascination and eventual scrutiny of Obama's candidacy. (p. 182)

Survey research has concluded that racial attitudes had a much larger effect on 2008 presidential votes than any other recent presidential election (Tesler and Sears, 2010). However, this did not necessarily work against Barack Obama. According to Remnick (2010), "the diversity of Barack's background, not that he was African American per se, was essential" (p. 133) and served him well in the areas where the electorate was younger and more racially and ethnically diverse. National polling research reveals that racial perceptions played a role in the votes of some U.S. citizens, this was especially the case in states such as Alabama, Arkansas, Louisiana, and Mississippi. These anti-Obama ballots, however, were relegated as non-difference makers given Obama's success in boosting black turnout and securing white votes outside the deep South (Kenski et al, 2010). The reality is that race—especially as Barack Obama projects a multidimensional racial identity—helps him far more than it hurts him (Remnick, 2010; Sugrue, 2010). This includes support from some Caucasians whose 'colorblind' support might be generated by the need to refute the stereotype that all white people are racist (Aronson and McGlone, 2009).

During his first term as President, Obama's focus on international and national financial crises, health care, and two different wars overwhelmed any particular racial issues (Sugrue, 2010). As such, issues related to race remain largely unaddressed in ways that some had hoped for. Some might suggest that this was strategic on President Obama's behalf because too much focus on race might threaten his attempts toward universal appeal (e.g., Joseph, 2010). Yet perceptions of President Obama as an out-group "Other" (e.g., non-U.S. born Muslim) continue to carry negative connotation for some (Hollander, 2000; Kalkan, Layman, and Uslaner, 2009; Tesler and Sears, 2010). Given all of this, Hall (2010) describes our current times as reflective of numerous teachable moments that must be embraced by everyday people.

[There is] no need to have a bunch of academic symposia or fancy commissions or panels on race ... [Instead] we should all make more of an effort to discuss with one another, in a truthful and mature and responsible way, the divides that still exist, the discrimination that's still out there, the prejudices that still hold us back ... conversations should be held not on cable TV but around kitchen tables and water coolers and church basements and in our schools and with our kids all across the country. (p. 2A)

From this perspective, one of the gifts of President Obama to the United States is "a chance to talk about race like adults" (Cooper, 2010, p. xii). This belief is at the core of the motivations for this particular research project. Participants' descriptions of "race matters," in terms of President Obama's presidency, and race relations in general, vary greatly. However, if taken as a collective representation of public perceptions, one conclusion is evident: The issue of race in the United States is negotiated differently and Barack Obama's election as the forty-fourth president is a testament to that reality. Within this consensus, the divergence of public perceptions lies within just how far the United States has progressed toward a "post-racial" society—a time when race no longer matters. While some participants in this study regard President Obama's election as an indication of a "post-racial" society, the majority understand it as reflecting progress to that goal, but not a sign that the United States actually has reached it. As one critic aptly put it: "Until we have a black president as inarticulate as President George W. Bush, racial progress has not really been achieved" (Gavrilos, 2010, p. 8).

Scholars have written critically on the idea promoted by the mass media that "The Age of Obama" signifies the emergence of a "post-racial" society (e.g., Joseph, 2010). Many agree that such an assessment is premature. In fact, Squires, Harris, and Moffitt (2010) make this statement explicit when they write: "events during and after the election demonstrate that declarations of a post-racial society were native and self-congratulatory" (p. xviii). One of the most powerful comments that I heard during all of the focus groups that I conducted is offered by an African American young woman attending a HBCU in Alabama. In her rejection that the United States has become a "post-racial" society, she explains how "*post-racial*" should not be the goal. Instead, the United States should strive to become a "*post-racist*" society instead. After some recent reading, I found that Dyson (2009) also makes this point when he distinguishes between a "post-racial" and "post-racist" outlook. Specifically, he explains how "a post-racial outlook seeks to delete crucial strands of our identity; a postracist outlook seeks to delete oppression that rests on hate and fear; and that exploits cultural and political vulnerability" (p. 4). As I teach others about issues of communication and diversity, this distinction will be invaluable in demonstrating some of the concerns with what seems to be an ideal to some.

Without question, Barack Obama represents a national symbol of racial progress. However, highlighting one person's achievement as "proof" that an entire race of people is no longer plagued by racial prejudice, discrimination, and racism is problematic (Gavrilos, 2010). Such conclusions fail to recognize the power that comes with systems of institutional and societal power. To paraphrase Gavrilos, one U.S. president of African American descent—out of forty-four—does not automatically erase all institutional barriers based on race. In fact, some might suggest that President Obama's election actually may work to promote new forms of racism (e.g., enlightened racism) that are grounded in the idea that African Americans are to blame for their own struggles since examples of African American professional success exist across public arenas (Jhally and Lewis, 1992).This type of conclusion is what makes claims that the United States has achieved a "post-racial" status so dangerous; they tend to create a climate that "blames the victim(s)."

Resisting "post-racial" messages as premature and overly optimistic should not negate the progress that has been made regarding race in the United States. The significance of President Obama's election is noteworthy for people of all ages and backgrounds. One middle-aged white man (an Independent voter) who participates in a focus group in Massachusetts describes this significance when he says:

> I'll go back to my daughter. The first president that she knows is Obama. She is not comparing him to anybody else. Other future presidents, for her, will be compared to Obama. So, I hope ... You know, big changes never really happen ... change occurs in these small, everyday steps. I hope that in 100 years this will be just one of those small, everyday steps that make us a better country.

These comments are offered within a recognition that the United States is moving in the right direction in terms of race, and that a "post-racial" society will occur with time. Other participants, however, are not as optimistic. One older white man (Tea Party member) from Nebraska is not as optimistic. Specifically, he states:

> The only way that we are going to get passed the racial stuff in our world is if we are invaded by aliens. And then it will no longer be "us" and "them." It will just be "us." In most people's minds, there has to be a "them." Somebody who is different.

This particular man fears that, as racial and ethnic diversity in the United States continues to increase, Whites will increasingly become more oppressed ("Are Whites Racially Oppressed," 2010). For many, President Obama reflects the reality that both men are likely correct. Sugrue (2010) argues that:

Obama represents the paradox of race in early twenty-first century America: he embodies the fluidity and opportunity of racial identity in a time of transition. He also captures the ambiguities of a racial order that denies racism yet is rife with racial inequality; that celebrates progress when celebration is not always warranted. (p. 136)

THE MEDIA MACHINE

"People tend to *underestimate* the influence of persuasive messages on themselves and *overestimate* the influence on others" (Kuehl, 2010, p. 176, italics in original). When it comes to media influences, this statement rings true as participants throughout the data collection process describe how the perceptions of friends, family members, and other acquaintances are impacted by various media sources. In many ways, their descriptions illustrate the inextricable relationship between media and perception: Media images influence personal perceptions *and* personal perceptions influence opinions on the media generally, and specific media outlets specifically.

Across different chapters, participants highlight the effective ways that Barack Obama benefits from intense mass media exposure, including a dominant presence within social media geared at young people, an important but seemingly unreliable voting bloc. President Obama's overexposure in the media triggers a designation as the very first "celebrity president" in the United States. Diverse participants perceptions on this status illustrate how the public generally perceives President Obama's media presence in similar ways (e.g., a sense of overexposure similar to other celebrities), yet view the reasons for, and effectiveness of, this heightened media presence in different ways. Recent publications by several communication scholars help to interpret these divergent opinions.

Barack Obama's distinction as the first "new media" candidate is well-documented (Cooper, 2010; Harfoush, 2009; Hendricks and Denton, 2010). In 2008, more information about candidates was more readily available through the media, digital technology, and the Internet than ever before. As such, technological advances allowed Barack Obama to send traditional messages to voters in new traditional ways that were more direct, cost efficient, and timely. According to Kenski et al. (2010), the presence of the Internet changed the nature of the election and promoted exposure to official and unofficial campaign messages to millions. By the end of the election, Democrats sent out more than one billion emails to supporters and had created over one million registrations for Obama's texting program (Vargas, 2008). These strategies created "a two-way interactive communication environment [where] supporters and volunteers felt empowered to strike out in new and creative fashions" (Cheney and Olsen, 2010, p. 51).

In a recent study, Dong, Day, and Deol (2010) analyze the messages that Obama's campaign sent via email, Twitter, and text. These were personally addressed to individuals, and contained a sense of "us," "you," and "we." Four principles explain the success of using social media: (1) New media use messages that are personal, interactive, instant, convenient, and resonated with the public; (2) Social networking is used to capture the hearts of young people; (3) Internet fundraising provides instant results, and (4) Taking advantage of new media forms reflects campaign best practices. Early activities of potential 2012 presidential candidates reveal that new media and social networking is going to play an increasingly significant role (Fouhy, 2011). Despite all of the advantages of new media technologies, they are not without some key disadvantages. As Kenski et al. (2010) aptly state, "Just as the digital world opened new ways in inform, engage, and mobilize, it expanded the opportunities to inflame and deceive" (p. 307). In this regard, social media—like the media overexposure of Barack Obama during and after his presidential campaign—is best understood as a double-edged sword, one that is full of ethical questions (Gordon, 2009; Shaer, 2009).

Barack Obama's designation as a "celebrity president," for some, equals or even overshadows the significance of the distinction of being the first U.S. president of African descent. His ability to reach diverse segments within and beyond the United States creates a sense of familiarity and connection for many individuals unlike any other previous president. Associations with, and endorsements from, celebrities cement his status as a major player in political and social worlds (see Kuehl, 2010; Pease and Brewer, 2008). Like that which exists with other celebrities, individual connections with President Obama are like interpersonal relationships despite the fact that they are based solely on mass-mediated exposure (Gregg, 2005). The public's enticement with him is based on an attraction that is part intellectual, part social, and part physical (see, for example, Forrest and Foster, 2006; Logan, 2010).

The double-edged nature of the media can be seen within Barack Obama's celebrity status. Since he reached celebrity status, he is treated more like a tabloid celebrity and not a U.S. president (Kuehl, 2010). For some, this weakens his credibility as an expert, political, and government official and leads to questions regarding his ability to lead (Corsi, 2008; Freddoso, 2008). Critics are quick to point out that, like with many celebrities, the public's obsession with President Obama is based on a media-inspired collective movement with little critical thought (Spicer, 2010). As seen within participant comments, certain media outlets (e.g., FOX News) are quick to use his celebrity status and other points of criticism to fuel anti-Obama sentiment.

Recent research by Tesler and Sears (2010) provides strong evidence that FOX News watchers are more likely than others who watch other news programs to believe accusations like that President Obama was not born in the United States. Of course, given my comments earlier, it still remains unclear if this specific media source is influencing public perceptions or if viewers seek out news programming that reinforces pre-existing opinions. One thing remains clear, however, people's perceptions are largely informed by what they want or expect to see. This statement best reflects the most effective means to understand the diverse public perceptions gathered in this study. During one California focus group, a traditionally aged Middle Eastern American male college student reflects on the diversity among participants. His explanation uses an effective analogy to explain how individual perceptions are influenced by larger societal messages:

> It's like that whole experiment when you put a baby boy and sit him in front of the room . . . They did that in my psychology class. And the teacher had us analyze what we saw and people were like, "Yeah, the boy is more aggressive, he's crawling, he's doing stuff, he's more active." And, at the end, we found out that it was really a girl dressed in more masculine colors. So, it is just that . . . it's the same experiment. People see what they want to see. It also shows the power of identity—race, gender, age, etc.—and how that all affects how we see and interpret things.

Existing research in the field of communication (e.g., Allen, 1998; Orbe and Camara, 2010; Warren, Orbe, and Greer-Williams, 2003) has explored how perceptions are informed by issues of race and gender. My research on public perceptions of President Obama described within this book extends this existing research by illustrating how race and gender intersect with other aspects of identity—including age, educational status, political affiliation, and geographical location—something that resists in attempts to understand a diverse world in overly simplistic ways (Crenshaw, 1991).

CONCLUDING THOUGHTS

As stated in chapter 1, this book is about public perceptions of Barack Obama's communication generally, and his presence as the first U.S. president of African descent who is also deemed as the first "celebrity president." The insights featured through the book hold great potential in helping readers recognize the diversity of perception that exists between and within various social and cultural groups in the United States. As such, I hope that it assists in promoting an understanding that resists simple distinctions based on mass generalizations that seem to dominate most media coverage. In this regard, I trust that it complements other research that does not solely rely on statistical data to understand public perceptions of President Obama (e.g., Logan, 2010; Yoo, Zimmerman, and Present, 2010).My ultimate desire is that this book will be read by an audience as diverse as the participants that contributed to it. As such, an increased understanding of the great diversity of public perceptions—both between and within different cultural groups—can enhance intergroup relations, political persuasion efforts, and traditionally bipartisan political divisions.

Despite the strengths of the research described in this book, my findings should be understood within several inherent limitations. First, the insights featured in my analysis should be appreciated for their descriptive power, not as conclusions that should be generalized to the entire U.S. population. Second, while the participant pool included significant diversity in terms of age, sex, race and ethnicity, socioeconomic status, education, political affiliation, and geographical region, findings could have been enhanced by data that was collected from more participants from diverse backgrounds and a larger number of states. Third, and finally, the findings summarized in this book reflect structural themes created through one specific interpretive lens. This is to say that, while I worked diligently to embrace the qualitative methodological principles described in chapter 2 that foster a rigorous methodological design, another researcher with different personal, cultural, and political orientation may have generated different insights. In explicitly unconscious ways, I have worked to produce thematic insights that reflect the diversity of public perceptions gathered in the last six months of 2010. My hope is that this research will be read within the context of other existing studies of Barack Obama and contribute to a more in-depth understanding of perceptions of his communication style, the role of various mass media outlets, as well as identity politics in the United States on a larger level.

Without question, this final chapter has been the most difficult to write and seemingly impossible to complete since public perceptions of President Obama are shifting as his presidential term continues. In fact, I fought the temptation to conduct additional focus groups at key points during the analysis and writing process which lasted from January to May, 2011 including President Obama's funeral address following the Arizona shooting that killed several and wounded Rep. Gabrielle Giffords, bipartisan compromise on the budget to avoid a governmental shut-down, the official announcement of his re-election campaign, and the death of Osama bin Laden. To paraphrase several focus group participants, "Only time will tell how President Obama will be ultimately perceived by the public." Currently, numerous unanswered questions remain, in all likelihood too many to list here. As I conclude, I offer several questions that are prompted by the findings of my recent study:

- What impact will President Obama's biracial heritage have on how the millions of bi- and multiracial U.S. Americans self-identify, or are identified by others? Will his presence work to increase multiracial identities that resist the "one-drop rule" (Frazier, 2002; Lewis, 2006; Walker, 2001)?
- How will President Obama's communication style be evaluated by the public? Will public perceptions continue in their diversity, or will time and distance create any consensus?
- Will President Obama's more androgynous communication style contribute to new understandings of "presidential communication," or will it be rendered ineffective like past presidents (Kimble, 2009)?
- What impact will specific events, like President Obama's decisive leadership in the death of Osama bin Laden (Baldor, 2011), have on public perceptions (Balz, 2011)?
- How will future elections at the national, state, and local levels maximize the use of advanced new media technologies while minimizing negative effects (Harfoush, 2009; Hendricks and Denton, 2010)?
- Will reaching a "celebrity status"—like Sarah Palin, Mike Huckabee, and Donald Trump have reportedly attempted (Douthat, 2009; Peters and Stelter, 2011)—become the norm for future successful presidential candidates?
- Given the historic nature of the 2008 election (Remnick, 2010), will Barack Obama's election serve as a bridge for other presidential candidates who are not white or male? Or will his election be an exception to the long-standing presidential norm?
- How will American politics be impacted by the existence of intensified bipartisanship and an increasingly resistance by increasing numbers of voters to identify with one political party (Goldberg, 2010)?
- What role will race and other forms of portrayals that define President Obama as an "Other," play in the 2012 election? How will these issues impact his communication, and equally as important, public perceptions of his communication (Orbe and Urban, 2011)?

Recent news articles have indicated that issues of difference will not impact the election in significant ways, especially since accusations regarding his religious faith, allegiance to the United States and birth certificate have dissipated (Horowitz, 2011; Wax, 2011). Additionally, some recent research (e.g., Hajnal, 2007) reports that the general public, especially white voters, appear less interested in the race of elected African American officials and more focused on their political track records. Yet, others (e.g., Joseph, 2010) remain skeptical and insist that Barack Obama's presidency be understood in a contemporary reality where race still matters. With an eye on these conclusions, but staying true to the scholarly principles that serve as the core of this book project, I am more interested in what everyday people across the United States have to say about the subject. These diverse perceptions work to create multiple communication realities that ultimately will provide the most powerful responses to the larger question: What effect will Obama's rise to power have upon the United States, upon history, and upon the world (Cooper, 2010)?

Appendix A

Appendix A: Self-Reported Participant Demographic Data

	New England (CT, MA, RI)	East North Central (MI, OH, IL, IN)	South Atlantic (VA, NC)	West North Central (NE)	Pacific (CA)	East South Central (AL)	Totals/ (Percentages)
Age:							
>20	6	8	0	2	2	2	20 (6%)
20–30	30	73	18	6	24	39	190 (57%)
31–40	5	34	6	1	10	4	60 (18%)
41–50	8	16	0	3	10	2	39 (11.7%)
51–60	7	6	5	1	3	4	26 (7.8%)
61–70	2	3	11	0	2	0	18 (5.4%)
71–80	2	0	0	0	0	0	2 (.6%)
Gender:							
Female	39	69	20	7	23	36	194 (58.2%)
Male	21	49	20	6	28	15	139 (41.7%)
Race/ Ethnicity:							
African Amer.	13	24	6	1	12	33	89 (26.7%)
Asian Amer.	2	2	3	2	2	0	11 (3.3%)
Euro Amer.	29	75	29	10	10	14	167 (50.1%)
Latino/a	7	9	0	0	18	3	37 (11.1%)
Middle East.	0	2	1	0	6	0	9 (2.7%)
Native Amer.	1	3	0	0	0	0	4 (1.2%)
Bi/Multiracial	7	2	0	0	3	1	13 (3.9%)
Unreported	1	0	1	0	0	0	2 (.6%)

(Continued)

Appendix A: Self-Reported Participant Demographic Data *(Continued)*

	New England (CT, MA, RI)	East North Central (MI, OH, IL, IN)	South Atlantic (VA, NC)	West North Central (NE)	Pacific (CA)	East South Central (AL)	Totals/ (Percentages)
Education:							
>12th Grade	3	0	0	0	0	0	3 (.9%)
H.S. Graduate	12	14	2	2	18	2	50 (15%)
Some College	26	102	21	7	21	40	217 (65.1%)
B.A./B.S.	11	0	8	1	7	7	34 (10.2%)
Post-Grad	8	2	9	3	5	2	29 (8.7%)
SES/Class:							
Lower	15	13	6	2	8	8	52 (15.6%)
Working	5	6	5	1	14	4	35 (10.5%)
Lower/Mid	10	4	4	0	0	0	18 (5.4%)
Middle	20	73	17	8	18	29	165 (49.5%)
Upper/Mid	6	18	1	2	2	7	36 (10.8%)
Upper	0	4	0	0	6	0	10 (3%)
Unreported	4	0	7	0	3	3	17 (5.1%)
Political Affil.							
Democrat	32	42	15	3	17	22	131 (39%)
Republican	7	25	9	5	5	8	59 (17.7%)
Independent	15	11	5	2	12	7	52 (15.6%)
Libertarian	0	1	0	1	0	3	5 (1.5%)
Tea Party	1	0	2	2	5	0	10 (3%)
Green Party	0	1	1	0	0	0	2 (.6%)
Unaffiliated	5	28	5	0	4	10	52 (15.6%)
Unreported	0	9	3	0	9	1	22 (6.6%)
Total	60	118	40	13	51	51	333

Appendix B

FOCUS GROUP TOPICAL PROTOCOL

Topical Protocol
1. Perceptions of President Obama's communication (effectiveness and appropriateness)
2. Perceptions of how President Obama communicates about race
3. Changes in perceptions over time

Opening Questions
1. Can you describe your perceptions of President Obama as a communicator?
2. How would you evaluate how President Obama has dealt with race issues?
3. Have your perceptions of the President changed over time? If so, how?

Hypothetical Questions
1. Can you describe the first time that you were introduced to Barack Obama? What were your first impressions of his communication? Have your perceptions of him changed over time?
2. In general, would you describe President Obama as an effective or ineffective communicator? Can you provide a specific example of when he was effective and/or ineffective?

3. In general, would you say that President Obama is an appropriate or inappropriate communicator? Can you provide a specific example of when he was appropriate and/or inappropriate?
4. Would you rate President Obama's effectiveness as a communicator differently in different context (e.g., giving speeches, interacting with the media, meeting with citizens, etc.)?
5. When it comes to issues related to race, how would you describe President Obama's communication?
6. What role do you think that race played in the 2008 Presidential election? Can you provide specific examples?
7. Do you think that the general public sees President Obama as an African American U.S. president, or a U.S. president that happens to be African American?
8. Have your perceptions of President Obama changed over time? If so, can you describe how and why?
9. If I were to ask these questions to other people that you know, what would they say? Would their responses be similar or different than your own?

References

ABC apologizes for tweet of Obama calling Kanye a "jackass." (2009, September 15). *Seattle Post-Intelligencer.* Retrieved on April 12, 2011 from docs.newsbank.com.ezaccess.libraries.psu.edu/s/InfoWeb/aggdocs/AWNB/12AC1262DFB49F78/OEB90CA9CF65E92A?s_lang.

Allen, B. J. (1996). Feminist standpoint theory: A black woman's re(view) of organizational socialization. *Communication Studies, 47*(4), 257–271.

Allen, B. J. (1998). Black womanhood and feminist standpoints. *Management Communication Quarterly, 11*, 575–586.

Anderson, K., and Jack, D. C. (1991). Learning to listen: Interview techniques and analysis. In S. B. Gluck and D. Patai (Eds.), *Women's words: The feminist practice of oral history* (pp. 11–27). Boston: Routledge Kegan Paul.

Are whites racially oppressed? (2010). Retrieved on March 7, 2011 from www.cnn.com/2010/US/12/21/white.persecution/index.html?hpt=C1.

Aronson, J., and McGlone, M. S. (2009). Stereotypes and social identity. In T. Nelson (Ed.), *Handbook of stereotyping, prejudice, and discrimination* (pp. 153–177). New York: Psychology Press.

Ashe, B. D. (2010). Post-soul president: *Dreams from my father* and the post-soul aesthetic. In H. Harris, K. Moffitt, and C. Squires (Eds.), *The Obama effect: Multidisciplinary renderings of the 2008 campaign* (pp. 103–115). Albany: SUNY Press.

Asim, J. (2009). *What Obama means ... for our culture, our politics, our future.* New York: William Morrow.

Baldor, L. C. (2011, May 8). "No guarantees" as Obama risked much for mission. *Kalamazoo (MI) Gazette*, p. A17.

Balz, D. (2011, April 5). Can Obama recapture magic of 2008?: President hopes to breathe life back into his army of volunteers. *The Washington Post*, p. A6.

Carter, R. (2008, September 1). The macho factor. *Orlando Sentinel*, p. A18.

Cheney, M., and Olsen, C. (2010). Media politics 2.0: An Obama effect. In H. Harris, K. Moffitt, and C. Squires (Eds.), *The Obama effect: Multidisciplinary renderings of the 2008 campaign* (pp. 49–64). Albany: SUNY Press.

Cho, S. (2009). Post-racialism. *Iowa Law Review, 94*(5), 1595–1599.

Connaughton, S. L. (2004). Multiple identification targets in examining partisan identification: A case study of Texas Latinos. *Howard Journal of Communications, 15*(3), 131–145.

Connell, R. W. (2005). *Masculinities* (2nd ed.). Cambridge, MA: Polity Press.

Cook, W. L., and Douglas, E. M. (1998). The looking glass self in family context: A social relations analysis. *Journal of Family Psychology, 12*(3), 299–309.

Cooper, D. (2010). Preface. In H. Harris, K. Moffitt, and C. Squires (Eds.), *The Obama effect: Multidisciplinary renderings of the 2008 campaign* (pp. xi-xiv). Albany: SUNY Press.

Cooper, F. (2010a). *Masculinities, post-racialism, and the Gates controversy: The false equivalence between officer and civilian.* Suffolk University Law School Faculty Publications. Paper 60. Retrieved on January 26, 2011 from lsr.nellco.org/suffolk_fp/69.

Cooper, F. (2010b). Our first unisex president?: Obama, critical race theory, and masculinities studies. In H. Harris, K. Moffitt, and C. Squires (Eds.), *The Obama effect: Multidisciplinary renderings of the 2008 campaign* (pp. 153–174). Albany: SUNY Press.

Cooper, F. (2006). Race, sex, and working identities: Against bipolar black masculinity: Intersectionality, assimilation, identity performance, and hierarchy. *U.C. David Law Review, 39*, 853–904.

Cooper, H. (2009, July 23). Obama criticizes arrest of a Harvard professor. *New York Times*, p. A20.

Cooper, H., and Goodnough, A. (2009). In a reunion over beers, no apologies, but cordial plans to have lunch sometime. *New York Times*, p. A10.

Corsi, J. R. (2008). *The Obama nation: Leftist politics and at the cult of personality.* New York: Threshold Editions.

Crenshaw, K. (1991). Mapping the margins: Intersectionality, identity politics, and violence against women of color. *Stanford Law Review, 43*, p. 1241.

Cushman, E. (2005). Face, skins, and the identity politics of rereading race. *Rhetoric Review, 24*(4), 389–395.

Darsey, J. (2009). Barack Obama and America's journey. *Southern Communication Journal, 74*(1), 88–103.

Dong, Q., Day, K. D., and Deol, R. (2010). The resonant message and the powerful new media: An analysis of the Obama presidential campaign. In H. Harris, K. Moffitt, and C. Squires (Eds.), *The Obama effect: Multidisciplinary renderings of the 2008 campaign* (pp. 75–88). Albany: SUNY Press.

Douthat, R. (2009, November 23). They chose celebrity. *The New York Times*, p. A27.

Durgee, J. F. (1987). Point of view: Using creative writing techniques in focus groups. *Journal of Advertising Research, 26*(6), 57–65.

Dyson, M. E. (2009). *Can you hear me now?: The inspiration, wisdom, and insight of Michael Eric Dyson.* New York: Basic Books.

Evans, B. (2010, July 25). Racial sensitivity takes a new twist: Teachable moments turns President Obama into the student. *Kalamazoo (MI) Gazette*, p. A23.

Fiske, S. T., Bergsieker, A. M. R., and Williams, K. (2009). Images of Black Americans. *Du Bois Review: Social Science Research on Race, 6*, 83–101.

Flores, L. A., Moon, D., G., and Nakayama, T. K. (2006). Dynamic rhetoric's of race: California's racial privacy initiative and the shifting grounds of racial politics. *Communication and Critical/Cultural Studies, 3*(3), 181–201.

Forrest, K., and Foster, B. L. (2006). 25 beautiful people: Barack Obama. *Washingtonian Magazine*, March 1. Accessed April 5, 2010 from www.washingtonian.com/ articles/ people/2295.html.

Fouhy, B. (2011, April 24). Tweet, "friend" and "Tube" way to the White House. *Kalamazoo (MI) Gazette*, p. A18.

Fram, A. (2010, November 28). Tea party is more like "Me, the people." *Kalamazoo (MI) Gazettte*, p. A18.

Frank, D. A. (2009). The prophetic voice and the face of the other in Barack Obama's "A More Perfect Union" address. *Rhetoric and Public Affairs, 12*(2), 167–194.

Frank, D. A., and McPhail, M. L. (2005). Barack Obama's address to the 2004 Democratic National Convention: Trauma, compromise, consilience, and the (im)possibility of racial reconciliation. *Rhetoric and Public Affairs, 8*(4), 571–594.

Frankenberg, R. (1993). *White women race matters: The social construction of whiteness.* Minneapolis: The University of Minnesota Press.

Frazier, S. (2002). *All that apply: Finding wholeness as a multiracial person.* Downers Grove, IL: InterVarsity Press.

Freddoso, D. (2008). *The case against Barack Obama: The unlikely rise and unexamined agenda of the media's favorite candidate.* Washington, DC: Regnery Publishing.

Gavrilos, D. (2010). White males lose presidency for first time: Exposing the power of whiteness through Obama's victory. In H. Harris, K. Moffitt, and C. Squires (Eds.), *The Obama effect: Multidisciplinary renderings of the 2008 campaign* (pp. 3–15). Albany: SUNY Press.

Goldberg, J. (2010, December 7). Politics without labels?: What a silly concept? *USA Today*, p. 9A.

Gordon, R. (2009). Social media: The ground shifts. *Nieman Reports, 63*(3), 7–9.

Gregg, P. (2005). *Parasocial relationships' similarity to interpersonal relationships: Factor analyses of the dimensions of parasocial interaction.* Minneapolis: University of Minnesota Press.

Guy, K. (2010, March 12). Don't blame racism for Obama's ratings. *Sun Sentinel* (Ft. Lauderdale, FL), p. 21A.

Hajnal, Z. L. (2007). *Changing white attitudes toward black political leadership.* Cambridge: Cambridge University Press.

Hall, M. (2010, July 30). Obama urges a dialogue on race after Sherrod case. *USA Today*, p. 2A.

Hall, S. P., and Carter, R. T. (2006). The relationship between racial identity, ethnic identity, and perceptions of racial discrimination in an Afro-Caribbean descent sample. *Journal of Black Psychology, 32*(2), 155–175.

Harfoush, R. (2009). *Yes we did! An inside look at how social media built the Obama brand.* Berkeley, CA: New Riders.

Harris, H. E. (2010). The webbed message: Re-visioning the American Dream. In H. Harris, K. Moffitt, and C. Squires (Eds.), *The Obama effect: Multidisciplinary renderings of the 2008 campaign* (pp. 65–74). Albany: SUNY Press.

Harris, H. E., Moffitt, K. R., and Squires, C. R. (Eds.) (2010). *The Obama effect: Multidisciplinary renderings of the 2008 campaign.* Albany: SUNY Press.

Hendricks, J. A., and Denton, R. E. (2010). *Communicator-in-chief: How Barack Obama used new media technology to win the White House.* New York: Rowan and Littlefield.

Hertzberg, H. (2009). *Obamanos: The birth of a new political era.* New York: Penguin Press.

Hillary Clinton's February 19 speech. (2008). *The New York Times.* Retrieved April 10, 2011 from www.nytimes.com/2008/02/19/us/politics/19text-clinton.html.

Hollander, B. A., (2010). Persistence in the perception of Barack Obama as a Muslim in the 2008 presidential campaign. *Journal of Media and Religion, 9*(2), 55–66.

Horowitz, J. (2011, May 8). More steer clear of birther ideas. *Kalamazoo (MI) Gazette,* p. A20.

Horton, D., and Wohl, R. R. (1956). Mass communication and para-social interaction: Observations on intimacy at a distance. *Psychiatry, 19,* 215–229.

House, A., Dallinger, J. M., and Kilgallen, D.-L. (1998). Androgyny and rhetorical sensitivity: The connection of gender and communication style. *Communication Reports, 11*(1), 11–20.

Hunt, R. G. (1970). *Strategic selection: A purposive sampling design for small numbers research, program evaluation, and management.* Buffalo: State University of New York Press.

Hurst, S. R. (2010, January 15). Post-racial America? Not yet. *Kalamazoo (MI) Gazette,* p. A8.

"I could have calibrated those words differently." (2009, July 25). *New York Times,* p. A15.I.

Ifill, G. (2009). *The breakthrough: Politics and race in the age of Obama.* New York: Doubleday.

Isaksen, J. (2011). Obama's rhetorical shift: Insights for communication studies. *Communication Studies, 62*(4), 456–471.

Italie, H. (2010, January 27, 2010). Critics assess Obama's speech-making. *Kalamazoo (MI) Gazette,* p. 7.

Jackson, D. (2010, August 14). Obama's comments on mosque near Ground Zero draw strong reactions. *USA TODAY,* p. A2.

Jackson, J. L. (2009). Media reform, 2008's presidential election, and the sportification of politics. *International Journal of Communication, 3*(1), 42–46.

Jhally, S., and Lewis, J. (1992). *Enlightened racism: The Cosby Show, racism, and the myth of the American Dream.* Boulder, CO: Westview Press.

Jones, S. (2010). The Obama effect on American discourse about racial identity: Dreams from my father (and mother), Barack Obama's search for self. In H. Harris,

K. Moffitt, and C. Squires (Eds.), *The Obama effect: Multidisciplinary renderings of the 2008 campaign* (pp. 131–152). Albany: SUNY Press.

Joseph, P. E. (2010). *Dark days, bright nights: From black power to Barack Obama.* New York: Basic Books.

Joseph, R (2011). The conundrum of the Obama bumper sticker: Reading overtly and inferentially racist images of Barack Obama. *Communication Studies, 62*(4), 389–405.

Kalkan, K. O., Layman, G. C., and Uslaner, E. M. (2009). Bands of others?: Attitudes toward Muslims in contemporary American society. *Journal of Politics, 71*(3), 847–862.

Katz, J. (2006). *The macho paradox: How some men hurt women and how all men can help.* Naperville, IL: Sourcebooks.

Kenski, K., Hardy, B., and Jamieson, K. H. (2010). *The Obama victory: How media, money, and message shaped the 2008 elections.* New York: Oxford University Press.

Kimble, J. J. (2009). John F. Kennedy, the construction of peace, and the pitfalls of androgynous rhetoric. *Communication Quarterly, 57*(2), 154–170.

Kinder, D. R., and McConnaughy, M. C. (2006). Military triumph, racial transcendence, and Colin Powell. *Public Opinion Quarterly, 79*(2), 139–165.

Kohut, A. (2008, November 13). *High marks for campaign, a high bar for Obama.* Pew Research Center for the People and the Press. Washington, DC: Pew Research Center.

Krueger, R. A., and Casey, M. A. (2000). *Focus groups: A practical guide for applied research.* Thousand Oaks, CA: Sage.

Kuehl, R. A. (2010). Oprah and Obama: Theorizing celebrity endorsement. In H. Harris, K. Moffitt, and C. Squires (Eds.), *The Obama effect: Multidisciplinary renderings of the 2008 campaign* (pp. 175–189). Albany: SUNY Press.

Laney, M. (2010, August 17). Calling Obama the Antichrist is misguided and harmful. *Kalamazoo (MI) Gazette,* p. A9.

Leanne, S. (2009). *Say it like Obama: The power of speaking with purpose and vision.* New York: McGraw-Hill.

Lee, R., and Morin, A. (2009). Using the 2008 presidential election to think about "playing the race card." *Communication Studies, 60*(4), 376–391.

Lewis, E. (2006). *Fade: My journeys in multiracial America.* New York: Carroll and Graf Publishers.

Logan, E. L. (2010). The feminist (?) hero versus the black messiah: Contesting gender and race in the 2008 democratic primary. In H. Harris, K. Moffitt, and C. Squires (Eds.), *The Obama effect: Multidisciplinary renderings of the 2008 campaign* (pp. 250–265). Albany: SUNY Press.

MacGillis, A. (2009, April 29). Communicator in chief has a tone for every situation. *The Washington Post.* Retrieved on January 24, 2011 from www.washingtonpost.com/wp-dyn/content/article/2009/04/28/AR2009042893535.html.

Maira, S. (2009). Obama as enigma: A "new" regime for Muslim and Arab Americans? In L. Burnham (Ed.), *Changing the race: Racial politics and the election of Barack Obama* (pp. 40–44). Washington, DC: Applied Research Center.

Mattera, J. (2010). *Obama zombies: How the liberal machine brainwashed my generation.* New York: Threshold Editors.

McCracken, G. (1988). *The long interview.* Newbury Park, CA: Sage.

Mitchell, K. S., Kuftines, S. A., and Brod, H. (2009). Introduction: How does citizenship mean. *Text Performance Quarterly,* 29, 201–204.

Mitchell, W.J.T. (2009). Obama as icon. *Journal of Visual Culture,* 8, p. 125.

Moffitt, K. R. (2010). Framing a first lady: Media coverage of Michelle Obama's role in the 2008 presidential election. In H. Harris, K. Moffitt, and C. Squires (Eds.), *The Obama effect: Multidisciplinary renderings of the 2008 campaign* (pp. 233–249). Albany: SUNY Press.

Moon, D. G. (1999). White enculturation and bourgeois ideology. In T. K. Nakayama and J. N. Martin (Eds.), *Whiteness: The communication of social identity* (pp. 177–197). Thousand Oaks, CA: Sage.

Morgan, D. L. (1997). *Focus groups as qualitative research.* Thousand Oaks, CA: Sage.

Moskowitz, D., and Stoh, P. (1994). Psychological sources of electoral racism. *Political Psychology,* 15(2), 307–329.

Ng, K. (2010a). Beyond the candidate: Obama, YouTube, and (my)Asian-ness. In H. E. Harris, K. R. Moffitt, and C. R. Squires (Eds.) *The Obama effect: Multidisciplinary renderings of the 2008 campaign* (pp. 75–88). Albany: SUNY Press.

Ng, K. (2010b). Epilogue. In H. Harris, K. Moffitt, and C. Squires (Eds.), *The Obama effect: Multidisciplinary renderings of the 2008 campaign* (pp. 266–269). Albany: SUNY Press.

Nimmo, D., and Saunders, K. R. (Eds.) (1981). *Handbook of political communication.* Beverly Hills, CA: Sage.

Obama, B. (2006). *The audacity of hope: Thoughts on reclaiming the American dream.* New York: Crown Publishers.

Obama: Kanye is a "jackass." (n.d.). Retrieved on February 25, 2011 from www.huffingtonpost.com/2009/09/14/obama-kanye-west-is-a-jackass_n_286623.html.

Obama plan: "Pitiful" or "compelling?" (2011, April 15). *USA Today,* p. A16.

Obama urges politicians to adopt 'spirit of common cause.' (2011, January 16). *Kalamazoo (MI) Gazette,* p. A15.

Orbe, M. (2000). Centralizing diverse racial/ethnic voices in scholarly research: The value of phenomenological inquiry. *International Journal of Intercultural Relations,* 24, 603–621.

Orbe, M., and Camara, S. K. (2010). Defining discrimination across cultural groups: Exploring [un-]coordinated management of meaning. *International Journal of Intercultural Relations,* 34, 283–293.

Orbe, M., and Harris, T. M. (2008). *Interracial communication: Theory into practice.* Thousand Oaks, CA: Sage.

Orbe, M., and Urban, E. (2011). "Race matters" in the Obama era. *Communication Studies,* 62(4), 349–352.

Our news: What matters in the community. (2010, August). Gangsta prez? *Essence,* p. 97.

Overberg, P. (2010, November 4). 2010 Republican gains by region. *USA Today,* p. 10A.

Owens, W. (1984). Interpretive themes in relational communication. *Quarterly Journal of Speech*, 70, 274–287.

Parker, K. (2010, June 30). Obama: Our first female President. *The Washington Post*, p. A17.

Pasek, J., Tahk, A., Lelkes, Y., Krosnick, J. A., Payne, B. K., Akhtar, O., and Tompson, T. (2009). Determinants of turnout and candidate choice in the 2008 U.S. presidential election: Illuminating the impact of racial prejudice and other considerations. *Public Opinion Quarterly*, 73(5), 943–994.

Patterson, R. E. (2011). The "Beer Summit" and what's brewing: Narratives, networks, and metaphors as rhetorical confinement in the age of Obama. *Communication Studies*, 62(4), 439–455.

Patton, M. Q. (2002). *Qualitative evaluation methods*. London: Sage.

Pearson, J., and Davilla, R. (2001). The gender construct: Understanding why men and women communicate differently. In L. P. Arliss and D. J. Borisoff (Eds.), *Women and men communicating: Challenges and changes* (pp. 3–14). Prospect Heights, IL: Waveland Press.

Pease, A., and Brewer, P. R. (2008). The Oprah factor: The effects of a celebrity endorsement in a presidential primary campaign. *Harvard International Journal of Press Politics, 13*(4), 386–400.

Peters, J. W., and Stelter, B. (2011, April 3). Trump for President in 2012? Maybe. Trump for Trump? Without question. *The New York Times*, p. A16.

Pew Research Center (n.d). *Growing number of Americans say Obama is a Muslim*. Retrieved on March 31, 2011 from pewforum.org/Politics-and-Elections/Growing-Number-of-Americans-Say-Obama-is-a-Muslim.aspx.

Philpot, T. S., Shaw, D. R., and McGowen, E. B. (2009). Winning the race: Black voter turnout in the 2008 presidential election. *Public Opinion Quarterly*, 73(5), 995–1022.

Plouffe, D. (2009). *The audacity to win: The inside story and lessons of Barack Obama's historic victory*. New York: Viking.

Pollock, M. (2004). *Colormute: Race talk dilemmas in an American school*. Princeton, NJ: Princeton University Press.

Puchta, C., and Potter, J. (2004). *Focus group practice*. Thousand Oaks, CA: Sage.

Radhakrishnan, R. (2009). Recognizing Obama: Image and beyond? *Journal of Visual Culture*, 8(2), 150–154.

Remnick, D. (2010). *The bridge: The life and rise of Barack Obama*. New York: Alfred A. Knopf.

Robbins, L. (2009, July 24). Officer defends arrest of Harvard professor. *New York Times*, A19.

Robinson, E. (2010, January 15). Reid spoke the truth, even if it was crudely put. *Kalamazoo (MI) Gazette*, p. A17.

Rowe, A. C. (2010). For the love of Obama: Race, nation, and the politics of relation. In H. Harris, K. Moffitt, and C. Squires (Eds.), *The Obama effect: Multidisciplinary renderings of the 2008 campaign* (pp. 221–232). Albany: SUNY Press.

Rowland, R. C., and Jones, J. M. (2007). Recasting the American dream and American politics: Barack Obama's keynote address to the 2004 Democratic National Convention. *Quarterly Journal of Speech*, 93(4), 425–448.

Rush, E. (2010). *Ne*gro*phi*li*a: From slave black to pedestal, America's racial obsession*. New York: WND Books.

Sack, K., and Elder, J. (2000, July 14). Poll finds optimistic outlook but enduring racial division. *The New York Times*, p. A1.

Sargent, G. (2010, June 8). Obama's ass-kicking, in context. *The Washington Post*. Retrieved May 5, 2011 from voices.washingtonpost.com/plum-line/2010/06/obamas_ass-kicking_in_context.html.

Seelye, K. Q. (2009, July 23). Obama wades into a volatile racial issue. *The New York Times*. Retrieved May 5, 2011 from www.nytimes.com/2009/07/23/US/23race.html.

Shaer, M. (2009, September 16). Moral of Obama, Kanye incident? Nothing is off the record anymore. *The Christian Science Monitor*. Retrieved March 4, 2011 from www.csmonitor.com/Innovation/Horizons/2009/0916/moral-of-Obama-kanye-incident-nothing-is-off-the-record-anymore.

Sidoti, L. (2011, January 16). Things looking up?: Voters are, a little. *Kalamazoo (MI) Gazette*, p. A16.

Smith, Z. (2009). Speaking in tongues. *New York Review of Books*, 56, p. 24.

Spicer, R. (2010). The Obama mass: Barack Obama, image, and fear of the crowd. In H. Harris, K. Moffitt, and C. Squires (Eds.), *The Obama effect: Multidisciplinary renderings of the 2008 campaign* (pp. 190–208). Albany: SUNY Press.

Spitzberg, B., and Cupach, W. (1989). *Handbook of interpersonal competence*. New York: Springer-Vulga.

Squires, C., Harris, H., and Moffitt, K. (2010). Introduction. In H. Harris, K. Moffitt, and C. Squires (Eds.), *The Obama effect: Multidisciplinary renderings of the 2008 campaign* (pp. xvii-xx). Albany: SUNY Press.

Staley, C. C. (1990). Focus group research: The communication practitioner as marketing specialist. In D. O'Hair and G. Kreps (Eds.), *Applied communication theory and research* (pp. 185–202). Hillsdale, NJ: LEA.

Steele, S. (2008). *A bound man: Why we are excited about Obama and why he can't win*. New York: Free Press.

Steele, C. M., and Aronson, J. (1995). Stereotype threat and the intellectual test performance of African Americans. *Journal of Personality and Social Psychology*, 69, 797–811.

Stolberg, S. G., and Connelly, M. (2009, April 28). Obama is nudging views on race, a survey finds. *The New York Times*, p. A1.

Sue, D. W. (2004). Whiteness and ethnocentric monoculturalism: Making the "invisible" visible. *American Psychologist*, 59, 761–769.

Sugrue, T. J. (2010). *Not even past: Barack Obama and the burden of race*. Princeton, NJ: Princeton University Press.

Sweet, D., and McCue-Enser, M. (2010). Constituting "the people" as rhetorical interruption: Barack Obama and the unfinished hopes of an imperfect people. *Communication Studies*, 61(5), 602–622.

Terrill, R. E. (2009). Unity and duality in Barack Obama's "A More Perfect Union." *Quarterly Journal of Speech*, 95(4), 363–386.

Tesler, M., and Sears, D. O. (2010). *Obama's race: The 2008 election and the dream of a post-racial America*. Chicago: University of Chicago Press.

Todd, C., and Gawiser, S. (2009). *How Barack Obama won: A state-by-state guide to the historic 2008 Presidential election*. New York: Vintage Books.

Urban, E., and Orbe, M. (2010). Identity gaps of contemporary U.S. immigrants: Acknowledging divergent communicative experiences. *Communication Studies*, 61(3), 304–320.

van Manen, M. (1990). *Researching lived experience: Human science for an actional sensitive pedagogy*. London, Ontario: State University of New York Press.

Van Natta, D., and Goodnough, A. (2009, July 27). After call to police, 2 Cambridge worlds collide in an unlikely meeting. *New York Times*, p. A13.

Vargas, J. A. (2008). Obama raised half a billion online. *Washington Post*. washingtonpost.com/44/2008/11/20/obama_raised_half_a_billion_on.html.

Vaughn, S., Schumm, J. S., and Sinagub, J. (1996). *Focus group interviews in education and psychology*. Thousand Oaks, CA: Sage.

Vorauer, J. D. (2005). Micommunications surrounding efforts to reach out across group boundaries. *Personality and Social Psychology Bulletin*, 31, 1653–1664.

Vorauer, J. D., Hunter, A. J., Main, K. J., and Roy, S. A. (2000). Meta-stereotype activation: Evidence from indirect measures for specific evaluative concerns experiences by members of dominant groups in intergroup interaction. *Journal of Personality and Social Psychology*, 78, 690–707.

Walker, R. (2001). *Black, white, and Jewish: Autobiography of a shifting self*. New York: Riverhead Books.

Warren, J. W. (2000). Masters in the field: White talk, white privilege, white biases. In F. D. Twine and J. W. Warren (Eds.), *Racing research, researching race* (pp. 135–164). New York: New York University Press.

Warren, K. T., Orbe, M., and Greer-Williams, N. (2003). Perceiving conflict: Similarities and differences between and among Latino/as, African Americans, and European Americans. In D. I. Rios and A. N. Mohamed (Eds.), *Brown and black communication: Latino and African American conflict and convergence in mass media* (pp. 13–26). Westport, CT: Praeger.

Washington, J. (2010, February 1). Do blacks want to transcend race? *Kalamazoo (MI) Gazette*, p. A10.

Wax, E. (2011, May 8). Demanding full death certificate? *Kalamazoo (MI) Gazette*, p. A20.

Wertz, F. J. (2005). Phenomenological research methods for counseling psychology. *Journal of Counseling Psychology*, 52, 167–177.

West, C. (1993). *Race matters*. Boston: Beacon Press.

West, M., and Carey, C. (2006). (Re)enacting frontier justice: The Bush administration's tactical narration of the old west fantasy after September 11. *Quarterly Journal of Speech*, 92(4), 379–412.

Wickham, D. (2010, July 27). Obama team "a basket case" on race issues. *USA Today*, p. 11A.

Wijeyesinghe, C. L. (2001). Racial identity in multiracial people: An alternative paradigm. In C.L.W. and B. W. Jackson (Eds.), *New perspectives on racial identity development* (pp. 138–143). New York: NYU Press.

Winfield, B. H. (1997). The first lady, political power and the media: Who elected her anyway? In P. Norris (Ed.), *Women, media, and politics* (pp. 166–179). Oxford: Oxford University Press.

Wiio, O. (1978). *Wiio's laws—and some others.* Espoo, Finland: Welin-Goos.

Wolfgang, M. (2009). *Yes we can: Barack Obama's proverbial rhetoric.* New York: Peter Lang.

Yoo, G. J., Zimmerman, E. H., and Preston, K. (2010). Mothers out to change U.S. politics: Obama mamas involved and engaged. In H. Harris, K. Moffitt, and C. Squires (Eds.), *The Obama effect: Multidisciplinary renderings of the 2008 campaign* (pp. 209–220). Albany: SUNY Press.

Zezima, K. (2009, July 30). Caller says race wasn't mentioned to officer in Gates case. *New York Times,* p. A20.

Index

2004 Democratic National Convention speech, 51–52, 130
2009 MTV Music Awards. *See* MTV
2010 midterm elections, 60, 65, 113, 186–187
2012 election, 53, 187, 219, 221, 222–223

Akhtar, O., 6
Allen, B. J., 220
"A More Perfect Union" ("race speech"), 8, 70–71
Anderson, K., 25
Aronson, J., 215
Asim, J., 3, 5, 109
"Audacity of Hope," 7
Axelrod, David, 49, 67

Baldor, L. C., 222
Beck, Glenn, 172
Bergsieker, A. M. R., 213
BET, 172
Biden, Joe, 8, 80, 151, 164
bipartisan politics, 56, 59–60, 126, 210, 221, 222
birth certificate issues, 5, 220, 222
black allegiance to Obama, 120–122, 214

black church, 6
black opposition to Obama, 124–127, 214
black pride, 113–117
Blumenthal, Richard, 35
BP oil spill, 77–81, 84, 210, 213
Brewer, P. R., 5, 219
Bush, George W., 33, 34, 66, 67, 76, 77, 80, 85, 130–131, 136, 176, 182, 197–198, 199, 204, 210, 215

Camara, S. K., 21, 220
Carter, R., 212
Casey, M. A., 23
Cheney, M., 219
Cho, S., 9
Clinton, Bill, 8, 33, 135, 139, 197–198, 204
Clinton, Hillary, 37, 54, 105, 194, 212
CNBC, 82, 161
CNN, 82, 162, 172, 184, 203–204
color-blind society, 8, 117–120, 135, 146–148, 215
communication competence, 69, 210–211
Connaughton, S. L., 6
Connell, R. W., 212

Connelly, M., 5, 8
Cook, W. L., 120
Cooper, D., 215, 218, 222
Cooper, F., 149–151, 212–214
Cooper, H., 150–151
Corsi, J. R., 7, 109, 211, 219
Crenshaw, K., 220
Crowley, Jim, 149–163, 196, 214
Cupach, W., 69
Cushman, E., 6

Dallinger, J. M., 214
Darsey, J., 5
Davilla, R., 214
Day, K. D., 219
Denton, R. E., 17, 218, 222
Deol, R., 219
Dong, Q., 219
Douglass, E. M., 120
Douthat, R., 222
Durbin, Dick, 49
Durgee, J. F., 24
Dyson, M. E., 216

The Ellen DeGeneres Show, 191
Emanuel, Rahm, 49

Facebook. *See* social media
Farrakhan, Louis, 213
Fiske, S. T., 213
Flores, L. A., 6
Forrest, K., 219
Foster, B. L., 219
Fouhy, B., 219
FOX News, 95, 161, 172–174, 177, 198–199, 219–220
Fram, A., 5, 9
Frank, Barney, 49
Frank, D. A., 5
Frazier, S., 222
Freddoso, D., 6, 7, 211, 219

Gates, Henry Louis, 45, 149–163, 214
Gavrilos, D., 216, 217

Gawiser, S., 3, 5, 8, 109, 130
Goldberg, J., 222
Goodnough, A., 150, 151
Gordon, R., 219
Greer-Williams, N., 220, 223
Gregg, P., 219
Guy, K., 9, 151

Hajnal, Z. L., 222
Hall, M., 215
Hannity, Sean, 172
Hardy, D., 6, 7, 17, 210, 213, 215, 218, 219
Harfoush, R., 218, 222
Harris, H. E., 6, 209, 216
Harris, T. M., 21
The Harvard Crimson, 150
hate crimes, 143–144,
Hawaii (time in), 41,
healthcare (as political issue), 65, 150, 180
Hendricks, J. A., 17, 218, 222
Hertzberg, H., 3
Hitler, Adolf (comparisons to), 5, 48
Hollander, B. A., 5, 215
House, D., 214
Huckabee, Mike, 222
Hunt, R. G., 17
Hurst, S. R., 8

Ifill, G., 3, 5, 8
Illuminati, 193
Indonesia (time in), 41
international perspectives, 76, 206
international relations, 74
Internet, 41, 66, 170, 180–183, 190, 193, 209, 218–219
Isaksen, J., 8, 213
Italie, H., 210

Jack, D. C., 25
Jackson, D., 85
Jackson, Jesse, 38, 93–94, 104, 123, 212
Jamieson, K. H., 6, 7, 17, 210, 213, 215, 218, 219

Index 241

The Jay Leno Show, 192
Jhally, S., 217
job creation (as political issue), 65. *See also* U.S. unemployment
Jones, J. M., 5
Jones, S., 214–215
Joseph, P., 8, 109, 215, 216, 222
Joseph, R., 213

Kalkan, K. O., 215
Katsman, Abraham, 7
Katz, J., 212
Kennedy, John F., 33, 185, 186, 187
Kenski, K., 6, 7, 17, 210, 213, 215, 218, 219
Kilgallen, D. L., 214
Kilpatrick, Kwame, 213
Kimble, J. J., 222
Kinder, D. R., 6
King, Dr. Martin Luther, 8, 110
Krosnick, J. A., 6
Krueger, R. A., 23
Kuehl, R. A., 218, 219
Kuftines, S. A., 209

Laney, M., 5
Latino voters, 113
Layman, G. C., 215
Leanne, S., 4, 6, 34
Lee, R., 6
Lelkes, Y., 6
Lewis, E., 222
Lewis, J., 217
Limbaugh, Rush, 172, 175
Logan, E. L., 212, 221

MacGillis, A., 7, 210
Maher, Bill, 213
Maira, S., 209
Mattera, J., 17, 211
Matthews, Chris, 9
McCain, John, 36, 37, 53, 103, 122, 125, 143, 195, 202, 212
McCue-Esner, M., 210

McConnaughy, M. C., 6
McCracken, G., 27–28
McGlone, M. S., 215
McGowen, E. B., 6
McMahon, Linda, 35
media bias, 171–174, 179–180
media conspiracy, 86, 177–180, 200–201
methodological descriptions for study: data analysis, 27–29; data collection, 23–24; focus group discussions, 23–25; focus group transcription, 26–27; Human Subjects Institutional Review Board, 19, 27; participant demographics, 20–23, 225–226; participant recruitment, 18–19; site coordinators, 19–20; topical protocol, 25, 227–228
Mitchell, W. J. T., 209
Moffitt, K., 214, 216
Moon, D. G., 6
Morgan, D. L., 24
Morin, A., 6
mosque near Ground Zero (as political issue), 85–87, 210
MSNBC, 9, 172
MTV, 81, 84, 92–93, 191, 195, 210

Nakayama, T. K., 6
National Public Radio (NPR), 55, 182, 203–204
national surveys, 5, 8, 215. *See also* public opinion polls
Newsweek, 4,
The New York Times, 150–151
Ng, K., 209, 210
Nimmo, D., 6
Nobel Peace Prize, 202–203
NPR. *See* National Public Radio

Obama, Barack: as anti-Christ, 5, 125–126, 140–141, 174; approval ratings, 62; communication critics, 43–49, 54, 61–62, 77–87, 86, 126, 130, 159–160;

Obama, Barack (*continued*)
  communication styles, 55–60, 72–76;
  communicator characteristics, 34–43,
  210–211; expectations for presidency,
  63–67; family (children), 111, 114,
  116–117, 182, 200, 202; as feminine
  communicator, 72–76, 212–214, 222;
  grandparents, 41, 103–104; as media
  celebrity, 190–193; as mouthpiece
  (political puppet), 47–49, 54, 66,
  134; as Muslim, 5, 98, 140, 173, 215;
  parents, 41, 97, 103–104, 214; as
  post-racial, 92–95; presidency as step
  toward post-racial society, 105–108;
  race as political asset, 100–105,
  145–148, 214; race as political deficit,
  98–100, 132–134, 214; self-talk about
  racial identity, 95–97; as Socialist,
  5, 137–140, 189; use of language,
  36, 40, 42, 47, 57, 79–84, 85–86,
  151–153
Obama, Michelle, 114–116, 182
Olsen, C., 219
The Oprah Winfrey Show (Oprah
  Winfrey), 12, 187, 193–195
Orbe, M., 21, 24, 27, 220, 222
O'Reilly, Bill, 175
Overberg, P., 24
Owens, W., 28

Palin, Sarah, 222
Parker, K., 72, 212
Pasek, J., 6
Patterson, R. E., 151
Patton, M. Q., 24–25
Payne, B. K., 6
PBS, 203–204
Pearson, J., 214
Pease, A., 5, 219
Pelosi, Nancy, 49
Peters, J. W., 222
Philpot, T. S., 6
Potter, J., 23
Preston, K., 221

public opinion polls, 5, 8. *See also*
  national surveys
Puchta, C., 23, 25

Radhakrishnan, R., 209
rap music (rap artists), 106, 113, 191–
  192, 193, 200, 213
Reagan, Ronald, 33, 74
Reid, Harry, 8
Remnick, D., 6, 210, 214, 215, 222
Robinson, E., 8
Romney, Mitt, 53
Roosevelt, Franklin D., 81
Rowe, A. C., 215
Rowland, R. C., 5
Rush, E., 7, 109, 211

Sargent, G., 77
Saturday Night Live, 190, 202–203
Saunders, K. R., 6
Schumm, J. S., 23
Seacrest, Ryan, 205
Sears, D. O., 215, 220
Seelye, K. Q., 150
Shaer, M., 219
Sharpton, Al, 38, 123, 213
Shaw, D. R., 6
Sherrod, Shirley, 9
Sidoti, L., 5
Simpson, O. J., 121
Sinagub, J., 23
social media, 5, 122, 180–183, 190,
  203–204, 218–220, 222
South Park, 202–203
Spicer, R., 5, 211, 219
Spitzberg, B., 69
Squires, C. R., 6, 216
Staley, C. C., 24
Steele, S., 7, 213
Stelter, B., 222
The Steve Harvey Morning Show,
  203–204
Stolberg, S. G., 5, 8
Sugrue, T. J., 9, 109, 215, 217–218

Sweet, D., 210
Swift, Taylor, 81–82

Tahk, A., 6
tax policies, 124–125, 136–138, 139, 173, 179
Tea Party (members), 9, 20, 43, 56, 66–67, 137–138, 141–142, 217
teleprompter usage, 44–46
Terrill, R. E., 5
Tesler, M., 215, 220
Thomas, Clarence, 121
Todd, C., 3, 5, 8, 109, 130
Trump, Donald, 222
Twitter. *See* social media

Urban, E. L., 27, 222
USA Today, 209
U.S. economy (as political issue), 58, 64, 65, 136–138, 142
U.S. unemployment, 71–72. *See also* job creation
U.S. wars (as political issue), 73, 75
Uslaner, E. M., 215

van Manen, M., 27
Van Natta, D., 150
Vargas, J. A., 218
Vaughn, S., 23

Walker, R., 222
Wall Street reform, 47, 65
Warren, K. T., 220
Washington, J., 9
Washington politics, 35, 53, 126, 187
The Washington Post, 72
Wax, E., 222
Wertz, F. J., 18, 24
West, Kanye, 81–85, 196, 198, 210
white opposition to Obama, 129–145, 214
white support of Obama, 145–148, 214, 215
Wickman, D., 9
Wiio's Law, 211–212
Williams, K., 213
Winfield, B. H., 214
Wolfgang, M., 34
Woods, Tiger, 114
Wright, Jeremiah, 8, 45, 70–72, 178, 213

Yoo, G. J., 221
YouTube, 175, 183, 187, 192, 195

Zezima, K., 150
Zimmerman, E. H., 221

About the Author

A native of New London, Connecticut, and a product of New London Public Schools, **Mark P. Orbe** is an internationally known educator, author, and consultant and trainer. With a bachelor's degree in organizational communication (Ohio University, 1986) and a master's degree in higher education administration (University of Connecticut, 1989), Dr. Orbe has worked as a student affairs administrator at several colleges and universities. In 1993, he received his doctoral degree in interpersonal and intercultural communication from Ohio University and began his first faculty position at Indiana University, Southeast. To date, he has presented over eighty papers at regional, national, and international academic conferences and published over one hundred books, articles in scholarly journals, and chapters in edited books. Recognized as an award-winning teacher, researcher, and public servant, Dr. Orbe actively seeks out opportunities—across the United States and abroad—to utilize his expertise beyond the walls of the university. Through his consulting company, Dumela Communications, he has worked with a number of corporate, educational, healthcare, and community-based organizations in terms of promoting communication competence in an increasingly diverse society. At present, Dr. Orbe is professor of communication and diversity in the School of Communication at Western Michigan University, where he holds a joint appointment in the Gender and Women's Studies Program.